Studies in Economics Ethics and Philosophy

Wilfried Ver Eecke

Ethical Dimensions of the Economy

Making Use of Hegel and the Concepts
of Public and Merit Goods

 Springer

Prof. Wilfried Ver Eecke
Georgetown University Washington D.C.
214 and 37th New North and O Streets
Washington, DC 20057
USA
vereeckw@georgetown.edu

ISBN 978-3-540-77110-4   e-ISBN 978-3-540-77111-1

DOI 10.1007/978-3-540-77111-1

Studies in Economic Ethics and Philosophy ISSN 1431-8822

Library of Congress Control Number: 2008921519

Production: le-tex Jelonek, Schmidt & Vöckler GbR, Leipzig
Cover design: WMX Design GmbH, Heidelberg

Printed on acid-free paper

9 8 7 6 5 4 3 2 1

springer.com

For my grandchildren Maya, Josie, Michael, Edmund, Charles and Ellen,
who are the way of the future.

Acknowledgments

The following chapters are based on previously published articles that have been reworked more or less extensively for this volume.

Ch. 1 appeared in (1981) as: The Economy and Values. In *Absolute Values and the Search For the Peace of Mankind. Proceedings of the Ninth International Conference of the Unity of the Sciences. Conference: Miami Beach 1980* (pp. 123–40). New York: The International Cultural Foundation Press. I thank the International Cultural Foundation for their generous permission to the authors to let them make use of their chapters.

Ch. 2 appeared in (1979) as: Relation Between Economics and Politics in Hegel. In D. Verene (Ed.), *Hegel's Social and Political Thought* (pp. 91–101). New York: Humanities Press. I gratefully acknowledge the original publication of this chapter in a book published by Humanities Press and Harvester Press Ltd in England.

Ch. 3 appeared in (1983) as Hegel on Economics and Freedom. *Archiv Für Rechts-und Sozialphilosophie*, *69*(2), 189–215. I thank the journal *Archiv Für Rechts-und Sozialphilosophie* for their policy to let authors use their articles.

Ch. 4 appeared in (1983) as: Ethics in Economics: From Classical Economics to Neo-liberalism. *Philosophy and Social Criticism*, *9*, 145–68. I wish to thank the journal *Philosophy and Social Criticism* and Sage Publications for permission to use the article.

Ch. 5 appeared in (1998) as: The concept of a 'merit good.' The ethical dimension in economic theory and the history of economic thought or the transformation of economics into socio-economics. *Journal of Socio-Economics*, *27* (1), 133–53. I wish to thank the *Journal of Socio-Economics* and Elsevier for permission to use the article.

Ch. 6 appeared in (1999) as: Public Goods: An Ideal Concept. *Journal of Socio-Economics*, *28*(3), 139–156. I wish to thank the *Journal of Socio-Economics* and Elsevier for permission to use the article.

Ch. 7   appeared in (1988) as: American Capitalism: A Philosophical Reflection. *Philosophy and Theology*, *3* (2), 105–32. I wish to thank
the journal *Philosophy and Theology* for the permission to use the
above article.

Ch. 8   appeared in (1996) as: A refundable tax credit for children: Self-
interest-based and morally based arguments. *Journal of Socio-
Economics*, *25* (3), 383–394. I wish to thank the *Journal of Socio-
Economics* and Elsevier for permission to use the above article.

Ch. 9   appeared in (1996) as: The limits of both socialist and capitalist
economics. In *Institute for Reformational Studies*. *Study Pam-
phlets.* (Vol. 348, pp. 1–12). Potchefstroom: Potchefstroom Univer-
siteit. I wish to thank the *Institute for Reformational Studies and
its current successor the *Centre for Faith and Scholarship* for the
permission to use the above pamphlet.

For some of the work I received financial support from the A. von Hum-
boldt Foundation in Germany and the following entities at Georgetown
University: the Center for Advanced Study of ethics, the Center for Busi-
ness-Government Relations, the office of the Dean of Faculty, the office of
the Academic Vice-President (GUROP), the Graduate School and the Philosophy Department .

Along the way I received editorial assistance from Thane Naberhaus, Carol
Taylor, Christiana Coletti, Reva Harris, David O'Mara, Alexander Skall,
William Remley, and Charles Mackel; and bibliographic assistance of
Bridget Johnson and Christiana Coletti. For the final revision I received
help from Megan Hughes. I benefited from two discussion groups, one
organized by Bruce Douglass and one by Michael Novak. I am grateful
for comments on the final draft by Albino Barrero, Richard Hattwick and
Guido Deboeck and for suggestions for improvements by Mark Nowacki,
Luc De Wulf and Henri Ghesquiere. Joint teaching with my colleague of
the economics department, Henry Briefs, proved to be encouraging and instructive. Finally, I benefited from comments from many colleagues who
read my work or attended papers I presented.

Table of Contents

Introduction

Overview

This book is a philosophical reflection (using mainly Hegel, in addition to Adam Smith, Kant, Marx and Catholic Social Thought)[1] about the socio-political dimension of economics. In it I both agree and disagree with the slogan that "the least government is the best government." I agree with the slogan, in particular as it applies to the economic domain. Adam Smith taught us that rational and self-interested individuals, left by themselves, create a more efficient and reliable economic system than one in which the government has a heavy role as was the case in his time with the mercantile system (Smith, 14, 651). Ludwig von Mises demonstrated the same idea for the communist command economy (Hayek 1935, 87–130). I disagree with the above mentioned slogan if it is interpreted as suggesting that we can best forget about the role of the government for a good functioning economy. Instead, I will argue that the government has an important function in creating the proper regulations and the wise institutional arrangements which will allow the economy to flourish in a more efficient, fair and humane way.

This book is interdisciplinary in nature. It is a philosophical and ethical reflection on economics. Hence, I make use of philosophical ideas, often but not exclusively those of Hegel. I reflect philosophically on economic concepts. I analyze the influence of moral and ethical ideas upon economics, and I argue that there is an important role for the government in providing the proper institutions for the economy to work, to work efficiently,

---

[1] It is true that Catholic Social Thought is part of a theological tradition, and some might feel that it therefore has no place in a philosophical reflection on the economy. However, religious and theological thought rooted in the natural law tradition is recognized as a legitimate part of philosophy under the name of natural theology (theologia naturalis). Thus the *Cambridge Dictionary of Philosophy* distinguishes supernatural theology from natural theology. About the latter, the *Dictionary* states that it "uses the methods of investigation and standards of rationality of any other area of philosophy" (Audi 1995, 795). In so far as Catholic Social Thought is rooted in natural law and is thus part of natural theology, it has a recognized and legitimate place in philosophical debates.

and to work humanely. Philosophers, economists, political scientists, and theologians might be interested in different parts of the book. At the end of this introduction, I provide some guidance for what sections may interest different readers. I consider each chapter a separate part of the book and able to be read on its own.

The book is divided in two parts. Part I consists of normative reflections on the economy and contains three sections. Section I reflects on the interconnections between the multiple discourses on the economy. Section II presents Hegel's claim that the economic order is an ethical institution and defends his ontological view of the economy against the one of Adam Smith who considered the economy to be a natural system (Smith, 651). I use Adam Smith's views on property as an ad hominem argument against Adam Smith himself. I also stress that the neo-liberal program for the economy demands a Hegelian view of the ontology of the economic domain. Section III is a dialogue with economists about their concepts of public and merit goods. These two concepts point to economic phenomena where collective action is desirable or necessary. This chapter defends a Hegelian ontology of the economic domain through analysis of technical concepts used by economists themselves.

Part II of the book consists of sections, each containing an application derived from the normative analysis. In Section I, I gather the views of authors belonging to different academic disciplines pointing to failures in late capitalism, in particular the failure of American capitalism. I use Hegel to highlight the structural challenges facing a society which relies on the free market and a constitutional government. I point to one area – child support – where the U.S. approach can be called inefficient and unjust. In Section II, I reflect on the challenges faced by communist societies wanting to transform their command economies into a free market economy. Relying on a Hegelian ontology of the economy I argue that attention must be paid to both to pure economic changes as well as to changes in the socio-political sphere. In Section III, I draw attention to an overlap of ideas found in Catholic Social Thought and in the publications of some recent Nobel Prize winners in economics (Buchanan, Sen, Stiglitz). These two quite different methods of thinking defend the crucial structuring role of the government for a well functioning economy.

Throughout the book I develop four major ideas or themes. First, I defend the ontology of the economic domain as proposed by Hegel and the neo-liberals: the economic order belongs to the domain of values. Hegel does so by calling the economy an ethical institution. The neo-liberals do so, because they believe that the economy can be regarded as a tenuous human institution worth supporting and defending since it promotes the value of economic efficiency. This ontology is different from Adam

Smith's who saw the economic domain explicitly as a natural system that would be efficient so long as princes and governments did not foolishly intervene with it.

The writings of Adam Smith provide arguments for the proposition that the economic domain is a human arrangement and can thus be expected to contribute positively to ethical goals. Smith's arguments – which undercut his own ontological views of the economic domain – can be found in his reflections about the need for property arrangements (Smith, 670), his arguments for some government control of the banking system (Id., 308, 313) and his claim that the government (or in Adam Smith's terminology: the sovereign) has important functions to perform for the proper and efficient working of the economy (Id., 651, 740, 768).

Hegel's claim that both property rights and economic efficiency are means toward and objective forms of human freedom implies that instituting property rights and pursuing efficiency should not be done in a way that violates the foundational principle of freedom. Allowing some people to starve to death in order to either promote social economic efficiency or uphold property rights becomes unacceptable because it destroys the freedom that it is supposed to nurture. Thus, I derive a justification for one of the goals of the modern welfare state: the creation of a safety net for all.

Using a further Hegelian argument, I point out, however, that welfare measures violate a principle of the free market. As that principle is itself a harsh principle (produce, produce efficiently and produce what others want or you will go bankrupt and/or starve to death), the violation of it for the benefit of the least well off will unavoidably produce resentment in those on whom taxes are imposed. This is natural, since paying for the welfare of others appears to give to these others the privilege of escaping the harsh principle of the free market: produce or you will go hungry. Resentment results from the perception that some are allowed to escape the harsh principle of the free market at the expense of the ordinary taxpayer, while at the same time this taxpayer remains subject to this harsh principle and furthermore is asked to pay so that others may be exempt from its demands. Resentment, therefore, limits the possibility of the modern state in helping the economic domain achieve the ethical goal of providing properly for all.[2]

If the claim, that the economic order is not a natural system but a useful human institution is valid then an inevitable question arises: "What is the contribution to the human good of the emerging new economic order so well described by Adam Smith?" Hegel answers that the emerging new economic order can deliver something that the utopian political ideals of

---

[2] Resentment also has the positive function of pushing society to eliminate any wasteful spending for the poor.

Rousseau cannot, i.e. a form of radical individualism that does not destroy the institutions which necessarily organize the lives of individuals. Hegel makes his point in two steps. First, he shows that Rousseau's utopian ideas necessarily lead to Robespierre's terror. Second, he accepts Adam Smith's concept of the invisible hand which connects constructively radical individualism in economics with social productivity. Hegel goes beyond Adam Smith by looking for the many ways in which the economic domain educates the individuals for his social destiny. Hegel adds to Adam Smith's notion of the "invisible hand" the functions of the corporation, work, and the work sphere (Stände), all of which help to transform selfish economic individuals into social beings. One important positive consequence of the socialization process imposed by the economic order on economic individuals is the formation of socio-economic groups and structures. Such group formation is, for Hegel, essential for effective political activity.

A second major idea developed in the book follows naturally from the ontological claim that the economic domain belongs to the ethical order. Indeed, if the ontological claim is true, it, then, follows that an economic analysis of the economic domain will inevitably hit upon ethical (moral) problems. As the government is often assigned the role of intervening in the economy on ethical grounds, it is inevitable that an economic analysis will also point to political problems. Thus, in analyzing the economic domain, it seems inevitable that moral, economic and political discourses will be intertwined. I argue that this occurs when economists introduce the technical concepts of "public good" and "merit good," when public documents (e.g., church documents about a just economy) advocate the use of moral criteria in the economy, when proposals are made to transform old command economies (Russia and Eastern Europe) into free market economies, and when academics analyze the failures of the American socio-economic system (Lowi) or all Western economic systems because interest groups have come to have too much influence (Briefs, Olson).

Let us develop the claims made by some academics. Goetz Briefs argues that the Western world has witnessed two parallel developments with undesirable moral consequences: one in economics and one in politics. The development in economics is the change from a competitive economic system where the competing units are individuals towards one where the competing units are interest groups. The development in politics is the change from a democracy which is metaphysically or religiously grounded (Calvin's Geneva) to a democracy that is philosophically grounded in some combination of Enlightenment philosophy and utilitarianism, and then to a pragmatic democracy that has given up most theoretical justification by becoming a bargaining democracy. A bargaining democracy in an era of interest groups means that the government will negotiate with and thus legitimize the existing powerful groups. Those individuals who are not organized or whose organization is not powerful will lose. According to Briefs, the third phase of democracy combined with the second phase of capitalism creates a societal organization that cannot pursue the common good.

Lowi derives similarly pessimistic conclusions about the American situation. He demonstrates that the federal government has expanded its function by including distribution and regulation among its tasks. In order to perform these enormously burdensome tasks, the Congress has changed its method of legislation. Instead of preparing detailed legislation after extensive public hearings and debates, Congress now often passes legislation without much debate, producing legislation that lacks detail. Congress creates an agency with the task of fleshing out the details. Agencies in turn flesh out the details by negotiating with the relevant powerful interest groups. According to Lowi such a process cannot lead to justice because justice requires just rules and the current process does not pay enough attention to the creation of rules. Lowi proposes a new form of government: judicial democracy. In such a democracy, the government would curtail its tasks and demand from Congress specific legislation after thorough and public debate.

Where Briefs and Lowi focus on the moral failures of contemporary socio-economic systems, Olson investigates the loss of economic efficiency in democratic societies with multiple interest groups. Interest groups take a long time to form. Once they are successful, they tend to stay in business. Their business is to protect the interests of their members even against innovations if they are perceived as harmful to their members. In resisting some innovations interest groups create a growth retardant and thus produce economic inefficiency.

One example of a policy which is simultaneously inefficient and unjust is the method of child support in the United States. Because part of the support is given as a deduction against taxable income and another part is given as a non-refundable credit against tax liabilities, this method of child support has the perverse result of providing fewer tax dollars per child to support children in poor families than for children in more wealthy ones.

Next, I turn to Hegel who points to structural dangers in modern society, particularly dangers resulting from the relationship between the economic and the political order. Hegel perceived the need for a proper representation of economic interests in the political system, but he also understood the threat that the excessive influence of economic interests can play in the political process. A part of Hegel's solution to the challenge is now unacceptable, i.e. the demand for a hereditary monarchy and a hereditary upper house in parliament in order to guarantee that not all politicians are dependent upon the economic domain. At the same time, the alternative in the United States is not meeting the challenge for which Hegel thought that his solution was a viable answer. A reading of Hegel allows us to see the structural origin of the unacceptable situation as analyzed by Briefs and Olson for all Western societies and as analyzed by Lowi for the United States in particular.

A third major idea of the book is the claim that economic goods and services need to be distinguished as private, public and merit goods. Private goods are goods where property rights are effective. For example, if people want to enjoy bread they have to pay for it, and, having paid for it, nobody else is entitled to enjoy it. The competitive free market is generally credited with being an efficient mechanism for the production and distribution of private goods. There is a tendency to ask the government only to enforce property rights in the handling of private goods. By introducing the idea that the government should institute banking regulations and introduce and enforce anti-trust regulations, the neo-liberals have assigned the government positive tasks beyond the one of enforcing property rights.[3]

The terms of the debate about the role of the government change when economists discover that there are goods and services that have characteristics, which do not fit the category of private goods. Economists have discovered that some goods and services have technical or factual characteristics which make them exceptions to the idea of private goods. Such goods and services have been termed public goods and defined as goods characterized by non-rivalry in consumption and unenforceability of compensation. Let me clarify. Indeed, a good such as a street light in a back alley has the factual (technical) property that if one neighbor buys a back alley light all the other neighbors can enjoy the same light without the first neighbor losing any utility of that light (non-rivalness in consumption). At the same time the first neighbor who bought the light cannot extract a payment from the second neighbor (appropriation of legitimate payment is impossible; compensation is unenforceable). In many cases such public goods will not be bought because one person alone cannot afford to do so even though the price of the good is less than what the community jointly is willing to pay for. Thus, the competitive free market mechanism will often fail to optimally provide public goods. Some economists then argue that such a failure of the market mechanism leaves open the possibility for government initiative.

---

[3] There are disagreements among the neo-liberals of the Chicago school on what regulations the government should provide. For one famous proposal about regulations of money supply see Friedman, 1962, 37–55.

A libertarian thinker, Aaron Wildavsky, and his student, Jesse Malkin, sharply criticize this line of thinking. These authors argue that the economic profession uses at least five different definitions for the concept of public good and, thus, does not possess an agreed upon definition. And, as different countries treat different goods as public goods, they conclude that the concept of public good is not an objective concept but rather a social construct where different countries, by an act of political will, declare different goods to be public goods.

I argue against such a relativistic view of the concept of public good. Using a phenomenological method, I argue that economists have noticed many exceptions to the definition of private goods and used many labels for these exceptions. The many different labels used to describe anomalies that cannot be fully analyzed by the concept of private good can be reduced to the two separate characteristics which then can be used to define the new concept of public goods (non-rivalness in consumption (a second person can enjoy the good without the first person losing any enjoyment herself and non-enforceability of payment or non-appropriability (the first person cannot recuperate payment from others who enjoy the good he provided). The non-rivalness in consumption presents an opportunity for gain if some form of collective action is taken.   However, the non-appropriability makes it difficult to finance the public good even if collective action is undertaken.   Samuelson analyzes the difficulties that face a collective action undertaken by the government.   Olson analyzes the difficulty faced by those who want to provide the public good by means of private groups (interest or pressure groups). On the basis of the argument that all labels for the concept of public good can be reduced to two characteristics, I conclude that the concept of public good has a specific objective content. Since the financing method has problematic aspects in both the case of government initiative and in the case of private initiative, countries might decide to try solving the financing difficulty in different ways, given that there is theoretically no perfect solution.   However, the fact that there is no perfect solution for the financing method does not mean that the concept of public good itself becomes completely arbitrary.

The concept of public good identifies a potential gain if collective action can be undertaken. The technical concept of public good thus points to a challenge, even though it does not point to a unique solution. It is important to notice that the possible role of the government with respect to public goods is restricted to helping the individual consumers realize a potential for gain which they cannot always realize by themselves.   If the government can obey the Pareto principle (no one is made worse off and at least one is made better off), then economic thinking argues that the government's role in providing public goods is self-justifying.

A problem arises because in some cases the requirement that nobody must be harmed in the provision of a public good fails. Somebody will be hurt or will claim to be hurt. The normative idea behind the concept of public good is that any one harmed in the provision of a public good should receive compensation. Thus, if a farmer experiences a loss because his land is confiscated for the construction of a highway, then the people wanting the highway must be willing to compensate the farmer. If the farmer cannot be satisfied either because the farmer is asking an outrageous price or because there is no appropriate mechanism for calculating and providing compensation, the implementation of the public good is regrettably deficient. This is the case because, in the provision of public goods, the aim of the government is to help consumers capture an opportunity for gain without hurting anyone.

Musgrave has pointed out that some governmental activities in the economy do not fit the definition of public goods. He gives as examples: obligatory education, free school lunches, and sin taxes on alcohol. He defines merit goods (descriptively) as goods that are so meritorious that the appropriate authorities are justified in declaring that the goods' level of consumption in the free market is unacceptable. If the judgment is that the level of consumption is too low (education, school lunches) then we are in the presence of a merit good. If the judgment is that the level of consumption is too high (alcohol), then we are in the presence of a demerit good. The descriptive definition of the concept merit good leaves open the question of the meaning of "meritorious." But, even if the idea of meritoriousness remains unspecified, the concept of merit good implies that the government has the right to interfere with consumer wishes in the case of legitimate merit goods. Sometimes the idea of a legitimate merit good is interpreted politically as having been voted upon in a legitimate way.

The introduction of the concept of merit good by Musgrave creates a paradox for the economic profession. On the one hand, Musgrave demonstrates convincingly that a new concept is needed in order for economic theory to be complete, otherwise there would be some economic activities without a conceptual home. On the other hand, the new concept of merit good contradicts a basic assumption of economic theory. Indeed, economic theory is the science of how to maximize the utility of consumers whereas the concept of merit good is about justified interference with consumer sovereignty. The concept of merit good accepts the proposition that the wishes of consumers as expressed in free market transactions are unacceptable and ought to be interfered with. That implication of the concept merit good makes many economists feel uneasy about it. In chapter 3 I argue that Hegel used the idea of merit goods without using the label. In his book, *Hegel als Ökonom (Hegel the Economist)*, the German philosopher-economist, Birger Priddat, makes the same claim.   The history of economic thought shows that economists who describe the total economy introduce the distinction between the three concepts of private, public and merit good without using all three labels.   From Adam Smith, Henry Simons and a study by Christian Scheer about education, I construct a Kantian argument that the idea of merit good has been part of the history of economic thought even though the label was only introduced in 1956.

My dialogue with the history of economic thought has two additional results. First, it shows that the idea of merit good has a much wider applicability than the creator of the concept, Musgrave, is defending. The concept not only applies to a limited number of concrete economic activities, but it also captures the institutional arrangements imposed on consumers and producers in order to make the market work and make it work efficiently and humanely. Second, one can borrow from the history of economic thought the idea that merit goods can be systematically divided into meaningful and distinct categories, such as government interventions connected to property rights; government interventions aiming at making economic transactions more efficient – banking regulation and anti-trust laws; government policies aiming at improving the education of all people and finally those aiming at creating a safety net. One, thus, obtains an idea of the different kind of institutional arrangements for which the government is responsible. The defense of the different categories does not imply that agreement exists about the method of governmental regulation or intervention. In this book I do not analyze which regulations in the different domains are the wisest. I only defend the idea that there are specific domains in which the government has a regulatory duty.

A fourth idea covered by the book is the relation of religious ethics to economics.   Given my thesis that economics belongs to the domain of values and the fact that values, morality, and ethics are an integral concern of organized religion, I felt it necessary to reflect on church pronouncements about the economy. I address two aspects in the relationship between religion and economics.

First, there is the question as to whether the method of religious thinking is appropriate in economic matters. I argue that an ethical discourse about the economy, such as a church document supporting a more just economy, is subject to risks. It can be abstract and therefore ineffective; it can point to very concrete economic goals while being naive and/or technically inconsistent. And finally in advocating specific changes, it might show itself to be one-sided, partial, or even partisan. I argue that two church documents, *Justice for All* (A Pastoral Letter from the U.S. Bishops); and *Centesimus Annus* (An Encyclical from John Paul II) avoid these pitfalls.

Second, I study the effective role that religion plays or could play in economic theory. Thus, Hegel teaches us that resentment is a feeling which will necessarily emerge when the government tries to help the economy achieve the ethical task of providing enough goods and services for a decent way of living to all, including the poor, the disabled, and the unemployed. This Hegelian argument allows me to make the claim that governments making a transition from a command economy to a free market economy will need help to let their free market economy achieve the ethical goal of providing for all. Governments making the transition to a free market economy will, therefore, not only have to introduce freedom in economic transactions, they will also have to introduce freedom of religion. I even argue that those governments will have to allow or promote the institutionalizing of religion in order to have their effective help in dealing with the social question that arises with particular sharpness in a free market economy. Those governments will not only have to allow or possibly promote the organization of religion, they will also have to allow (promote) the organization of independent unions, of the association of lawyers and of economists if they want help in promoting a safe working environment, an independent judiciary, and free trade policies. Given the importance of religion in Hegel's thought and given the sensitivity to the moral and ethical dimension in economics in both Hegel and church documents about the economy, it is not surprising to find some similarities in their views of the economy. Both praise the free market for its productive achievements. Both regret the inability of the free market to solve the problem of poverty. Both refuse to abandon the ethical goals they assign the economy, even if they see that the goals are not reached or might not be reachable. Both prefer to maintain the tension between the ethical ideal and the reality rather than provide unrestrained praise for the existing arrangements. Both give the political order an oversight role.

The interdisciplinary nature of the book may attract different audiences. Readers mainly interested in Hegel should read Chapter 2 for a presentation of the crucial function of economics in the architectonic of Hegel's philosophic system, Chapter 3 for a summary of Hegel's view of the economy, Chapter 4 for a dialogue between Hegel and part of the history of economic thought, and Chapter 7 for the use of Hegel to critically analyze the American method of relating politics and economics.

Readers mainly interested in political economy should read Chapter 4 for a dialogue between Hegel and part of the history of economic thought, Chapter 5 on merit goods, Chapter 6 on public goods, Chapter 9 on recommendations for a transition from a command economy to the free market, and Chapter 10 for the argument on the similarity between the ideas of Catholic Social Thought and those of three Nobel prize winners due to the fact that all stress the need of government to provide the free market with a proper institutional framework.

Readers interested in practical conclusions derived from philosophical principles should read Chapter 7 where I critically analyze the structure of American capitalism, Chapter 8 where I show that the US method of child support is both inefficient and unjust, Chapter 9 where I develop some recommendations for the transition to the free market in formerly communist countries, and Chapter 10 where I review arguments from quite different traditions about the need of the government to regulate and organize economic activity.

Readers mainly interested in ethics and morality should read Chapter 1 where I demonstrate the interconnection between a moral and an economic discourse about the economy, Chapter 3 and 4 where I argue for ethical tasks in the economy, Chapter 7 and 8 where I point to moral deficiencies in the American economic system, and Chapter 10 where I provide ethical arguments (rooted in the nature of economic reality) for a role of the government in the economy.

Readers mainly interested in a philosophic discussion of the role of religious ethics in economics should read Chapter 1 where I point to the risks inherent in religious discourse about the economy, Chapter 7 where I underline a limited similarity between the position of Hegel and that of the Catholic Bishops' Pastoral on the economy, Chapter 9 where I argue for the need of freedom of religion as part of the transition from a command economy to the free market, and Chapter 10 where I show that technical economic analysis develops ideas that are consonant with Catholic Social Thought in that both see the importance of responsible political decisions for a well functioning economy.

Readers with eclectic interests might find in the abstracts to each chapter more detailed information on the chapter than can be given in the title. Hopefully, the abstracts will prove useful for guiding those with eclectic interests.

Part I

Normative Reflections on the Economy

Section I

Multiple Discourses on the Economy

1. The Interconnection of Moral and Economic Theory

Abstract

The economic reality is discussed, analyzed, and judged from different points of view. At least three points of view have considerable weight today: the economic, the political and the moral. Each of these three points of view gives rise to a special kind of discourse. Such discourses have their own style, their preferential subject matter, their own priorities, and their own methodological requirements. In this chapter I will reflect upon two of these three discourses: the moral and the economic discourse on the economic reality, and I will demonstrate that they are unavoidably intertwined. The moral discourse must refer to specific economic problems in order to be relevant. Doing so makes a moral discourse on the economy technically vulnerable and possibly one-sided. The economic discourse on the economy, too, becomes unavoidably entangled in moral or ethical questions due to the problems with public and merit goods. Thus, this chapter explicitly introduces the claim that ethics and economics are interconnected, a claim which Hegel's philosophy takes for granted, because Hegel includes the economic domain (civil society) among his three ethical institutions.

I. The Moral Discourse on Economic Reality

Among the documents that discuss the economic reality and opt for a moral point of view, one can enumerate pronouncements of the World Council of Churches, encyclicals of popes, and statements of different conferences of Catholic Bishops. To illustrate this kind of discourse, I will use the document, "The Economy: Human Dimensions," which the Catholic Bishops of the United States issued in 1975. In this document we find the following statements:

Unemployment is the great peacetime physical tragedy of the nineteenth and twentieth centuries, and both in its cause and in the imprint it leaves upon those who inflict it, those who permit it, and those who are its victims, it is one of the great moral tragedies of our time. (Byers 1985, 469)

It is the moral, human and social consequences of our troubled economy which concerns us and their impact on families, the elderly and children. (Ibid.)

Economic prosperity is to be assessed not so much from the sum total of goods and wealth possessed as from the distribution of goods according to norms of justice. (Ibid., 470)

The right to have a share of earthly goods sufficient for oneself and one's family belongs to everyone. (Ibid.)

A just and equitable system of taxation requires assessment according to ability to pay. (Ibid., 471)

Unemployment frequently leads to higher rates of crime, drug addiction, and alcoholism. It is reflected in higher rates of mental illness as well as rising social tensions. (Ibid., 472)

The distribution of income and wealth are important since they influence and even determine our society's distribution of economic power. Catholic social teaching has condemned gross inequality in the distribution of material goods. (Ibid., 473)

It is not enough to point up [sic] the issues in our economy and to propose solutions to our national problems while accepting uncritically the presupposition of an economic system based in large part upon unlimited and unrestrained profit. (Ibid., 474)

Finally, in the Appendix, we find a call for the following:

... minimum wage legislation; unemployment insurance and protection against sickness and old age; minimum age limit for working children; legal enforcement of the right of labor to organize; a national employment service; public housing; and a long-term program of increasing wages. (Ibid., 475)

We find a call as well for "prevention of excessive profits and progressive taxes on inheritance, income, and excess profits" (Ibid.).

These quotations should be enough to raise three kinds of questions about such a moral discourse on the economic reality. Indeed such a moral discourse is unrealistic. If everyone has the right to have a sufficient share of earthly goods for himself and his family, how can such a right be realistically reached, enforced or implemented if, in fact, there are not enough goods to go around? Second, such a moral discourse gives advice that is systematically inconsistent. A moral discourse on the economic reality is concerned with the human misery that results from unemployment. In the same document, though, one finds a call for minimum wage legislation, unemployment insurance and other social services. Some economic theorists, however, teach that such programs, *ceteris paribus*, result in a higher cost of labor, which, in turn, diminish the demand for labor and, thus, increase unemployment. Although concern for social services stems from the same compassion for human misery, as does concern for unemployment, the moral discourse of this Catholic Bishops' document displays no understanding of the possible incompatibility of the implementation of social services and the decrease in unemployment.

Finally, the moral discourse of the Bishops shows a systematic bias in favor of what one could call a socialist ideology. Thus, the Bishops' discourse questions the profit motive, advocates progressive taxation, and stresses the role of the government in guiding economic activity and in securing the economic well-being of all. The Bishops do not speak about the need for entrepreneurial initiative or courage, about the duty to respect the employer, or the necessity to give a fair day's work for a good wage.

If one ponders over these three kinds of questions, does one not have to conclude that the moral discourse on economic reality risks becoming a discourse which is naively unrealistic, technically inconsistent, and ideologically biased? I believe that, indeed, any moral discourse on economic reality runs these three dangers. Still, I would not want to conclude, as some colleagues would, that a moral discourse on the economic reality is invalid. On the contrary, I would argue that while these three risks are inherent in a moral discourse, the moral discourse still has its legitimacy. Let me address consecutively the three risks of a moral discourse about the economy.

The first risk of a moral discourse is that it sounds naively unrealistic. However, one should remember that the moral discourse is not about facts alone; it is also about a *telos*. Typical of this aspect of the moral discourse is that it can be valid even though it is not descriptively true of the reality. Thus, the moral imperative that one should not kill another person for personal enrichment can be valid, even though robberies and murders occur. Or put in another way, the belief that there will always be robberies and murders does not mean that the moral prohibition against murder becomes naive utopianism. Therefore, the function of a moral discourse is not to accurately describe reality. Realism in this sense of the word is not a requirement for a valid moral discourse. A moral discourse should point to a different dimension than the one that exists in fact and should communicate that this other dimension poses a challenge to human beings because they can distinguish between a *telos* and a fact.

The second risk of a moral discourse is that it is technically inconsistent, in the sense that ineffective attempts advocated to reach the morally desirable *telos* lead to situations worse than the original situations one tried to correct. For example, the right to have a share of earthly goods sufficient for oneself and one's family by means of legislation on minimum wages and social programs might lead to less real income for the labor force.[4] This risk is, indeed, real. The theoretical solution is a methodological awareness of the legitimate domain of different discourses on the same reality. Such an awareness exists in the document under discussion as illustrated by the following text:

> Our concern, however, is not with technical fiscal matters, particular economic theories or political programs, but rather the moral aspects of economic policy and the impact of these policies on people. (Byers, 469)

The trouble with this solution is that the moral discourse intends and must intend to influence the real by making people aware of a moral *telos*. But, how can one do so effectively if one does not make suggestions about the ways to implement the moral *telos*? However, if one were to go that route, a moral discourse on economic reality cannot honestly avoid talking about the wage level or the need for social insurance systems. The moral discourse, however, can avoid the risk of technical mistakes only by avoiding part of the moral intention, which is to make suggestions about the implementation of a moral *telos* in the reality.[5] Clearly such a risk is something of which the moral discourse must be aware. The implementation program should be presented as a second part of the moral discourse. Technical debate over implementation should be allowed, invited and stimulated as part of the implementation of the moral *telos*. The moral discourse cannot present any implementation program as necessarily identical with the moral *telos*, which motivated the implementation program. Similarly, economic discourse is false in questioning the moral *telos* which

---

[4] Crucial for this argument is the concept of the "Phillips curve." For a discussion of this idea, see: Michael Evans 1969, 263–274; Rees; Prasch & Sheth.

[5] The avoidance of problems connected with an implementation program for moral concerns might go neatly together with an economic theory à la Samuelson, which assumes without proof the existence of an ethical welfare function for determining society's bliss function. The neatness of the combination of these two special forms of discourses derives from the fact that the two discourses abstain from real dialogue. I will argue that the economic and moral discourses are much more interdependent (Bator, 28).

motivated an implementation program on the sole ground that the implementation program is economically inconsistent. It is not because social programs indirectly increase the cost of labor and, thus, augment unemployment that it is illegitimate to talk about the relation between unemployment and crime rates, drug addition, and alcoholism (Byers, 472). The moral discourse has its own legitimacy regardless of the dangers involved in suggesting implementation programs for moral concerns.

The third risk of a moral discourse is the most puzzling and most dangerous. This third risk, too, is an essential problem of moral life and is already clearly formulated in Hegel's *Philosophy of Right*. Hegel argues that moral life is not the solution to the problem of free will, since moral life requires the individual to identify with the good *as he sees it* (Hegel 1967 a, # 132).[6] Therefore, moral life unconditionally binds one to do what is but conditionally correct and good. Moral discourse, therefore, necessarily runs the risk of systematic bias. Such a bias often occurs in moral discourse on the economic reality. Thus, neo-liberals such as Hayek or Friedman see self-responsibility and initiative as the central elements of a moral discourse on the economic reality. Clearly, these virtues are virtues connected with the entrepreneurial class. The question one can pose to these neo-liberals is: are these virtues the supreme virtues of moral life, or are they just refined forms of self-interest?

On the other hand, the statement by the Catholic Bishops of the United States in "The Economy: Human Dimensions" concentrates on the right of labor to organize, the right to just and minimum wages, the right to a sufficient share of wealth, and the right to progressive taxes on inheritance, income, and excessive profits. It decidedly concentrates its moral discourse on the plight of labor, the poor, and the needy. One could ask: should not a moral discourse on economic reality take into account all economic subjects – rich and poor, the successful and the needy? To this objection, I find a possible answer in the statement by the Bishops. They state, "We hope in these limited reflections to give voice to some of the concerns of the poor and working people of our land" (Byers, 469). As for the possible objection that the statement limits itself to a subgroup of economic subjects, one can read the following answer:

> ...we are guided by the concern for the poor and afflicted shown by Jesus, who came to 'bring good news to the poor, to proclaim liberty to captives, new sight to the blind, and to set the downtrodden free.' (Ibid., 470)

---

[6] Hegel's *Philosophy of Right* subsequently referred to as *PR*. When quoting Hegel, I will give, where possible, paragraph numbers, signaled by the sign #.

In that text, the Bishops of the United States in 1975 make an appeal to their ultimate authority for explaining the possible systematic bias of their moral discourse on economic reality.

Given that Christianity aims at providing a universal message, which is valid for all human beings, one might therefore expect a tension in Christianity between its preference for the poor and its claim to universality. One can observe such a tension in the change of formulation of the principal norm for judging an economic policy as just or unjust in the first draft and the final version of the Catholic Bishops' Pastoral on the economy. Thus, in the first draft, the Bishops write:

> In addition, our perspective and our conclusions are shaped by an overriding concern for the impact of decisions and policies on the lives of people, especially the poor. *Our fundamental norm is this: Will this decision or policy help the poor and deprived members of the human community and enable them to become more active participants in economic life?* (Catholic Social Teaching and the U.S. Economy. First Draft, # 21, 343)

In the first draft of the Pastoral, the fundamental norm of justice is restricted to the impact a decision or a policy has on only part of the population: the poor and deprived people. The formulation of the fundamental norm of justice seems to be positively concerned only with part of humanity. The Catholic Bishops seem to feel that the above first formulation of the fundamental norm of justice was defective, and they change it in the final version into a text which affirms both the particularism and the universalism present in Christianity. Thus, the final version reads:

> The quality of the national discussion about our economic future will affect the poor most of all, in this country and throughout the world. The life and dignity of millions of men, women and children hang in the balance. Decisions must be judged in light of what they do *for* the poor, what they do *to* the poor and what they enable the poor to do *for themselves*. The fundamental moral criterion for all economic decisions, policies and institutions is this: They must be at the service of *all the people, especially the poor.* (Economic Justice for All. U.S. Bishops' Pastoral Message and Letter, # 24, 415)

The tension in the Christian conception of justice is even illustrated in the double criterion enunciated in the final version of the Bishops' Pastoral – not just in the change in formulation from the first draft to the final version. On the one hand, the paragraph in the final version proclaims that decisions must be judged according to what they do *for* and *to* the poor. On the other hand, the paragraph announces that economic decisions must be in the service of *all people, especially the poor.* The tendency to make the poor the sole concern of justice is a bias sometimes present in the Christian moral vision of the economy.

II. The Economic Discourse on Economic Reality

In Western economic discourse, by habit or by argument, a normative status is given to the free market: i.e., the free exchange of goods between individual decision-makers. Such a predilection for the free market, though, creates two problems. The first arises because there are goods which have technical characteristics that preclude the market mechanism as an efficient exchange mechanism for them. In the literature, these goods are usually called public goods. Special characteristics of these goods are, among others, their indivisibility, lumpiness, jointness of supply, external economics (or dis-economics), and decreasing marginal production cost. An example of such a good is a bridge that allows many people to save time when they have to cross the river even if only one firm paid for the bridge. By extension, one can argue that beautiful landscapes, street lights, clean air, railroads, etc., are public goods.[7]

The second difficulty arises because there are goods which are so important that appropriate authorities act as if they have the right to influence the production and/or consumption of these goods. The appropriate authorities act as if they can violate the principle of consumer sovereignty which is the foundation of the free market system. Some interesting examples are: obligatory education, obligatory inoculation, and taxation of tobacco and liquor in order to diminish their consumption. Clearly, such goods are not private goods. They are not public goods because in the case of public goods, the appropriate authority (the state) only helps individuals reach an optimum that they want but cannot achieve by themselves. The justification for government action concerns helping individual consumers whose preferences the state respects. This kind of help is called "voluntary exchange theory of taxation." In the case of obligatory education, etc., the government acts not to help consumers reach a maximum according to the preference-ordering of individuals; on the contrary, the government acts with the intention of interfering with the preferences of individuals because it considers these particular goods meritorious or demeritorious. In

---

[7] For some interesting survey articles, see Head 1974. The problem of public goods will be discussed explicitly in chapter 6 of this book. I will also make use of this concept when clarifying Hegel's views on the function of the state in the economic domain (Chapter 3).

his classic book, *The Theory of Public Finance,* Musgrave labels desires or wants for these goods "merit wants" (Musgrave 1959, 13–16).[8]

The presence in the economy of goods called "public goods" introduces questions such as the government's right to deny the individual rights because the economic theory of public goods implicitly assumes the right of the government to make use of the power to tax or the power to invoke the right of pre-eminent domain. The presence of merit goods introduces the question whether the government has the right to decide what are good and what are bad consumer wishes. In Chapters 5 and 6, I will more fully develop the necessity of value-considerations imposed on an economic discourse which happily or reluctantly accepts the concepts of public and merit good.

Conclusion

The reflections in this chapter started with the fact that there are several possible discourses on economic reality. I concentrated on the moral and the economic discourse. It is possible to argue that these two discourses operate at two different levels. Nevertheless, because morality wants to be effective in the world, moral discourse on the economic world needs to go beyond mere moral exhortations. Moral discourse needs to provide moral approval for certain economic policies and disapproval for certain other economic policies, even at the risk of being technically vulnerable.

The second puzzling thought is that the economic discourse cannot be complete without including in its own discourse ethical considerations. Economic discourse can then be value-free only if economists accept that their discipline is incomplete by excluding the concepts of public and merit good.

In the rest of the book, I will use Hegel as a guide for articulating the ethical dimensions of the economic domain and doing so in a way that avoids as much as possible the dangers of the one-sidedness of a purely moral discourse. Hegel does so by taking freedom as his norm.

---

[8] The problem of merit goods is discussed explicitly in chapter 5 of this book. I also make use of this concept when clarifying Hegel's views on the function of the state in the economy (Chapter 3). For an anthology containing all the texts written by the creator of the concept, Richard Musgrave, a selection of secondary literature, and some important applications, see Ver Eecke 2007.

2. Economics and Politics in the Architectonic of Hegel's Thought

Abstract

This chapter analyzes the relationship between economics and politics as it appears in Hegel's *Phenomenology of Mind,* the *Philosophy of Right,* and the *Encyclopedia of the Philosophical Sciences.* Hegel realizes that Western civilization was striving towards greater institutional protection of individual freedom. He interprets both Rousseau's utopian democracy and the claim for universal suffrage as unacceptable expressions of that tendency. He interprets the terror of Robespierre as the logical consequence of Rousseau's utopian ideals. Hegel learned from the Scottish economists that the new economic order provides a better institutional protection of individual freedom because it can tolerate and turn to its own advantage a form of radical individualism that proved disastrous for the political domain. Hegel therefore gives the emerging free market a central place in the good society as described in his *Philosophy of Right.* Hegel's challenge was to show the educating function of the new economic order.

I. The Rejection of the Rousseau-ian Direct Democracy

The passage in *The Phenomenology of Mind,* which analyzes the Rousseau-ian democratic ideal, has the title: "Absolute Freedom and Terror" (Hegel 1967 c, 599–610). This passage is preceded by an analysis of the Enlightenment and followed by an analysis of the moral vision of the world. I will, first, draw attention to how Hegel connects his analysis of "Absolute Freedom" with these two other moments in the culture of Western Civilization and will then analyze Hegel's specific argument according to which the ideal of "absolute freedom" must necessarily fail.

A. Hegel's Analysis of the Enlightenment Period, Absolute Freedom, and the Moral Vision of the World

The Enlightenment period produced a very critical intellectual attitude towards the political institutions of its time. However, few political institutions changed during this period. The Enlightenment created an intellectual climate whereby the actual political institutions were deprived of their traditional theocentric justification. Instead, it was thought that political institutions could find justification and legitimacy only in what they meant for the people.

Hegel connects this relationship between the Enlightenment and the political reality with the new image (notion) that consciousness developed about itself. He discusses the Enlightenment period in his *Phenomenology of Mind* as part of the section on *Spirit*. In this section, consciousness has already reached the insight that, as a self, the ego gets its form from social institutions. Thus, social institutions are not a dead reality. Instead, they are a formative part of the living reality. This can be explained, Hegel thinks, because social institutions (objective spirit) have three interdependent aspects. First, the social institutions have objective reality. They exist. Second, the social institutions have a meaning for the people. It is this meaning to which the people appeal. It is this meaning, too, which is transformed into an ongoing project of improvement and defense of the existing institutions. Third, as a result of the continuous projects related to social institutions, the existing institutions are at any time also a human product (Boey 1970, 57 ff).

Addressing the first aspect of social institutions, i.e., that they have objective reality, the Enlightenment did not advocate their destruction. Rather, it allowed the continuation of the existing institutions. However, such a moderate approach does not allow consciousness to claim that it is fully in control of itself. Indeed, as the substance of the self is produced by social institutions, consciousness cannot claim to be self-created. The subject and the social substance out of which it is made, therefore, do not yet coincide. On the other hand, as we will see, the social substance is not fully alien to the subject, either. The subject is capable of imposing a predicate upon the substance: it must be *useful for the subject*.

The Enlightenment period concentrated its efforts on the second aspect of social institutions. Indeed, Enlightenment philosophy affirms that the meaning of these institutions is to be found in the service they can render to the individuals as they live together in a historical community. Institutions are to be responsive to individuals. Individuals are not supposed to be required to have blind faith in the validity of institutions. Responsiveness, or in Hegelian terms, *utility,* is the concept, the notion, by which the individual in the Enlightenment period reconciled himself to the fact that his self is formed by social institutions. In other words, the possibly alienating dimension of the influence of social institutions upon the self is overcome by consciousness affirming the principle that those social institutions have to be *useful for the self.*

The willingness of consciousness to require nothing more from social institutions than their utility in order for consciousness to be at peace with itself as a social being is a fact that Hegel expresses as follows, "Consciousness has found its notion in the principle of utility" (Hegel 1967 c, 599).

The ideals behind the French Revolution propelled a movement created by consciousness to address actively the relationship between itself and the social institution–the first and third aspect of a social institution. In order to be at peace with itself as a social being, consciousness now requires that the social reality be *not just useful, but its own product.* If this can be achieved, the ego, as a social self, would be a product of its own enterprise. Such a requirement means that consciousness aims at "absolute freedom," i.e., it aims at producing the social reality which, in turn, gives content to consciousness itself.

But an individual's social self is not independent of the social self of others. When consciousness insists upon self-determination of the social self, it is unavoidable that a consciousness will conflict with other consciousnesses for the determination of the social reality.

Hegel's dialectical solution to this problem consists of the willingness of consciousness to withdraw from the social reality while finding a way to determine itself as a self. For this to be possible, consciousness must not define itself any longer as a social self, but as a moral self. Indeed, moral self-determination allows for the self-determination of the self without necessarily having to impose upon others the content of the moral self that one accepts as unconditionally binding for oneself.

Thus, it is the lack of full self-determination as a social self which forces consciousness to move from the Enlightenment attitude to the aspirations of the French Revolution. It will be the insight that terror is unavoidable if consciousness insists on such a full self-determination of the self as a social self, which will force consciousness to move from the disillusioned aspirations of the French Revolution to the moral vision of the world (Smith 1989, 85 ff.).

B. The Rousseau-ian Direct Democracy

For Hegel it is not enough to show that a particular self-image, a notion, of consciousness is unsatisfactory. He looks for indications that consciousness is, de facto, already further than its own notion.

Hegel makes precisely this move when he comments that the autonomy of the social reality in the Enlightenment period is but an empty semblance because consciousness considers itself to be the legitimizing ground for any social organization.[9] If there is still an "in-itself" dimension to the social reality, it exists legitimately only as a reality *for somebody else* – for consciousness.

The consciousness that serves as the legitimizing ground for the social reality is individual consciousness. It is, however, in its function of being the representative of all consciousnesses that individual consciousness is the legitimizing ground of social reality. Consciousness must conceive of itself as a universal subject in order to conceive of itself justifiably as the legitimizing ground for all social reality.

Consciousness is not just thought. Consciousness is also will.[10] The social reality is not just something that exists. It is also something that is constantly produced. Now, in order for consciousness as will to be the ground of social reality – itself seen as a product – it is necessary that this consciousness participates in the making of this social reality. Inasmuch as consciousness considers itself to be the universal subject – and not an individual universal, an incarnated universal – each individual must require that the social self be its own product. This can occur only if the existing distinctions in social groups, social classes, or governmental functions are abolished.

This results in the *legitimate* social reality being reduced to what an individual (as self-conceived universal) actually wills. Nothing that is not actually willed by an individual is acceptable or legitimate.

This consequence permits the formulation of a first objection to a Rousseau-ian direct democracy. Indeed, if only that which is *actually* willed is legitimized, then what was willed in the past remains legitimized only if the individual still wills it now. Something that exists objectively has no legitimacy independent of the actual will of the individual as a representative of universal consciousness.[11] But the ground for legitimacy is the way individual consciousness conceives of itself as a representative of universal

---

[9] Ibid., 601, "individual consciousness conceives the object as having no other nature than that of self-consciousness itself."

[10] Ibid., 600–601, "this will is not the empty thought of will."

[11] Ibid., 602–603, "in which it [consciousness] lets nothing break away and assume the shape of a detached object standing over against it."

consciousness. This conception (notion) of consciousness, conceived one day, cannot be normative for consciousness the next day.

Here Hegel's argument is essentially an anthropological argument. The social-political argument is a derivative argument. Indeed, Hegel argues that a consciousness, which requires only its actual will as the legitimizing ground for commitment, submission, or obedience to an objective reality, has created a legitimacy requirement that is so strong that consciousness is *not even obliged to loyalty to past commitments made by itself.* Indeed, nothing objective is legitimate. Only the *actual* will produces legitimacy.

If consciousness is not bound by past commitments made by the individual himself, how can it be bound to commitments made by others? This anthropological argument has implications for the socio-political reality. For Hegel, a Rousseau-ian anthropology does not allow the creation of a constitution, i.e., the production of a binding thought; it also does not allow the organization of an effective government.

Hegel expands this last argument building on the assertion that the universal, in order to be able to act, must incarnate itself in a particular individual. Indeed, to act is to do something determinate, something particular. Only an individual can do so. For the universal to be effective, it is necessary that an individual takes it upon himself to represent *effectively* the universal. But the Rousseau-ian anthropology does not possess a theory of mediation. Thus, if one individual performs the tasks of the universal, others are necessarily excluded. Even worse, the grounds by which other individuals are excluded from participating in the determination of the universal are also precisely the reasons by which each individual can claim to have a right to be the head of the government. Thus, the government must necessarily and automatically be seen by the other individuals as a faction. The other individuals, in turn, must be seen by the head of the government as a necessary threat to his claim to being the universal (Ibid., 604–605).

The problem can be formulated as follows, as the effectiveness of the universal requires that the universal be tied to an individual, participation in the universal by other individuals requires that all these individuals adhere to a theory of mediation between individual and universal. One crucial element of such a theory is that it imposes a distance between the universal and the individual who happens to represent the universal, and that is precisely what Rousseau's direct democracy lacks.

II. Rejection of Universal Suffrage

In his *Philosophy of Right,* Hegel rejects universal suffrage as a satisfactory mediation between the universal and the individual. The abstract reason for this rejection is that the individual remains an individual even when performing this act of universal significance, i.e., casting his vote.

Hegel's abstract argument can be supported by two more concrete arguments. First, universal suffrage must be inefficient in large countries, since the influence of the individual performing the act by which the universal is determined remains an individual. Thus, the act pertaining to the universal, e.g., voting, must have meaning for the individual who performs this act. This is clearly not the case in universal suffrage in large countries. The act of casting one's vote is likely to makes no difference in the outcome of large elections. Indeed, one's vote makes a difference only if all the other votes end up in a tie. Thus, an individual might be rational in not going to the ballot box.[12]

Second, universal suffrage does not guarantee proportional representation of the different spheres of interests in parliament. Thus, participating in universal suffrage might legitimize a parliament – the instrument of the universal – which does not fairly represent the different spheres of interests. Universal suffrage is thereby reduced to a formal ritual that produces a formal legitimation of the universal without guaranteeing that the universal is tied to the individual as an individual. Such a universal is, for Hegel, a farce, and such a legitimacy is but an abstract legitimacy.

Thus, Hegel's rejection of universal suffrage rests, first, on his insistence that the individual have an effective and guaranteed interest in participating in the universal, and, second, on his further insistence that any arrangement which is not able to guarantee that, structurally, the interests of all individuals will be fairly considered is unacceptable.

The Rousseau-ian governmental theory is rejected because it forgets that the universal agent is an individual, and thus, excludes other individuals. Universal suffrage is rejected because even the voting citizen remains an individual and might find it in his interest as a individual not to participate in the universal or, worse, to sell his vote. Therefore, the universal becomes a farce.

---

[12] *PR,* comment to # 311, 202–203. This passage in Hegel has drawn enthusiastic attention from public choice theoreticians (Buchanan 1974, 99–101).

III. Hegel's Own Solution

Hegel's solution must be built on mediation, since his rejection of other solutions rests upon their lack of mediation between individual and universal
so that the individual who incarnates the universal leaves no place for other
individuals, this danger becomes obvious when this individual takes care
of his own interests under the cloak of the universal. The second danger is
that the individual is given such an insignificant participation in the universal that the individual does not bother to participate, and he, thereby,
becomes a mere individual and the universal an empty universal. Hegel's
solution – even if it may not be acceptable for practical or theoretical reasons – addresses both problems.

A. The Individual Representing the Universal

In his political theory, Hegel makes sure that he does not restrict the benefits of the universal to one individual. He does so by limiting the function
of the individual representing the universal. Indeed, the king is almost a
figurehead, someone who is allowed to put the dots on the "i's" (Ibid., addition to # 280, 289).

Furthermore, Hegel subscribes to the theory of separation of powers.
He would divide the functions of the state between the legislature, the executive, and the crown (Ibid.,# 273). This is an institutional guarantee
against total identification of one individual with the universal.

Third, the executive itself is restricted by the imposition upon government employees of a hierarchal structure of answerability and, more im-
portantly, by the barriers erected to protect lower societal units, e.g., corporations, associations, from interference by the executive (Ibid., # 295).

Fourth, the legislature, too, is restricted and made answerable. Indeed,
the legislature is to be composed of representatives of the different estates
(the word used by Hegel for interest group being "estates") (Ibid., ## 301–
302). These representatives must mediate the interests of their interest
group with the representatives of other interest groups.

Finally, Hegel restricts even the domain of the universal itself, i.e. the
rights of the state. This restriction occurs in two directions. First, it occurs
by the affirmation that the state is transcended by art, religion, and philosophy. These are all values which require freedom of thought and ex-

pression for the individual.[13] A second restriction of the state occurs in the objective domain of spirit itself. Hegel remarks that the freedom of the individual within the state is ultimately not guaranteed institutionally if the economic order[14] does not contain economic centers of decisions independent of the state. Thus, a form of free market economy is here seen to be the long-term institutional guarantor of the freedom of the individual.[15]

B. The Universal Made Available to the Individual

Hegel defends a second form of mediation between the individual and the universal. This second argument is built upon Hegel's insight that the universal can be reached in degrees. Reaching the universal is for the individual not an all or nothing proposition. The economic order is credited by Hegel for providing several levels of universality to an individual. The economic order creates the possibility of reaching a minimal form of universality to those individuals who do not participate directly in the universality of the state. Furthermore, the economic order educates all participating individuals in the direction of universality, as will be seen in the analysis of the different levels of universality offered by the economic order.

The first and best-known form of universality connected with the economic order is the universality that an individual gives himself through his work. This idea is already present in the *Phenomenology's* analysis of the slave and stoicism. The universality produced in work is a dual one. It is the objectivity of the result of my work – remember Horace saying about his poems, *"Exegi monumentum aere perennius."*[16] It is also the objectiv-

---

[13] This kind of limitation of the function of the state is made quite explicitly in Hegel's *Encyclopedia,* where the state is said to be transcended by absolute Spirit, which includes art, religion, and philosophy.

[14] Hegel's term is "civil society" and, thus, suggests that the economic order includes, besides contractual exchanges, also institutional arrangements. In this chapter I will continue to use the expression "economic order" where Hegel uses the term "civil society" because the weight of my analysis consists in understanding what the specific contribution of the economic order is for Hegel's theory of modern freedom.

[15] "If the state is represented as a unity of different persons ... then what is really meant is only civil society ... In civil society each member is his own end, everything else is nothing to him" (addition to #182). See also Hegel's criticism of Plato's conception of the state in #185.

[16] "I erected a monument that is more durable than bronze" (Horace, Carm. 3, 30, 1). The monument to which Horace is referring is his poetry. This aspect of work is referred to in Hegel (Hegel 1967 c, 238; See also, Smith, 14).

ity of the skills connected with producing these works (poems made Horace a poet for the Roman community) (*PR*, ## 187 & 197).

The second form of universality offered by the economic order is the one achieved by an individual when he participates, through his labor, in the system of social needs (*PR*, # 182). Thus, in order to satisfy his own needs, he is willing to produce what is demanded by others. This idea comes from the economists of Hegel's time. Among economists it is often referred to as the theory of "the invisible hand" (Smith 1937, 423). Again, there are two aspects to this form of universality. The first is *the guaranteed production* of those goods that are demanded by the individuals.[17] The second is the willingness of the individual to choose a kind of work, to acquire a skill that is socially demanded. Thus, the individual ties himself actively to, or accepts passively, that he is tied to the vicissitudes of the economic order (Ibid., # 200).

The third form of universality offered by the economic order is the one which results from the insertion of the individual into a subgroup of the economic order. Hegel discovers this form of universality in different places. He discovers it when he talks about professional groupings, corporations, and pressure groups.[18] He naturally talks about them in his own terminology, but this does not alter the substance of the argument.

A professional group, a corporation, or a pressure group provides *an individual universal* that an individual can identify with and work for (*PR* ## 206, 207, and additions to ## 201, 206, 207). In the case of professional groups, Hegel distinguishes between the agricultural, commercial, and bureaucratic professions. Each has its own difficulties, rewards, aspirations, and virtues. It is the acquisition of the special skills and virtues needed to overcome the difficulties related to the individual profession which is the measuring rod of social recognition. It is the capability of the individual to *be content with the recognition and rewards* of the chosen profession which transforms the individual into a universal. Instead of Mister X, one is now either a farmer, merchant, or government official.

A similar argument is developed by Hegel for the case of an individual willing and capable of identifying with his corporation or union. Indeed, Hegel talks about the place where one earns one's income, and about the guild (*PR* ## 251, 253, and addition to # 255)

---

[17] Ibid., # 199, the idea of a "universal permanent capital."

[18] The words used by Hegel are, *"Korporation"* and *"Stand."* For an analysis of the function of the corporation in Hegel's system, see Smith 1989, 140 ff.

C. The Transition from Economics to the State

The previous forms of universality present cases where the individual inserts himself into the universal. Hegel also mentions, however, two cases where the universal is imposed upon the individual, yet the imposition is justified, not by the requirement of the universal but by the self-interest of the individual. These two cases are the judicial system and the police.

The individual in the economic order has the will to acquire the goods he needs through his participation in the economic order. This requires the protection of the goods he acquires against claims of others. This is what the judicial system does (Ibid., ## 209, 230).

The term "police" has for Hegel a broader meaning than it has today. Hegel's definition covers law enforcement, the production of public goods, and the provision of welfare and could thus be well translated as "public authority." The general argument used by Hegel is that some acts of individuals have influence upon other individuals. This can be good or bad. The police have a right and duty to restrain individual acts which harm other individuals too much, intentionally or accidentally. The exact delineation of legitimate police interference is a matter that cannot be determined philosophically, according to Hegel.

Similarly, those goods that benefit many individuals or that are necessary for the private activity of individuals should be made available whether or not individuals have a private incentive to provide them. If private incentive is failing, the police should provide it, according to Hegel (*PR* addition to # 236). This argument is similar to the justification provided by economists for governmental provision of public goods (Samuelson 1955).[19]

---

[19] The problem of public goods as it relates to Hegel is taken up in chapter 3; and as it relates to the science of economic, it is taken up in chapter 6.

Conclusion

The economic order provides Hegel[20] an opportunity to find a solution to the political problem of reconciling the individual with the universal, without having to adhere to utopian political ideals.[21] The full articulation of that solution will require an in-depth analysis of the structural arguments offered in the *Philosophy of Right*, from which I borrowed the ideas to sketch the Hegelian solution. This is the purpose of the next chapter.

---

[20] An economist, David Levine, credits Hegel as being the first to reflect systematically on the idea that economics is a "separate and notable realm" in society (Levine 1995, 12).

[21] One should notice that Rousseau's ideas are more complex than Hegel makes us believe. Indeed, Rousseau allows for a legislator—a man of genius—who is able to see what is in the public interest and who, also, is able to suppress his own self-interests. But as Lionel Gossman argues (Gossman 1961), Rousseau involves himself in a contradiction. He holds that, on the one hand, the people have the fundamental right to legislate by enacting the laws proposed by the legislator. On the other hand, the legislator was needed because Rousseau believes that the people—a blind multitude—were unable to discern what is best for the public interest. How is this ignorance lifted by the legislator? Thus, Hegel's basic objection to Rousseau remains valid. (This note was suggested by W. Desan and R. Parise).

Section II

Hegel and Political Economy

3. The Ethical Function of the Economy

Abstract

Hegel tried to understand the new economic order that had emerged after the feudal, the mercantilist, and the physiocratic systems. That new order became known as the free-market economy. Helped by his reading of the Scottish economists, Hegel demonstrated a sophisticated understanding of the connection between the new economic order and the aspirations to freedom in the Western tradition.[22]

The question as to what the relation is between economics and freedom focuses on the most relevant philosophical question one could ask about Hegel's understanding of the economy. Hegel understood history as the attempt to create the institutions that can protect and provide freedom for people living together as bodily subjects—that is, as subjects who have a consciousness, but also, as subjects who have humble needs imposed by the fact that their consciousness is embodied. Hegel's most extensive and systematic treatment of the economic order is presented in his *Philosophy of Right*. Hegel calls a right the objective realization of freedom (Hegel 1967 a, # 29). By including his discussion of the economic order as a major section in the *Philosophy of Right*, it is legitimate to suppose that Hegel

---

[22] Some publications that elucidate the depth and sophistication of Hegel's analysis of the new economic order are, Angehrn 1977, 226-240; Avineri 1974, esp. chs.5, 7; Chamley 1963; Cullen 1979; Denis 1984, 7–36, 51–90, 153–162; Dubouchet 1995; Dudley 1997, 47–59; Fleischmann 1964, 207–254; Harada 1989, 110–167; Hardimon 1994, 189–205; Henrich & Horstmann 1982, 132–138 ; Jarczyk & Labarrière 1986, esp. 229–246; Jermann 1987, 166–182; Kainz 1974, 32–43; Kraus 1931/1932, 9–34; Lucas & Pöggeler 1986, 149–174; Lukacs 1973, chs.2:5 and 3:5,6,7; Maker 1987; Marx 1977, esp. intro.,ix–lxiii; Pelczynski 1984; Priddat 1990; Reyburn 1967, 214–225; Riedel 1975, esp. Vol. II, 247–337; Roth 1989, 144–183, 221–223, 257–259; Smith 1989 esp.140–145; Steinberger 1988, 199–203, 232–34; Waszek 1988, 142–228; Whitebook 1978, 136–205 ; Winfield 1988, esp. chs 12–14; Winfield 1990, esp. Part II; Wood 1990, 237–255. In his classic *History of Economic Analysis*, Schumpeter refers seven times to Hegel, including four pages where he describes German philosophy as part of the intellectual scenery for the crucial period in the development of economic thought from 1790 to 1870 (411–415). Ludwig von Mises, on the other hand, belittles Hegel for his "dialectic mysticism" and for inspiring the Marx and his mistaken doctrine (Mises 1963, 74).

wanted to analyze the economic order (the free market) as an embodiment of freedom.[23] In this chapter I will first analyze Hegel's concept of freedom. Second, I will present Hegel's arguments that can be construed as being in favor of the free market. Finally, I will study what Hegel sees as the proper relation between the state and the free market.

I. Hegel's Concept of Freedom

Typical of Hegel's treatment of freedom is his determination to see it as concrete and positive.[24]   By trying to define freedom in this way, Hegel discovers a paradox. Freedom is free will. Human will, however, is the will of a self-consciousness. Hegel defined a self-consciousness in his *Phenomenology of Mind* as follows:

> Self-consciousness is primarily simple existence for self, self-identity by exclusion of every other from itself...That which for it is other stands as unessential object, as object with the impress and character of negation. (Hegel 1967 c, 231)

The idea that the will of a self-consciousness is negativity because it is exclusion of anything objective is repeated in the introduction to the *Philosophy of Right*. There, Hegel gives several descriptions of this aspect of the will. He writes, "the will contains the element of pure indeterminacy or that pure reflection of the ego into itself." In more concrete terms, Hegel writes that this pure indeterminacy means "the dissipation of every restriction and every content either immediately presented by nature, by needs, drives, and impulses, or given and determined by any means whatever." In the same place Hegel describes this aspect of the will more abstractly as "the unrestricted infinity of absolute abstraction or universality, the pure thought of oneself" (*PR*, # 5).

This aspect of the will is responsible for the misidentification of freedom as negative freedom, and for the misguided feeling that acts of destruction are means to affirm the self (Ibid., # 5 remark).

However, a will that restricts itself to the moment of negation, dissipation, or indeterminacy, lacks the moment of self-determination. The will must therefore be "the dissipation of restriction" and "the positing of a determinacy as a content and object" (Ibid., # 6). This is the paradox of the

---

[23] Hegel talks about more than economics since he uses the term "*bürgerliche Gesellschaft*," translated into English as "civil society."
[24] For a book-length treatment of this problem, see Seeberger 1961.

will and freedom. Hegel tries to find a solution for this paradox by searching for an object of the will that is, at the same time, also the dissipation of the restriction of the will. Such a will Hegel would call a will that determines itself (Ibid., # 7 remark). To find such a will, Hegel analyzes different types of wills, and demonstrates their deficiency. Thus, he analyzes the immediate or natural will, the arbitrary will, and the eudaemonic will.

The immediate or natural will is a will that accepts as object immediately existing things such as impulses, desires, and inclinations. The practical problem with this kind of will is that it has before itself a "multiplicity of impulses, each of which...exists alongside other desires...and each of which is...aimed at all kinds of objects and satiable in all kinds of ways" (Ibid., # 12). The philosophic problem with this will, according to Hegel, is that it is not a will that wills itself as he sees the ideal will. This natural will accepts something other than itself (its impulses and drives) as its object. It thereby calls them "its impulses, its desires," but this relation hides the fact that there is no obvious rationality (or necessity) in accepting particular impulses or desires as objects of the will.

That lack of necessity is obvious in the fact that some desires are accepted and acceptable, whereas others are not accepted, and might not be acceptable. One might wish to have a drink or an airplane, or one might wish to kick someone. The natural or immediate will cannot distinguish between the rational acceptability of these different wishes because it accepts impulses, desires, and inclinations immediately[25] as motive for the will.

The arbitrary will[26] realizes the problem faced by the immediate will and overcomes these problems inasmuch as it accepts the necessity of the will to *choose and decide.* The will must choose and decide because the natural will faces a twofold indeterminacy; that is, which of the many impulses should be followed, and which object should be chosen to satisfy the chosen impulse. However, the freedom achieved by an arbitrary will is but limited freedom. It is a choice made by the will which maintains its distance from any content it decides to will. It wills a particular content

---

[25] In his philosophy, Hegel demonstrates that a solution to a problem using an immediate given will always be defective. A true solution will need to be mediated. That mediation will always involve a dialogue with what Hegel calls the universal. Hence, Hegel proceeds to show the deficiencies of the immediate will.

[26] The arbitrary will is the will which accepts that a proper will has to accept the duty that it must decide. It is called an arbitrary will because such a will does not yet require that its decisions must also be guided by principles. I found an example of such a will in the testimony of a successful businessman answering my question during a cocktail party as to what the most important characteristic was of a successful businessman. He answered: "A successful businessman must be able to make decisions. He can be wrong, but he cannot not decide, because otherwise thousands of people do not know what to do."

with the proviso that it could have refused to will this particular content because as arbitrary will it has the absolute right to decide what it alone wants to decide.

The object of an arbitrary will has so little necessity that Hegel can point to two contradictory positions in the history of thought concerning the proper relation between the will and, for instance, the impulses of human nature. One tradition holds that the impulses of human nature are ontologically good, and that corruption of human nature is the result of social influences. Within that tradition, an argument can be made that a human being should follow his *natural* impulses. This tradition was exemplified by Rousseau. Another tradition holds that the impulses of human nature are ontologically bad. In that tradition, an argument is made that a human being should distance himself from his natural impulses. These impulses should be controlled, educated, refined, or sublimated. The ontological view of this tradition's understanding of human nature is expressed by the concept of original sin.

Hegel's reference to the history of thought, thus, makes the point that the arbitrary will has respectable arguments for two contradictory attitudes towards possible objects of its will. The arbitrary will can only, therefore, be arbitrary; it has no full mastery of itself in the selection of an object of its volition (Ibid., # 18). However, there is progress in the transition from natural will to arbitrary will. The arbitrary will knows the truth about the natural will. Indeed, the natural will thought that it could describe its action as follows: follow your desires, your impulses. Actually, the natural will could not just follow its impulses; it has to choose between different impulses; it has to choose between different objects that could satisfy the chosen impulse. Thus, the natural will did more than it thought it was doing. Without thinking that it has to do so, the natural will has to choose. The arbitrary will knows it has to choose; it even conceives choice as its essence and its privilege.

The arbitrary will, however, has its own limitation that is addressed by the eudaemonic will. The eudaemonic will is one that must decide, one that must choose. However, this will knows that it cannot just decide on arbitrary grounds. Whatever the shortcomings of the criterion of happiness, the eudaemonic will accepts that it needs a criterion to decide, and that it needs to think constantly about how a particular object relates to the general criterion. Thus, the eudaemonic will introduces *thought* as a crucial dimension for the freedom of the will. Furthermore, the successful influence of thought on the decision-making process of the will requires an emotional maturation process. Hegel is aware of this requirement when he mentions that the eudaemonic will implies purification of the impulses. This concept of purification also allows us to see how the eudaemonic will synthesizes the contradictory extremes into which the arbitrary will can develop. The arbitrary will can accept impulses as good, or can reject them as bad. The eudaemonic will does both by accepting the impulses *after* their purification. As purified, the impulses are thus considered good. Yet the impulses are seen to be in need of purification; without this purification, the impulses are seen as bad.

However free the eudaemonic will may be, it is not fully free because its purpose is a subjective experience – that is, a personal experience of happiness. Indeed, the experience of feeling happy is an event that is willed by the eudaemonic will as a result of its acts. But the will cannot guarantee this result; it can only hope that the feelings of happiness will accompany, or follow, the acts of the will.[27] Thus, the eudaemonic will wants something that is not in its power to will. Such a will makes itself, by definition, a dependent will rather than an autonomous will.

There is, however, an essential truth in the eudaemonic will. The eudaemonic will wants to think the relation between, on the one hand, a concrete object of the will, and, on the other hand, the universal that is the proper object of the will. The eudaemonic will, however, takes as point of comparison not a real universal but a contingent universal – i.e., happiness. The solution to the limitation of freedom of the eudaemonic will is for a human being to create his existence by means of thought in order to be able to present to the will a real universal.

The history of philosophy is in agreement with this general line of Hegel's thinking. To be free requires that the will be given the proper object. This proper object has been identified, among others, as the unmoved mover, the Platonic ideas, happiness, or the contemplation of God. In each case identification of the proper object of the will requires thought. Thus, we should have no great difficulty in understanding and accepting Hegel's crucial thesis about the will and its relation to thinking: "it becomes clear that it is only as thinking intelligence that the will is genuinely a will and free" (*PR*, # 21 remark). Or, "true liberty ... consists in the will finding its purpose in a universal content, not in subjective or selfish interest. But such a content is only possible in thought and through thought" (*PM*, # 469).

Typical for Hegel, and thus less self-evident, is what he thinks thought must present as the true object of the will. For him, the proper object of

---

[27] In the *Philosophy of Mind*, Hegel formulates this as follows: "Happiness is ... that which only ought to be"(# 480). The implication is that what ought to be does not necessarily realize itself. Also, Hegel calls happiness a feeling (Ibid., # 479). And he defines feelings as contingent (*zufällig*) (e.g., ibid., # 447 and # 471). (Hegel's *Philosophy of Mind* is subsequently cited as *PM* followed by paragraph numbers.)

the will is none of the objects mentioned above. It is, rather, the absolute universal, the rational (*PR*, # 24 remark). Or, it is the "principle of right, morality and all ethical life" (Ibid., # 21 remark). What Hegel, therefore, has in mind as the proper object of the will is not something outer-worldly but rather some form of being-in-the-world.

But how can we understand that the will is free if it has as its object "the principle of right, morality and ethical life"? We can find help in another quotation from Hegel:

> The absolute goal, or, the absolute impulse, of free mind is to make its freedom its object, i.e., to make freedom objective as much in the sense that freedom shall be the rational system of mind, as in the sense that freedom shall be the world of its immediate actuality. In making freedom its object mind's purpose is to be explicitly, as idea, what the will is implicitly. The definition of the concept of the will in abstraction from the Idea of the will is 'the free will which wills the free will.' (Ibid., #27 remark)

The proper object of the will is, thus, to will freedom to be objective. More specifically, the proper role of the will is to will the embodiment of freedom. But in human society we find many forms of embodiments of freedom, including the constitution, prisons that protect us from criminals, and life-long tenure for judges and academics. Clearly, this enumeration is not complete and does not pretend to have a logic in its ordering. Hegel helps us by giving his own ordered enumeration. He orders all embodiments of freedom under three headings – the principle of right, morality, and ethical life – thereby reaffirming the enterprise of the *Philosophy of Right*. In that book, he writes, "An existent of any sort embodying free will, this is what right is" (Ibid., # 29). Thus, the *Philosophy of Right* is not just about the philosophy of law, it is about *rights.* In it, Hegel discusses abstract right, morality, and ethics; these are precisely the three embodiments of freedom that he also enumerates as the proper object of the free will. His claim that the proper object of free will is the principle of right, morality, and ethical life is thus backed by the structure of the whole book. Let us now analyze in what specific sense the will must will these objects so as to be free.

One finds a somewhat difficult summary defense of this thesis at the end of the introduction to the *Philosophy of Right* (Ibid., # 33). There, abstract right is presented as the expression of the immediate will, morality as the expression of a will reflected into itself, and ethics as the synthesis of these two important expressions of the will. Like many of Hegel's dense statements, this one does not help us very much either, except that from it we can see that Hegel might claim some form of dialectical completeness in his list of objects of the free will.

Abstract right is the immediate relation of the will to external things. It has its origin in a basic assumption of Hegel's philosophy: that the truth of subjectivity is *Entäusserung* (going outside itself). This Hegelian principle has its metaphysical roots in Hegel's understanding of history as the self-realization of the Trinity. In his vision, even God must come out of himself into history in order to realize himself. That principle can also be given a more easily accessible explanation: a subject can have many aspirations. Aspirations, however, are just aspirations. They need to be *realized* in order to become something more. Abstract right deals with the problems related to the first externalization of free will: property. In property, says Hegel, my free will becomes an object to my self (Ibid., ## 45–46). In willing abstract right, I therefore will property, which in turn means that I will the externalization of my freedom. This becomes obvious in contracts, which are an implication of property rights. In a contract, two parties demonstrate their power or their freedom over things in that they can decide, or refuse to decide, to exchange specific objects – for example, a house for two hundred thousand dollars. If the decision is positive, then a new owner moves into the house. He might like new wallpaper, even a new kitchen. If the decision is negative, the house might remain as it has been for several years. The seller, in selling his house, must accept the freedom of the buyer to change the house as he sees fit.

However, abstract right is but the realization of a limited form of freedom. Indeed, the right to property cannot be fully guaranteed. Criminals can steal, maim, and kill. Revenge is possible, but it is only a meager form of help. Indeed, revenge cannot always return what was taken, or undo what was done. Furthermore, revenge is a private act and, as such, it is wrong (Ibid., # 102).[28] Crime and revenge reveal the shortcomings of abstract right. The possibility of crime shows that abstract right does not take full account of particularity. Particularity then emerges as crime. The restoration of the universal by means of revenge in turn is deficient. Indeed, it is one person making another person respect the universal by imposing a privately determined punishment. What is lacking in abstract right is a proper relation between the universal and the particular. The person seeking revenge and the criminals are both antagonists. The former claims that

---

[28] A private act of revenge is not marked by the limits required by what Hegel calls the universal. In this case the universal requires that justice be restored. From the injured party it requires, among others, that they be satisfied with proportional punishment (the theft of a cow does not justify murdering the whole village of the thief). From the injuring party it requires that they can see the punishment as restitution of justice rather than as devious enrichment by the injured party. Dealing justly with crime will thus require that both the injured and the injuring party can move away from the private position of looking to private gains. Hegel points out that this came about historically if a community was able to introduce effectively the figure of the judge in order to deal with crimes.

abstract right provides the right to punish the criminal. But, the criminal does not recognize the right of abstract right. The solution can only come from a personal recognition of what abstract right stands for. In other words, the solution can only come in a recognition that the universal has a claim upon the individual or, again, that the fight emanating from abstract right becomes a right recognized by individuals (Ibid., # 104, and 332–334 translator's notes). Hegel sees this process as brought about by the labor of the individual. This labor he calls reflection.[29] An individual with such a commitment to the universal Hegel calls a (moral) subject.[30]

Morality is a higher form of freedom than the freedom embodied in property rights.[31] It is a higher form of freedom because property rights require an external enforcement (punishment, revenge) whereas morality is a commitment by the individual himself or, as Hegel says, morality is a "self-determination" (Ibid., # 104 and # 107). Hegel clarifies the difficult characterization of morality in his introduction to the *Philosophy of Right.* Morality is described there as the will, "reflected from its external embodiment into itself" (Ibid., # 33). We now understand this to mean that morality, compared with abstract right (this being an external embodiment of freedom as Hegel characterizes, for instance, property rights), involves an act of the individual that abstract right does not require – that is, a personal commitment to something (the good) that transcends the individual, rather than simply taking, using, and enjoying a transcendent object (property). Because the essence of morality is a personal commitment, or as the translator of the *Philosophy of Right,* T. M. Knox, calls it, "inner conviction," (Ibid., # 334 translator's notes) the moral point of view can be called a reflection of the will upon itself. It is this moment requiring an act of commitment from the will that Hegel calls *subjectivity.* He writes that it establishes the (free) will "as explicitly identical with the principle of the will"(Ibid., # 106, # 108 remark). Whatever the relation is between freedom and economics, we will therefore have to remind ourselves that the self determination of the will, the principle of subjectivity, will have to be respected in economics if the form of freedom reached in the moral point of view is not to be undone.[32]

---

[29] "reflected from" (Ibid., # 33); "as reflected in upon itself and self-identical"(Ibid., # 104, remark, # 105; *PM,* # 503).

[30] *PR,* # 33; "subjective individuality"; the identity between the moral point of view and subjectivity is stressed both in the main text and in the remark (Ibid., ## 104–5; *PM,* # 503).

[31] *PR,* # 106; ibid., # 33 and # 104 remark; see also Knox's comment in the translator's notes, 334.

[32] This idea has been defended also by some important economists such as Smith, Hayek, Mises and Friedman.

Even though Hegel stresses that morality is a higher point of view than that of the legal order, he states, as well, that the moral point of view is a one-sided view of the will. The one-sidedness derives from the fact that it requires a commitment of the individual to the good as that individual sees it (Ibid., ## 131–132). Such a point of view allows an individual to be wrong in what she thinks to be the good. In order to avoid this pitfall, Hegel claims, very logically, that the moral point of view needs guidance, and that guidance is provided by ethical institutions. These institutions require subjective commitments just as the moral point of view does. A subjective commitment to an ethical institution is, however, more than a mere moral commitment – it is a subjective commitment to institutional arrangements. The good to which one commits oneself is thus specified, but the specifications of ethical life have changed over time. In the *Phenomenology,* Hegel analyzes the specification of ethical life in Greece, in the Roman Empire, during the time of Charlemagne, that of Louis XIV, and the period around the French Revolution (Hegel 1967 c, 455–679). The family and the state are already recognized as ethical institutions in Greek antiquity. In his analysis of the culture of Charlemagne and Louis XIV, Hegel discovers economics as a crucial variable that plays havoc with the self-understanding of political figures. In his *Philosophy of Right,* Hegel gives a dialectical argument for all three ethical institutions – the family, the economic order, and the state (*PR*, # 33 and # 157).

To better understand Hegel's argument for his three ethical institutions, let us ponder once more what ethical life is for him. Hegel claims that ethical life is a union of objective customs, laws, or institutions, and individuals who see in these objective customs, laws, or institutions, the realization of their own essence (Ibid., ## 141–142, translator's notes 319; *PM*, # 514). Hegel's argument for his three ethical institutions, therefore, needs to demonstrate that each one of them is in some sense a self-realization of the individual. In the first ethical institution, the family, an individual realizes him or herself in an immediate way. Through the feeling of love and the unity created in marriage, the basis for the family, an individual finds purpose in her own life (*PR*, # 158). In the second institution, the economic order, the individual is left to herself to work for the satisfaction of her own needs. This private economic activity, though, is part of a whole that generally realizes itself without conscious attention by any particular individual. It is the whole (the GNP, or the gross national product, in modern terminology) which is the guarantee for the satisfaction of one's needs. Thus, obtaining a legitimate share of the GNP becomes one's purpose, given that one knows oneself to have needs and desires.

Given that the economic order realizes a unity that is not aimed at consciously, it is evident that the economic order will experience contingent developments that might be desirable or that might be undesirable. An economic subject is therefore not a fully autonomous subject. That full autonomy becomes possible only in the third ethical institution, the state (Ibid., ## 257–258, 260). Indeed, it is within the state that a human being discusses, agrees, and consciously realizes the rules by which he wants to organize his life in a community of human beings. These rules will have to promote the two other ethical institutions, the family and the economic order.

In this section of his book, Hegel teaches us that there is a systematic connection between freedom and economics. This connection can be formulated as follows: freedom is ultimately realized by the individual's insertion into the ethical institutions. One of these ethical institutions is the economic domain.

We also hit upon an idea that promises to be crucial when we have to determine, not whether the economic domain has a relation with freedom, but what kind of economic order is dictated by its relation to freedom. The idea is the following: the connection between freedom and the economic order is that freedom is realized in ethical institutions of which the economic domain is one. Furthermore, ethical institutions are the realization of freedom because of the deficiency of the moral point of view. Nevertheless, the moral point of view is an essential element of ethical life. One thing typical of the moral life preserved in the ethical world is the principle of subjectivity: the fact that the will wills itself as doing the good. This willing of itself according to Hegel is "the real aspect of the concept of freedom" (Ibid., # 106 remark). If this principle is applied to the ethical institution of the economic order, we must presuppose that the free market is the appropriate ordering of the economic order because it is an ordering that allows individuals to decide as they please. In the next section of this chapter, I will look for specific Hegelian arguments to demonstrate this thesis. One should notice, however, that the principle of subjectivity includes the intent of doing the good. The economic order must therefore intend to achieve the common good that it is supposed to achieve. Hegel will use this aspect of the principle of subjectivity to articulate an appropriate relation between economics and the state as he sees it. This will be the subject of the third, and last, section of this chapter. I now turn to arguments found in Hegel's writings which can be construed as demanding some form of free market economic system.

II. Hegel's Arguments in Favor of a Free Market

Hegel offers five different arguments that can be used to defend the free market as opposed to an economic system that would be fully subordinate to the political order. Hegel's first argument derives from his view of the economic order as an ethical system. As such, the economic order must incorporate the basic principle of morality as he understands it; that is, subjectivity, or free, self-determination. His second argument relates to his thought that the achievement of modern times was the recognition of the principle of subjectivity. In philosophy, that principle was introduced by Descartes. In religion, Luther introduced the same principle. The introduction of that same principle in economics, according to Hegel, accounts for the success of the new economic order. Hegel takes this success to be a proof for the truth of the principle of subjectivity. His third argument in favor of the free market derives from his understanding of the nature of labor. Hegel believes that there is an alienating dimension in labor. He believes that only free labor permits consciousness to give meaning to the alienating aspect of labor. His fourth argument is based on his hope that the free market, combined with a constitutional monarchy, might be able to provide a happy structural equilibrium for modern human beings who are torn between the contradictory requirements of self-interest and civic duty. His fifth argument is related to his correctly having perceived a problem between the rights of the state and the moral demands of the citizen. I will argue that dealing with this problem introduces a new argument for the free market. Let us develop these arguments separately.

The economic order is not, for Hegel, a morally neutral order: it is an ethical institution. It is not a natural system, as Adam Smith argued in his classic statement, "All systems of preference or of restraint, therefore, being thus completely taken away, the obvious and simple system of natural liberty establishes itself of its own accord."[33]

Hegel's understanding of the economic order as an ethical institution commits him to making a requirement that he must make of any ethical institution: each of the ethical institutions must realize the essential truth of the moral life that it is supposed to supplement. The truth of moral life is that the will intends to transcend its particularity and intends, instead, to do what is good. The right is that it be judged according to the knowledge and understanding it had of the worthiness or evil character of its deed. The moral will is thus a will that has the right to act as it thinks it must act.

---

[33] In the next chapter, I explicitly I argue against this ontology of the economic order using the writings of a group of economists such as Walter Eucken, Friedrich A. Hayek, and Henry C. Simons. See also Briefs 1957 a; Briefs 1983, 271–299.

The moral will is a self-determining will, which is what the modern principle of subjectivity is about (*PR*, ## 104, 132, 152).

The truth of the moral life – that is, the right to self-determination, combined with the duty to do the good – indeed, is given a crucial role by Hegel in determining the righteousness of marriage as "the free consent of persons ... to make themselves one person" (Ibid., # 162). In a more rhetorical passage, Hegel even calls it "the free surrender by both" (Ibid., # 168).

Similarly, Hegel defines the ethical character of the state by the dual aspect of free consent and free consent to a perceived transcendent good. Thus he writes:

> The state is the actuality of concrete freedom. But concrete freedom consists in this, that personal individuality and its particular interests not only achieve their complete development and gain explicit recognition for their right ... but, for one thing, they also pass over of their own accord into the interest of the universal, and, for another thing, they know and will their universal; they even recognize it as their own substantive mind; they take it as their end and aim and are active in its pursuit. (Ibid., # 260)

In the same way, Hegel argues that for the economic order to be an ethical institution, it must respect the principle of subjectivity. However, the economic order, organized as a free market, permits its members to will consciously only one of two requirements of subjectivity. Indeed, "homo economicus" is permitted to will only his interest; as Adam Smith wrote:

> Every man, as long as he does not violate the laws of justice, is left perfectly free to pursue his own interest in his own way, and to bring both his industry and capital into competition with those of any other man, or order of men. (Smith, 651)

The other principle of subjectivity, that the individual wills freely something of universal value, is only guaranteed indirectly. Again, let us quote Smith:

> He [every individual] generally, indeed, neither intends to promote the public interest, nor knows how much he is promoting it ... and by directing that industry in such a manner as its produce may be of the greatest value, he intends only his own aim, and he is in this, as in many other cases, led by an invisible hand to promote an end which was no part of his intention .... By pursuing his own interest he frequently promotes that of the society more effectively than when he really intends to promote it. (Ibid., 423)

Thus, the common good, or the universal value connected with economic activity, is only achieved by "an invisible hand." It is not willed consciously. Because of this, Hegel agrees that the economic order gives the impression of being "the disappearance of ethical life" (*PR*, # 181; *PM*, # 23). But Hegel corrects this impression by arguing that the economic order is not the essence of ethical life, but its *appearance* (*PR*, # 181). And from Hegel's logic, we know that the moment of appearance is a necessary moment (Hegel 1873: # 131, also # 112). We now come to the crucial aspect of the first argument for the free market. That aspect can be expressed in the form of a question. In what sense can we argue that the free market is a necessary moment in the system of ethical institutions, given that it is but the appearance of ethical life, not ethical life itself? Hegel's answer to this question is that the economic order educates individuals towards the full principle of subjectivity (*PR*, # 187). Indeed, the economic order allows everybody to follow his own interests, but if the economic subjects want to acquire the goods they wish to have, they must earn the right to claim such goods. The only way that the economic order can provide such claims is if one provides goods or services that others are willing to buy. Thus, economic subjects become interdependent (Ibid., # 183). This interdependence is not something these economic subjects are at liberty to accept or reject, because a human being is a bodily subject and, as such, needs goods and services for his survival.[34] The economic order as a free market system is thus desirable because it educates the members of the human community towards subjectivity, rather than compelling them to accept economic rules handed down by the political order. Such a compulsion would lack the moment of *free consent* to make the economic order an ethical order for anybody but those who decide upon the rules (Ibid., # 236 remark).

The second argument in favor of the free market is a more historical one.[35] Hegel believes that the modern era has created a society that is radically different from previous societies (Ibid., # 273 remark). It has done so because it has introduced the principle of subjectivity as a basic principle in different domains of human activity (Ibid., # 261 addition). This principle has arrived in economics with the replacement of mercantilism by the free market system. The question that arises from this argument is, "Why could the principle of subjectivity not be introduced into politics?" The political domain can then be seen as having legitimate authority to guide the economy.

---

[34] Thus Hegel can say that there is necessity or compulsion in the economic order (*PR*, # 184 and # 186).

[35] The arguments of this section were developed further in chapter 2 of this book and in Ver Eecke 1975a.

I will answer this question in several steps. First, I will point out that although the principle of subjectivity is respected in the organization of the modern state (otherwise it could not be an ethical institution), Hegel gives an explicit argument as to why the principle of subjectivity cannot be fully tolerated in the political domain. Second, I will give an argument for why the principle of subjectivity should be fully tolerated in the economic domain.

Hegel's idea which most obviously demonstrates that he wants to restrict the principle of subjectivity in the organization of the state is his rejection of popular suffrage.[36]

Let us, however, stress that Hegel's rejection of popular suffrage does not mean that he favors an authoritarian or totalitarian regime. On the contrary, his rejection of universal suffrage is to be understood as the rejection of an institutional arrangement that does not guarantee the representation of all legitimate interests in the decision processes of the state. Again and again, Hegel stresses that the state must recognize and promote the particular interests of the individual, and the values realized by the individual in lower ethical institutions such as the family or the corporation.[37] The sec-

---

[36] The argument merits direct quotation:

> To hold that every single person should share in deliberating and deciding on political matters of general concern on the ground that all individuals are members of the state, that its concerns are their concerns, and that it is their right that what is done should be done with their knowledge and volition, is tantamount to a proposal to put the democratic element without any rational form into the organism of the state, although it is only in virtue of the possession of such a form that the state is an organization at all.... The concrete state is the whole, articulated into its particular groups. The member of a state is a member of such a group, i.e., of a social class, and it is only as characterized in this objective way that he comes under consideration when we are dealing with the state. (*PR*, # 308 remark)

Arguing along the same lines, he writes:

> The idea of free unrestricted election leaves this important consideration entirely at the mercy of chance....As for popular suffrage, it may be further remarked that especially in large states it leads to electoral indifference, since the casting of a single vote is of no significance where there is a multitude of electors. Even if a voting qualification is highly valued and esteemed by those who are entitled to it, they still do not enter the polling booth. Thus the result of an institution of this kind is more likely to be the opposite of what was intended; election actually falls into the power of a few, of a caucus, and so of the particular and contingent interest which is precisely what was to have been neutralized. (Ibid., ## 260–261)

[37] Ibid., # 311 remark. A contemporary economist, James Buchanan, writes about this text that Hegel has a "very clear recognition of the voting problem in its modern meaning.... Hegel stated the problem clearly and recognized its implications for the democratic proc-

ond step we now have to take is to ask ourselves why it is that radical sub-jectivity cannot be tolerated in the political domain. One finds an answer to this question in Hegel's analysis of the French Revolution, which ap-pears in the *Phenomenology* under the title "Absolute Freedom and Ter-ror." It is the last passage in the section titled "Spirit in Self-Estrangement: The Discipline of Culture and Civilization."[38] That passage highlights the attempt by Western civilization to overcome the political alienation that emerges in the legalistic Roman Empire. Hegel saw in the French Revolu-tion and, more specifically, in Rousseau's utopian dream of direct democ-racy, the final attempt to do away with political alienation. Hegel's contri-bution shows the logical necessity of a type of absolute political freedom in the manner of Rousseau and the brutal terror that existed during the reign of Robespierre. Hegel's argument runs as follows: the utopian dream of direct democracy is that everyone can directly participate in the political decisions without the mediation of institutions. The result is that little or nothing can be decided. If the affairs of the state become pressing and a decision has to be made, it is necessary that one individual grasps power. But to grasp power is to be outside the legitimate political order and, thus, to be guilty. To maintain the ideal of direct democracy, the citi-zens are therefore obliged to try to overthrow the government. As long as the ideal of direct democracy prevails, there is no argument to which the government can appeal in order to justify itself or in order to declare the act of those who want to overthrow it illegitimate. Thus, says Hegel, "Be-ing suspected, therefore, takes the place, or has the significance and the ef-fect, of being guilty" (Hegel 1967 c, 606). Or, in other words, as Hegel concludes, "The sole and only work and deed accomplished by universal freedom is therefore death" (Ibid., 605).[39] The analysis of the French

---

ess" (Buchanan 1974, 100). The danger of universal suffrage is that the influence of one vote is negligible. Only if all other votes together create a tie does one's own vote make a difference. Under such circumstances, individual voters would serve their self-interest by selling their votes to powerful entities, such as corporations or rich politicians. According to Hegel, the common good would not be served by such a voting arrangement.

[38] I give here only a summary of the argument with the purpose of understanding how Hegel sees the free market economy as providing a helping hand for solving the philoso-phical problem of contemporary politics. For a more detailed analysis, not referring to the implications for the function of economics in contemporary society, see chapter 2 of this book.

[39] In a society in which, on the one hand, the population believes that the only legitimate form of government is a Rousseau type of direct democracy and in which, on the other hand, a powerful elite understands that direct democracy is too paralyzed to make the nec-essary decisions for the survival of the state it is unavoidable that a conflict will arise be-tween the general population and the powerful elite. According to Hegel, the conflict will take on dramatic proportions because of the prevailing philosophical beliefs. The powerful elite might be able to take decisions that serve the common good and the interests of the

Revolution teaches Hegel the following metaphysical insight: the principle of radical subjectivity in politics is not possible. It invites him to give an ontological reason: in politics, decisions must bind everyone but must ultimately be made by one person – even though many may participate in the decision (Ibid., 604). But political participation, in the form of representative government, for instance, is not the same as deciding by oneself. In the *Philosophy of Right,* Hegel then searches for a method by which political life can correctly incorporate the radical subjectivity which, if implemented without mediation – as in direct democracy – is catastrophic. Hegel's solution is to argue that the state, the universal, "does not prevail or achieve completion except along with particular interests and through the cooperation of particular knowing and willing."[40] These particular interests are achieved in the family and the economic order. Given the crucial nature of this argument, I quote Hegel directly on this matter:

> It is therefore to these ideal spheres [the family and civil society] that the actual Idea assigns the material of this its finite actuality – namely human beings as a mass – in such a way that the function assigned to any given individual is visibly mediated by his circumstances, his caprice, and his personal choice of his station in life. (*PR, # 262*)

It is now the purpose of the state to support and promote the particular interests of the individuals as they are realized in these two institutions (Ibid., ## 289, 261, 264–265). Hegel even calls these institutions "the firm foundation...of the state," (Ibid., # 265) and argues that the strength of the modern state finds its source in the free market, in saying:

> The principle of modern states has prodigious strength and depth because it allows the principle of subjectivity to progress to its culmination in the extremes of self-subsistent personal particularity. (Ibid., # 260)

Summarizing the second argument for the free market, one can state that Hegel demonstrated that radical subjectivity cannot be realized directly in the political domain, even though such a principle is necessary. Its realiza-

---

state and of society. The philosophical beliefs prevailing in society do not take good decisions as a reason for legitimizing a government. Only if all people participate in the decision process is an action by the state considered legitimate. The powerful elite thus knows that they are illegitimate in the eyes of the population. This elite also believes that the prevailing ideology unavoidably leads to societal disasters. The elite thus sees no way to placate an enemy whose ideology it beliefs will destroy the state. According to Hegel, the terror of Robespierre is the unavoidable outcome of the prevailing philosophy during the French Revolution. For a more detailed analysis see: Ver Eecke 1975 a.

[40] *PR, # 260.* The connection between the French Revolution and Hegel's concept of freedom is the object of two important essays (Ritter 1982; Hyppolite 1939, 321–352).

tion can, therefore, be only indirect, that is, in the duty of the state to tolerate and promote other institutions that embody the principle of radical subjectivity – the family and the free market system. The reward for such a
state is that it can count on "the citizen's trust" (Ibid., # 265).

Hegel's third argument that can be used to prefer a free market over a
government-controlled economy is based on his philosophical anthropology, particularly his view of labor. In *Hegel's Theory of the Modern State,*
(section: "Labour Alienation and the Power of the Market," chapter:
"Modern Life and Social Reality"), Avineri places Hegel's anthropological
reflection on labor within the context of the metaphysical question of the
relation between consciousness and nature. At first nature is external –
alien to consciousness. But, because consciousness is "embodied consciousness," this separation between consciousness and nature must be
overcome. It must be overcome because a human being is a needy subject
who requires nature to satisfy his or her needs. A more Hegelian argument
is that consciousness seeks to find recognition of itself in the other (Avineri 1972, 88). Consciousness does that by reducing nature to objects that
are useful for the satisfaction of its needs. Yet, this satisfaction is temporary. It has no permanence beyond the time that the satisfaction of consumption lasts.

Human beings appropriate nature in a more permanent way by the creation of property rights. Through property rights, human beings do not relate to objects for the sole purpose of destroying them for the satisfaction
of needs. Property rights do not destroy objects; they preserve them. In
Hegel's words, property rights allow consciousness to "translate his freedom into an external sphere" (*PR*, # 41), thus "property is...[an] embodiment of freedom" because "I as free will am an object to myself in what I
possess" (Ibid., # 45). The question then arises as to what is legitimate
property. One act that leads to legitimate property is the taking possession
of what belongs to no one (Ibid., ## 50–51). But in contemporary society,
there are few objects that belong to no one. Furthermore, taking possession of an object is connected with all kinds of accidental elements.

It is at this point that Hegel looks at labor to overcome the limitations
evident in the concept of property, and to serve as a permanent bridge between consciousness and nature. Avineri finds an explicit text to support
this thesis in Hegel's *Realphilosophie* (Avineri 1972, 88, quoted from
(Hegel 1967 b, 207)) "[only through labor] is the accidentality of coming
into possession being transcended." Hegel gives the same mediating function to labor in his *Phenomenology* and in the *Philosophy of Right*. In the
Philosophy of Right, Hegel writes:

When I impose a form on something, the thing's determinate character as
mine acquires an independent externality and ceases to be restricted to my

presence here and now and to the direct presence of my awareness and will. To impose a form on a thing is the mode of taking possession most in conformity with the Idea to this extent, that it implies a union of subject and object, although it varies endlessly with the quantitative character of the objects and the variety of subjective aims. (*PR, # 56*)

To "impose a form on something" is the shorthand definition for labor, used by Hegel several times in the crucial section "Lordship and Bondage."[41] If "to impose a form on something" can correctly be construed as Hegel's definition of labor, we have, in the above quotation from the *Philosophy of Right*, an even stronger statement than the quotation from the *Realphilosophie* mentioned by Avineri. Whereas in the latter, Hegel maintains that labor transcends the accidental nature of the problem of property in the *Philosophy of Right* he argues that work implies a union of subject and object. Labor is thus explicitly stated to be the solution of the problem of the separation of consciousness and nature. A close look at the crucial texts in "Lordship and Bondage" supports this same thesis.

Labor is described here as being the solution to the problem of how consciousness can become self-consciousness. In order to achieve that level, consciousness must affirm two truths that cannot be maintained simultaneously. Consciousness must affirm that it is other than anything objective, be it life, or any objective determination such as physiological, psychological or sociological characteristics. Consciousness must also accept that it is tied to the objective world. The first truth is often summarized as follows: consciousness must affirm itself as pure negativity. The figure of the master embodies this aspect in the right he has acquired to enjoyment (consumption) of the goods prepared by the slave (Hegel 1967 c, 235). He thus expresses himself as pure negativity inasmuch as he is a desire.[42] As such, his "satisfaction...is itself only a state of evanescence, for it lacks objectivity or subsistence" (Ibid., 238). Respect for objectivity emerges due to the fear of death. It has a terrible consequence in that the consciousness that experiences the fear of death must submit itself to the other consciousness in order to avoid risking its life. This other con-

---

[41] Here are some of the important phrases and sentences quoted from Hegel 1967 c: "The negative relation to the object passes into the form of the object;" "This negative mediating agency, this activity giving shape and form;" "Shaping or forming the object has not only the positive significance that the bondsman becomes thereby aware of himself;" "By the fact that the form is objectified, it does not become something other than the consciousness moulding the thing through work;" "without the formative activity shaping the thing;" "its formative activity;" (238–40) and "in the formative activity of work" (242).

[42] "Desire has reserved to itself the pure negating of the object and thereby unalloyed feeling of self" (Ibid., 238).

sciousness, the master, forces upon the first, the slave, the burden of service and labor. But Hegel writes:

> Labour...is desire restrained and checked, evanescence delayed and postponed; in other words, labour shapes and fashions the thing. The negative relation to the object passes into *the form* of the object, into something that is permanent and remains; because it is just for the labourer that the object has independence. This negative mediating agency, this activity giving shape and form, is at the same time the individual existence, the pure self-existence of that consciousness, which now in the work it does is externalized and passes into the condition of permanence. The consciousness that toils and serves accordingly attains by this means the direct apprehension of that independent being as its self. (Ibid., 238)

The first truth of consciousness (negativity), and the second truth of consciousness (respect for positivity) are thus synthesized in labor. It should be noticed, however, that labor is a synthesis of the two truths inasmuch as labor is performed by the slave but only after being threatened by the master. Hegel says as much:

> Thus precisely in labour where there seemed to be merely some *outsider's* mind and ideas involved, the *bondsman* becomes aware through this rediscovery of himself of having and being a 'mind of his own.' (Ibid., 239, emphasis added)

These texts of the *Phenomenology* will permit us to understand and to complement the important thesis attributed by Avineri to Hegel: "labour...[is] not only an actualization of man but also his possible emasculation," (Avineri 1972, 90) or "labour also brings forth conditions which frustrate man's attempt to integrate himself into his world" (Ibid., 90).

Avineri relates the emasculating and alienating aspects of labor to its social aspects (Ibid., 90 ff). Social aspects become more and more burdensome for the individual as the economic order becomes more industrialized and complex.[43] Indeed, this complexity increases the productive capabilities of human beings, but, at the same time, requires a division of labor. This, in turn, breaks the obvious link between the individual's labor and his concrete needs. Human beings cannot produce the goods that they need,

---

[43] Adam Smith saw the great productive advantages of the division of labor and glorified it by his example of the pin factory. Hegel points in the *Philosophy of Right* to several negative consequences of the division of labor (*PR*, ## 198, 243). The division of labor deprives the individual workman of the possibility of being proud of having made a finished product that he can see, admire, show to friends and bring home to his family for consumption. The division of labor also submits the individual worker to the possible arbitrary whims of supervisors.

instead they must produce goods and services for sale, i.e., commodities. Human beings must become part of a production system. One's own contribution to the production system bears no obvious relation to the basket of goods one needs. Furthermore, the value or worthlessness of one's own contribution depends upon movements, shifts, or changes in the system itself. This dependence is obvious in the involuntary unemployment connected with business cycles resulting in "whole masses...abandoned to poverty...a poverty that cannot do anything for itself" (Hegel 1967 b, 232-33; as quoted in Avineri, 1972, 97).

The text from the *Phenomenology* that we quoted earlier allows us to point to a form of alienation in labor that is not related to its social aspect, but to an ontological characteristic of labor. Indeed, labor is human toil. It therefore necessarily requires that "desire [be] restrained and checked" (PhG, 238).

However, consciousness is, by Hegel's account, not capable of this self-restraint. Consciousness needs to have experienced the importance of life through fear of death, and it needs a master who forces it to transform this general experience of the importance of life into the harsh task of daily toil (Ibid., ## 238–240; PM, # 435 addition). One therefore must accept, according to Hegel, that consciousness is at first aware of the repressive characteristics connected with the toil of labor. Only later does consciousness become aware of labor's positive function. For that to be possible, consciousness must have given up the illusionary thought that the idle life of the master is a true human existence. Hegel teaches us that labor might be the way for human beings to reconcile themselves to nature, but human beings will not naturally prefer this reconciliation, given that labor itself brings with it a social and an ontological alienation.[44]

At this point, the organization of the economic order makes a decisive difference. If people are confronted with a command economy – that is, an economy planned by a central command, as in some communist countries – they are able to interpret the alienation connected with work as political in origin. They do not have to accept it as the thorn of a rose, where the rose is the reconciliation of consciousness with nature. Free labor, that is, labor within the free market, does not have the option of interpreting the alienation of work as political in origin. Consciousness can therefore only interpret the alienation of work as the thorn of a rose, that is, as the act which brings about the reconciliation of consciousness with nature. Clearly, such a reconciliation requires self-discipline or, as Hegel calls it, an education *(Bildung)*. Free labor is ready for such education (PR, # 187

---

[44] For a study of this dual aspect of labor and how one philosophical tradition (the natural law tradition) had a hard time discovering the positive aspects of labor, see James B. Murphy (1994), particularly from Section IV on: "Labor as a Bonum Arduum."

and remark). Labor in a command economy finds an easy excuse to reject this kind of self-education.

In summary, Hegel's third argument in favor of the free market consists of his belief that the free market is more capable, than a command economy, of allowing individuals to experience the reconciling dimension of labor notwithstanding its alienating aspects. The reconciling dimension consists of the awareness that in work human beings transcend their dependence upon nature. To survive human beings must transform nature, e.g., make French fries from potatoes. That transformation is also the occasion for the human mind to imprint itself upon objects and thereby become visible. The free market rewards effective transformation of nature by creating demand for such products. The pain, boredom, and fatigue are understood as the unavoidable characteristics of work required to deal with human dependence upon nature. In a command economy, on the contrary, the emphasis is upon the power of political decisions. Pain, boredom, fatigue, and other nuisances of work can then be attributed to ineffective or bad political decisions. The population then feels justified in trying to avoid the negative consequences of the work experience as illustrated by the statement of a Polish intellectual after the fall of communism: "The communist state pretended that they paid us for our work; and we, in turn, pretended that we worked."

Hegel's fourth argument that can be used in favor of the free market is based on his hope that the free market, combined with a constitutional monarchy, might be able to provide a structural solution to the modern predicament of human beings. That predicament has been well-formulated by Rousseau as the distinction between a human *being (homme)* and a citizen *(citoyen)*. This distinction points to "the existence of two distinct spheres of aims, rights, and responsibilities, the separate spheres of private and public interest." The question posed by Rousseau concerned "how modern man could be restored to a unified condition, how the dualism of private and public, or civil and political life could be overcome."[45]

Hegel's attempt at solving the modern problem diagnosed by Rousseau is typically Hegelian. He affirms the necessity of both extremes, and then works toward proposing a synthesis.

It is well known that Hegel affirms the need of political life. "The state is the actuality of the ethical Idea"; or, "The state is the actuality of concrete freedom" (*PR*, ## 257 and 260).

What is important for our argument at this point is to remember that Hegel also affirmed the need for private life. More specifically, he argued

---

[45] The quotes about Rousseau are from Joseph O'Malley's introduction to Karl Marx's *Critique of Hegel's* Philosophy of Right, xl (Marx 1977). There, O'Malley masterfully uses the political ideas of Rousseau to contrast Hegel and Marx.

that private life and interests should have the right to full affirmation in a separate domain. "These institutions [the family and civil society] are the components of the constitution...in the spheres of particularity. They are, therefore, the firm foundation not only of the state but also of the citizen's trust in it and sentiment towards it" (Ibid., # 265). But for particularity and private interests to assert themselves, the state needs to allow the free market. This is very clear in the following comment:

> in ancient times the labour on the pyramids and other high monuments in Egypt and Asia...were constructed for public ends, and the worker's task was not mediated through his private choice and particular interest. This interest involves freedom of trade and commerce against control from above. (Ibid., # 236)

This quotation is not just a side remark of Hegel's. It fits into his overall vision of social and political life. One can infer this from his sharp criticism of Greek political life and of Plato's political philosophy. This criticism is at odds with his overall admiration for the political achievements of Greece.[46] Hegel's criticism of Greek political life can therefore not be understood as a rejection of the Greek democratic ideal. Instead, his criticism focuses on the Greek state's method of curtailing property rights and economic freedom. Thus he writes

> In order to avert from their state the danger threatening to freedom from the inequality of wealth, Solon and Lycurgus restricted property rights in numerous ways and set various barriers to the freedom of choice, which might have led to unequal wealth" (Ibid., 197)

This description of the factual relationship between the political and economic order receives a normative aspect in the following quotation:

> This is the beautiful happy life of the Greeks, which has been and is admired so much. The people are at the same time split up into citizens as well as constituting the one individual, the government. It inter-relates with itself alone. The same will is the individual and the universal. The alienation of the particularity of the will is its immediate preservation.... There is no protest here: everyone knows himself immediately as universal, i.e., *he gives up his particularity* without knowing it as such, as a self, an essence. (Hegel 1967 b, 249–50; quoted as translated by Avineri, emphasis added)

---

[46]

As free men the Greeks and Romans obeyed laws laid down by themselves, obeyed men whom they had themselves appointed to office, waged wars on which they had themselves decided, gave their property, exhausted their passions, and sacrificed their lives by the thousands for an end which was their own (Hegel 1977, 154–55).

This criticism is even more apparent in Hegel's remark on Plato:

> In ancient times, beautiful public life was the ethos of all, beauty [was] the immediate unity of the universal and the particular, a work of art in which no part separates itself from the whole...Plato's Republic is, like the Lacedemonian state, this disappearance of the self-conscious individual. (Ibid., 251)

Hegel also writes:

> In Plato's state subjective freedom does not count, because people have their occupation assigned them by the Guardians...but subjective freedom, which must be respected, demands that individuals have free choice in this matter. (*PR*, # 262 addition)

Or again:

> In Plato's *Republic,* the Guardians are left to allot individuals to their particular classes and impose on them their particular tasks.... The same particular character pertains to tasks imposed in the East and in Egypt in connection with collosal *[sic]* architectural undertakings, and so forth. In these circumstances the principle of subjective freedom is lacking, i.e., the principle that the individual's substantive activity...shall be mediated through his particular volition. (Ibid., # 299 remark, see also # 185 remark)

I can do no better than repeat Avineri's summary statement of Hegel's view about Greek political life:

> The polis is thus an entity which despite its apparent beauty enslaves the individual, and the democratic nature of its structure only accentuates the individual's total absorption in the political system. (Avineri 1972, 112)

The enslavement is the direct result of the absence of an intermediate institutional arrangement between the individual and the state, in which self-interests express themselves. Thus, the free market can be said to have been understood by Hegel as the institutional arrangement that liberated the modern citizen from the enslavement to the state that was typical of the Greek city-state. That liberation created the split in modern human beings that was so well formulated by Rousseau. It is clear from the above that Hegel does not intend to solve this predicament of modern human beings by eliminating the private or the public domain. Instead, he develops two lines of thought to identify a synthesis between these two domains. The first is that the private life as affirmed in the free market educates the individual and integrates him or her into a first form of public organization

(Kraus 1931/1932, 21). The free market educates the individual because it entices and even forces the individual as economic agent to pay attention to the wishes of others. It makes the individual into a social being against his own will. Furthermore, the economic order creates natural groupings that integrate individuals. Hegel mentions two such groupings: classes and corporations (*PR*, # 255 remark). Obviously, Hegel attaches great importance to classes because he wants political representation at the legislature to be representation along class lines. He also attaches great importance to the corporation evident from the following statement: "The sanctity of marriage and the dignity of Corporation membership are the two fixed points round which the unorganized atoms of civil society revolve" (*PM*, ## 527–528, 534; *PR*, ## 201 ff., 250 ff.).

The second line of thought developed by Hegel is that the state should be organized in such a way that the organization of the state guarantees that private interests, as they are already transformed and made rational, are promoted by the state (*PR*, ## 257–258, 260–261, 264).

These two lines of thought are Hegel's solution to the predicament of the modern individual so well seen by Rousseau. The free market is a critical aspect of Hegel's solution.

The fifth and last argument that can be used to argue in favor of the free market emerges in a reflection about the proper relation between the individual's right to morality and the right of the state to perform its duty. Hegel sketches the possible conflict between these two rights very well:

> The welfare of the state has claims to recognition totally different from those of the welfare of the individual. The ethical substance, the state, has its determinate being, i.e., its right, directly embodied in something existent, something not abstract but concrete, and the principle of its conduct and behavior can only be this concrete existent and not one of the many universal thoughts supposed to be moral commands. (Ibid., # 337 remark)

He continues:

> When politics is alleged to clash with morals and so to be always wrong, the doctrine propounded rests on superficial ideas about morality, the nature of the state, and the state's relation to the moral point of view. (Ibid.)

From these remarks, at least this is clear: the right of the state can clash with moral demands of individuals, and the state cannot be said to always be wrong. But in such a clash, the state has power. There is, therefore, something unequal about this clash. Individuals with moral convictions, conflicting with the ethical values behind the actions of the state, are the weaker parties. How can the right to morality of this weaker party be protected against a powerful state? Even though this difficulty emerges directly from a remark by Hegel, I have not found an answer in Hegel's texts. It is, however, possible to construct an answer in line with Hegel's thought. The right to morality can be protected, I submit, by making sure that the state does not have full control over the individual.[47] The free market economy is a mechanism that limits the coercive control of the state over individuals. The free market, once again, appears as an organization of the economic domain that has a philosophical function. Indeed, it guarantees the existence of income-earning potential outside the control of the state, thereby limiting the coercive power of the state and promoting the individual's right to morality.[48]

The above five arguments, which can be used in favor of the organization of the economic domain as a free market, might give the wrong impression that the state has no right to intervene in the economic order. I will use the third and last section of this chapter to correct this impression.

III. The Proper Relation between State and Free Market

The fact that one can find in Hegel's texts arguments useful to argue for the free market does not mean that he rejects a role for the state in the functioning of a free market economy.[49] In fact, Hegel sees several roles for the state. Some of these are well recognized, while others are more controversial. Let us start with the generally recognized roles.

A first role of the state is dealing with the problem of property rights. The protection of this right requires the creation and administration of a system of justice. This implies the creation of laws and the organization of power to enforce them (*PR*, # 209). In the history of economic thought, national defense and the administration of justice are normally connected

---

[47] Another protection, which does not immediately concern us here, would be the emergence of an institution at least semi-independent of the state and concerned with the individual's right to morality, e.g., organized religion.

[48] In the Soviet Union, the Academy of Science was unique in that it had a budget which the scientists, not the state, controlled. Hence, the state could bring judicial action against Sakharov for his moral criticism of the state, but the state did not have unrestricted ability to punish Sakharov economically by firing him, or by cutting his salary drastically. The financial independence of the Academy of Science is a partial explanation for why scientists more than politicians, managers, or bureaucrats were able to be the moral conscience of the Soviet Union. The Hegelian argument is that the free market makes most industries semi-independent from the state and thus one might expect to find moral voices to appear in many places in the capitalist society.

[49] The government can also interfere improperly in the economy. I discuss that problem as it relates to the United States in chapter 7 and 8 of this book.

with the idea of protection of property. Whereas administration of justice is understood to be a defense of property rights against threats internal to the state, national defense is connected with protection of property rights against threats from outside the state (Smith 1937, 651, 653 ff., esp. 659). It is important to notice, however, that Hegel does not reduce national defense or war to the defense of property. National defense exists for the defense of all institutions that promote freedom.[50]

A second generally recognized role for the state in the economic domain is what economic theory calls the provision of public goods.[51] Economic theory defines a public good by means of two characteristics.[52] The first is that the exclusion principle that is characteristic of private goods does not work. The second characteristic is that a public good can be enjoyed by more than one person. Goods having these two characteristics present several problems for the free market, among others, that of the free-rider problem. It means that with public goods, the free market does not have the capability of linking the enjoyment and consumption of a good with payment for its provision or its production. But if people do not pay for the enjoyment of public goods, less will be invested in such goods than is optimal.[53] Public goods will be underprovided in a free market system. In modern economics, the voluntary exchange theory of taxation proposes that the state help the free market achieve the optimum it cannot achieve by itself.[54] The state is supposed to ask all citizens who would enjoy a public good how much they would be willing to pay. If the total cost for providing the good is equal or less than what people are jointly willing to pay, then the government should provide the good or the service and use its power of taxation to collect the money necessary to finance the good. Everybody should be happy with this solution because the government will have to charge each citizen no more than he or she declared him or herself willing to pay. It is thus a happy (voluntary) exchange of taxes for public goods.

The concept of public good (or public bad) also covers goods that are partially private goods and partially public goods and gives rise to another problem with public goods. The partially public good connected with a

---

[50] If one restricts the role of the state to this first role, one is said to favor a "minimal state" or the "protective state".

[51] For a critical evaluation of my use of contemporary economic concepts to interpret Hegel, see Priddat 1990, 99 ff.

[52] We gave a preliminary definition in Ch 1 of this book. We provide a more thorough discussion of the definition of public goods in Chapter 6 of this book.

[53] One can find a pedagogically written survey essay on the economic problems of public goods in John G. Head's "The Pure Theory of Public Goods" (Head 1974, 68–92).

[54] For an explanation beyond the one summarized here on what economists mean by "voluntary exchange theory of taxation," see ibid., ch.7.

private good is technically called an externality.[55]   An externality can be either desirable (cultivating bees has the externality of increasing the fertilization of fruit trees in the country), or undesirable (using coal to produce heat pollutes the air for everybody).   The market mechanism, by overlooking externalities, does not charge the full social cost of a product with undesirable externalities and does not pay the full social benefit for a product with positive externalities.   Contemporary economic theory argues that externalities are a source of market failures.   Such market failures leave room for improvement by government intervention.   It is possible to argue that Hegel tried, in an imperfect way, to formulate the problem of public goods and externalities under the title "Police."[56]

The public good's argument for governmental help in the economic order can be formulated to include many areas of economic activity where there is a market failure.   The argument would allow the government the option of choosing the best method of dealing with such inefficiencies. These methods could include setting up state monopolies (guaranteeing money supply), creating public utilities (gas or electric companies), producing the service itself (water supply), or creating legal obligations (imposition of pollution standards).   The general argument for government intervention in the case of market failure attributed to public goods is implicitly present in Hegel's thought.[57]   The argument begins by acknowledging that there is an element of *compulsion* in the free market" (*PR*, ## 186, 199).   Indeed, to claim part of the social product, individuals must first produce something that others want.   If they do not produce anything, or produce what others do not want, they cannot claim part of the social product.   But to survive, individuals must make such claims.   The compulsion present in the free market entices or forces people to be efficient and useful in their economic activity.   Hegel then argues that if efficiency and utility are values that justify the impersonal compulsion of the free market, why would rational compulsion for that same purpose not be justified? Rational compulsion is here understood to be governmental intervention intended to correct the market inefficiencies.[58]

---

[55] For a full discussion of the economist's view of externality, see ibid., chs.7, 9.

[56] Thus *PR*, ## 232–234 could be said to be a reference to negative externalities.   In # 235 we find Hegel presenting the public goods argument for intervention by public authority.

[57] For a critical evaluation of this claim see Priddat 1990, 98 ff.   For a further defense of the concept of public good as a necessary tool for understanding correctly certain economic phenomena see chapter 6 in this book.

[58] In contemporary literature, two objections are made to the Hegelian conclusion that the government should step in to remedy market failures in public goods provision.   The first objection is that government provision of goods and services often involves inefficiencies which might be bigger than the market inefficiency it tries to remedy.   Thus, Head writes: "although serious market failure in public goods supply can readily be demonstrated, it

A third generally recognized role for the state in the economy is the enforcement of competition in the free market. This includes antitrust legislation and fair-trade laws.[59] It is possible that Hegel had this role in mind when he wrote:

> The differing interests of producers and consumers may come into collision with each other; and although a fair balance between them on the whole may be brought about automatically, still their adjustment also requires a control which stands above both and is consciously undertaken. (*PR*, # 236)

Hegel's argument, however, conflates three different arguments: collision, difficulty for individuals in obtaining necessary knowledge, and the political interest in the quality and price of goods in absolutely universal daily demand. Only the argument of collision has its proper place under the heading of the enforcement of the competitive character of the free market. The argument of lack of knowledge is mostly transformed into a public good argument; that is, if one provides the knowledge, everybody can enjoy it. It is thus an argument that belongs under the second role of the government. The argument that some goods that are used daily have a political significance is rarely employed unless one transforms it into a merit good argument. But this brings us to government interventions that are less universally accepted.

The merit good argument was introduced by the public-finance economist Richard Musgrave (Musgrave 1959, 13–14).[60] A merit good is one that the government considers so meritorious that it has the right to judge whether or not the level of production and consumption provided by the free market is acceptable. Musgrave gives the following as examples of merit goods whose level of provision by the market is considered unacceptable: education, inoculation against some illnesses, school lunches, and low-cost housing.[61] Typical of merit goods is that the government does not respect consumer sovereignty, thus representing a violation of the

---

should not too readily be assumed that government can do better" (Head 1974, 91). The second objection is that the concrete method of financing for government-provided public goods is often not voluntary as required by economic theory: rather the financing method is imposed by a political majority on a minority and thus involves some violation of property rights. Thus, Schmidtz would allow such violation of property rights for provision of public goods only when society's survival is involved (Schmidtz 1991, 159). We will go into more detail about these ideas in chapter 6 of this book.

[59] One can find an authoritative defense of this role of government in (Simons 1973, esp. chs. 3–4).

[60] We introduced a preliminary discussion of the concept of (de)merit good in chapter 1 of this book. We provide a fuller discussion in chapter 5 of this book.

[61] The same is true of demerit goods, such as tobacco and liquor. On these goods a "penalty taxation" is levied in order to discourage consumption.

principle of the free market. Clearly, the merit goods problem touches upon a very troublesome role of the government in the economic order. In the merit good debate, Musgrave and Head, among others, have argued for the legitimacy of considering some goods as merit goods. McLure forcefully rejected it. But, even Musgrave and Head acknowledge the difficulty of finding a tight argument for legitimizing merit goods (Musgrave 1959, 13–14; Head 1974, chs.10–11; McLure 1968, 474–483). Hegel's reflections on the free market provide an illuminating understanding of the merit good problem.

Hegel, as we have shown, gives solid arguments in favor of the free market. All his arguments relate to what he calls the principle of subjectivity; the right of the individual to decide for himself what is the good. This right is respected in the free market. The question arises as to whether the free market mechanism can achieve the goals it is supposed to achieve. According to Hegel, the economic system must, as we have seen, achieve three goals: it must provide the goods and services required to satisfy the needs of people; it must provide the opportunity to earn recognition in work; it must provide a preliminary form of social integration that is subsequently completed by the state.

The free market does not pursue these goods consciously. It relies upon a threat and an enticement in the market mechanism: the rule that one may claim goods and services only in return for goods and services that one produces for others. If one combines this rule with the fact that people have needs that they must fulfill, we can understand why Hegel calls this the inner necessity, or the compulsion behind the appearance of free choice (*PR*, ## 184, 186–187, 199). This compulsion, or inner necessity, does not, however, guarantee the achievement of the three purposes of the economic order. This inner necessity forces people to participate in the economic order, and puts a penalty upon them if they do not participate, or if they do not participate in it successfully. However, this penalty can strike individuals for reasons beyond their control. Hegel writes, "Not only caprice,...but also contingencies, physical conditions, and factors grounded in external circumstances...may reduce men to poverty" (Ibid., # 241). He further connects poverty with "a consequent loss of the sense of right and wrong, of honesty and the self-respect which makes a man insist on maintaining himself by his own work and effort, [of which] the result is the creation of a rabble of paupers."[62]

Concerning the goal of self-realization in the economic order, Hegel points out that there "is the subdivision and restriction of particular jobs.

---

[62] Because Hegel juxtaposes poverty and loss of sense of right and wrong, it is difficult to maintain that he does not see an inner link between the two (*PR*, # 244).

This results in the dependence and distress of the class tied to work of that sort, and these again entail inability to feel and enjoy the broader freedoms and especially the intellectual benefits of civil society" (Ibid., # 243). The free market therefore does not fully guarantee the achievement of any of the three goals (satisfaction of needs, self-realization in work, and social integration). It is at this point that Hegel makes his darkest diagnosis about the free market. He argues that private charity is not satisfactory because such help is contingent. It thus falls upon society and the state to organize relief or prevent the crises of distress (Ibid., # 242). This is the Hegelian argument for what is debated in economic theory as part of the problem of merit goods. It runs as follows: the free market system can and should be imposed on society because it promises to achieve three goals. If the free market cannot reach these goals, it might be useful to have charitable help from the wealthy, but it befalls the state to complement the charitable help in such a way as to remove the contingencies and arbitrary aspects that are present in charitable help. This is Hegel's argument for the merit good known as redistribution.[63]   Directly connected with this argument is Hegel's pessimistic judgment about the free market. He states that providing such help and relief is destructive in that it prevents the poor from earning self-respect by knowing that one has earned a living. Furthermore, by providing goods and services to the poor without their contributing to the social product, the state does "violate the principle of civil society" (Ibid., # 245). Resentment then becomes a plausible reaction from those who have to obey the principle of civil society and are required, furthermore, to pay for subsidies to the poor. Hegel then briefly entertains what could be called a Keynesian technique of helping the poor by giving them work, but he dismisses this solution as well. He then ends with the following statement: "It hence becomes apparent that despite an excess of wealth civil society is not rich enough; i.e., its own resources are insufficient to check excessive poverty and the creation of a penurious rabble" (Ibid).

---

[63] Priddat, too, uses the concept merit good to articulate Hegel's vision of the function of the state in the economy (Priddat 1990, 113). For a fuller development of the power of the concept of merit good for articulating systematically the role of government in the economy see chapter 5.

Conclusion

Hegel explicitly and categorically classifies the new economic order (the free market) as an ethical institution.[64] He thereby makes it an objective requirement for the realization of freedom in the modern world. Hegel, however, sees that the free market cannot deliver the three goals it is supposed to achieve as an ethical institution.[65] Therefore, it is necessary to conclude that, for Hegel, the free market is necessary, but that he maintains that it cannot deliver the contributions it is supposed to make for the realization of human freedom. Hegel defends the free market on solid grounds, without falling into the trap of giving it a salvific and sublimating role that it clearly does not have.[66] The Hegelian arguments are humble but realistic, and thus solid. They give the government an extensive function in the realization of human freedom. Specifically, the government has a role in the economic order that goes beyond the role described as the "minimal state", or even as the "productive state."[67] The government has the task of helping the economic order reach the three goals it is supposed to meet.[68]

---

[64] For an economist, appreciating Hegel's understanding that moral imperatives require institutional arrangements, including economic ones, see: Levine 1988, 126 and 145.

[65] These three goods are: satisfaction of human needs for all, possibility of self-recognition for all through work, and preliminary integration of individuals into the social order.

[66] Michael Novak praises democratic capitalism; though it mobilizes all vices; presumably it will sublimate them. "Its [democratic capitalism's] chief aim is to fragment and to check power, but not to repress sin. Within it every human vice flourishes. Entrepreneurs from around the world, it appears, flock to it and teach it new cultural specialties, of vice as well as virtue, of indelicacy as well as delicacy." He then mentions "massage parlors, pornography shops, pickpockets, winos, prostitutes, pushers, punk rock, chambers for group sex" (Novak 1982, 350). He also praises, democratic capitalism because it imitates *caritas*, the highest form of love, "by reaching out, creating, inventing, producing, and distributing, raising the material base of the common good....It makes communal life more active, intense, voluntary, and multiple....The highest goal of the political economy of democratic capitalism is to be suffused by *caritas*" (Ibid., 357). For a summary of the hopes put into the sublimating potential of the free market as they were already present in the eighteenth century, see Hirschman 1977a.

[67] In economic theory, the function of the "minimal state" is protection. It refers to the protection of life and property by police, courts, and army. The productive state refers to the state when it helps individuals produce public goods. Among others, see Buchanan 1975 b, 68–70.

[68] The correctness of this philosophical claim is supported by the analysis of the causes of the Asian economic miracle. Thus, Jose Campos and Hilton Root attribute a key role in the Asian economic miracle to reduced poverty, improved income distribution (Chapter 1) and different well thought out wealth-sharing mechanisms (Chapter 3). In their introduction Campos and Root summarize this aspect of the Asian economic miracle by the "principle of shared growth" and point out that "rapid economic growth has been associated with relatively low and declining levels of income inequality" (Campos & Root 1996, 1 and 8).

Hegel did not see how it was possible to do so successfully, but that did not prevent him from assigning the task to society and the state.

4. The Economic Order: A Human, Not a Natural Institution

Abstract

In this chapter I challenge the implicit (and sometimes explicit) claim of Adam Smith that the free market is a natural system which would emerge on its own if governments did not interfere. I argue instead that the free market is a tenuous human institution which needs support and protection. I build my claim upon Adam Smith's open avowal that property rights are necessary for the free market and upon the neo-liberal demand that governments must intervene in order to maintain the competitive nature of the free market so as to guarantee its efficiency. Hegel incorporates both claims that property rights and economic efficiency are necessary. For Hegel both are necessary for achieving freedom. I then point out that defending the above two claims with the philosophical argument that they contribute to freedom implies that both property rights and economic efficiency must not be allowed to undermine freedom. This provides the philosophical foundation for minimal welfare measures: society must make it possible for all to acquire the property necessary for exercising freedom or to enjoy the fruits of socially enforced efficiency. Hegel thereby teaches us that a philosophical reflection upon the writings of Adam Smith and the doctrines of neo-liberalism provide an argument in favor of some form of welfare state. Borrowing from Hegel, I then point out that any welfare state contradicts a basic principle of the free market: no one gets something for nothing. For this reason, I believe that alleviating poverty in a free market system is always going to be a tenuous affair.

I. Adam Smith's Ontology of the Economy

Adam Smith sometimes has been called the last British philosopher who was concerned with a full-fledged philosophical speculation about economics and economic man (Hirschman 1977a, 112). One of Adam Smith's achievements is that he tried to describe the ontological status of the economic domain.   In his writings he attacks the mercantilist and the physiocratic thought systems which preceded him. Smith argues that both gave undue preference to or imposed harmful restraint on some economic activities. Therefore, by implication, he must consider the economic system to be ontologically a *natural* system. The crucial quotation that expresses this view is:

> All systems either of preference or of restraint, therefore, being thus completely taken away, the obvious and simple system of natural liberty establishes itself of its own accord. (Smith, 651)

Such an ontological view of the free market system allows the economist to study the laws of this natural system in the same way as Newton studied nature.

If the economic domain were simply a natural system, clearly, ethics would have no place, or at most a marginal one, in economic theory. In this chapter I wish to argue against Adam Smith's view of the ontology of the economic domain. I will propose a different ontology which will allow me to argue that ethics must be central to economic theory.

There are at least two arguments that challenge Adam Smith's ontology. The first argument can be developed by reflecting on the function of property. The second argument can be developed by reflecting on the publications of a particular group of economists. The German label, neo-liberals, seems very appropriate for them.[69] The philosophical aspect of these two arguments will be developed by making use of Hegel's philosophy.

II. The Function of Property

In explaining how he views the ontology of the economic domain, Adam Smith writes the following:

> Every man, as long as he does not violate the laws of justice, is left perfectly free to pursue his own interest his own way, and to bring both his industry

---

[69] Given the ambivalence of the term liberalism in the U.S. as compared with the meaning of this term in Europe, including Great Britain, I am aware that the term neo-liberalism might share the same ambivalence. I therefore explicitly state that I take the term as a translation of the German term: "Neo-Liberalismus."

and capital into competition with those of any other man, or order of men. (Smith, 651)

One can therefore argue that even Adam Smith recognizes that there must be restrictions to free competition in the economic domain. Free competition must recognize the laws of justice, which protect life and property. But about property, Adam Smith writes, "Civil government, in so far as it is instituted for the security of property, is in reality instituted for the defense of the rich against the poor, or of those who have some property against those who have none at all" (Smith, 674).

Adam Smith therefore understands that property rights are not just a fact; they are a societal action taken in favor of some and against others. Given that property rights are not just a fact but also an action, it is possible to ask if that action is efficient, wise, prudent, or even just. All of these questions take the problem of property out of the domain of nature (facts, events) and relocate it into the domain of values. Rather than look upon property as a given, one can view property as something that requires justification.

What justification can there be for property rights? If one takes Stanley J. Benn's article in *The Encyclopedia of Philosophy* (Edwards 1967, vol. 6, 491 ff.) as a starting point, one learns that in the history of thought, several forms of justification have been given. Benn highlights four such approaches. The Church Fathers thought that a property owner was obliged to administer property for the benefit of all, given that property once belonged to all. Benn calls this the stewardship view of ownership. The second view is that of the natural law tradition of which Locke is a crucial spokesperson. In that tradition, individuals have a natural right to objects that were *res nullius* before they added their own labor to it. The third view is that of the utilitarian tradition. Hume already formulates the main argument of that tradition. The argument says that property should be upheld because it encourages "useful habits and accomplishments." The fourth approach is associated with the German philosophical tradition. Hegel formulates that view as follows: "Property is the first embodiment of freedom and so is in itself a substantive end" (*PR*, # 45).

The natural law and utilitarian traditions are vulnerable to some easy objections. The natural law tradition grounds the justification of property rights in the fact that labor has been added to a *res nullius*. Such a view might be sufficient to discuss property rights in a society where most things are *res nullius*. However, when property rights are established and productive relations are complex, the natural law tradition does not provide a guideline for deciding between competing claims for re-compensation (remuneration) on the basis of the contributions to the productive process of labor, management, and capital respectively.

The utilitarian tradition justifies property because it encourages "useful habits and accomplishments." However, this argument can be turned around by contending that whenever any violation of property rights encourages useful habits and accomplishments, property rights should be violated. Thus, the same principle can be invoked equally well to undermine as to defend property rights.[70]

One is left, then, with the view of the Church Fathers and of the German philosophical tradition. Both traditions tie the justification of property to a moral concept. The Church Fathers tie their justification to the concept of stewardship rooted in a religious view of the world; the German philosophical tradition ties it to the concept of freedom. Given the pluralist nature of contemporary society, a religious argument needs the backing of a philosophical argument in order to even appear to have universal validity. We are thus left with the argument of the German philosophical tradition.

In the next pages, I will try to clarify the relationship between property and freedom as it is worked out by one German philosopher, Hegel.

According to Hegel, a person's freedom has two dimensions. A person has inner freedom, and he has freedom realized in the world. Morality is the study of inner freedom. Yet, this is but a partial study of the problem of freedom. Hegel says elegantly that there is an additional part to the study of freedom in the following statement: "A person must translate his freedom into an external sphere" (*PR*, # 41). The first step to such an external freedom is to lay claim to external things. This is the right of appropriation of things which Hegel says is an absolute right of the individual. He does not make such a right conditional upon impregnating the thing with labor. Hegel simply says that things have no end in themselves. A person has a substantive end to make things his own. And, that argument he considers sufficient justification for possession. But possession is not yet property because property is more than mere possession.[71] Indeed, where possession is a fact, property is a right. What then is the justifica-

---

[70] Utilitarians might not think that such a situation is necessarily a bad thing since they are concerned with usefulness or utility and only concerned with property rights as a means to increasing utility. My objection to the utilitarian view of property is precisely that property is a concept that is not reducible to utility. Indeed, I would argue that a city faced with bandits who threaten to destroy the property of the whole city unless the city takes away the property of an enemy of the bandits should not violate the property rights of the enemy of the bandits. The city might try to buy the property of the enemy of the bandits in order to be able to satisfy the bandits by destroying then that property. However, buying out a person is recognizing and respecting his or her property rights.

[71] For a critical study about Hegel's alleged inconsistency in his use of the concepts of possession and property see Cristi 1978.

tion of property? It is that by being able to call an object mine, I become through my possession an object of my own will. In willing my possession, I will my freedom as external. In having my possession become property, I therefore have the possibility of having my willing of my own external freedom recognized by society.

Thus, a philosophical justification of property ties property to a crucial aspect of freedom of the individual. The realization of that aspect of individual freedom is permanently threatened unless society provides help. Protection of property is the help society can provide. Is it rational to claim that personal possession is so important that society can be called upon to protect it as property, while at the same time, claiming that personal possession is not important enough to call upon society to help individuals acquire such personal possession? If the justification is tied to the concept of freedom, then both must be argued for (Winfield 1988, 239)![72]

This argument does not specify how much property, nor what kinds of property, must be made available to an individual.

This kind of philosophical thinking about property, however, has the advantage that it can make sense out of the difficult economic concept of merit good.[73] Indeed, modern Western democracies have decided that some or all of the following goods, such as retirement benefits, unemployment benefits, educational opportunities, health-care, and housing possibilities are claims that individuals should have. By means of mandatory participation in such programs as social security and unemployment insurance or by direct subsidies, the government is indeed capable of insuring that these special kinds of property claims are guaranteed. The force of my argument here, however, is not that I have justified these kinds of merit goods, but simply that I have a philosophical framework in which to locate specific governmental activities. If one adopts a strict free market philosophy, one has no framework to even locate such governmental activities, even though they are economically relevant. In order to be complete, an economic theory will, therefore, have to rely on an economic philosophy other than a mechanistic view of the free market. That richer economic philosophy is emerging in the writings of a group of economists called the neo-liberals.[74] It is to them that I now turn.

---

[72] In their analysis of the Asian economic miracle, Campos and Root stress these two points. The successful Asian societies created "a secure political foundation for economic rights," and there was a "commitment to shared growth" (Campos and Root 1996, 175 and 177).

[73] For a comprehensive survey of the debate on the concept of merit good, see Head 1974. See also chapter 5 in this book in which I clarify, defend, and expand the concept of merit good.

[74] I purposefully restrict myself to the study of the neo-liberal movement because I want to emphasize that economic thought itself made a shift in the way it viewed the ontology of

III. The Neo-Liberal Economic Philosophy

The neo-liberal movement emerged in different countries. In Austria, Ludwig von Mises is the crucial figure. In Germany, it is the group of economists connected with the journal *Ordo* and centered in Freiburg which is important. In England, it is the "London School of Economics" and, in the United States, it is the Chicago school where Henry Simons is recognized as its founder.[75]

This movement was stimulated by different factors in each different center. Von Mises started a theoretical discussion with the Marxists about the essence of the economic domain, which he claims is the economic cal-⟨illegible⟩ (Mises 1975). On the other hand, Simons was disappointed with the chaos of regulations and subsidies that were practiced in the American economy and which made a mockery of the idea of a free competitive market (Simons 1948, 84).

It is true that some of the neo-liberals stress the continuity between the neo-liberal movement and the old liberal tradition (Simons 1973, 1; Hayek 1978, 134 ff.; Hayek 1960, 220 ff.). When it comes to an appreciation of the free market, though, the neo-liberals make an important correction to traditional liberal thought. Instead of maintaining that the free market is a natural system, they see it as a tenuous human institution. Furthermore, the neo-liberals see that the free market imposes a burden on its participants, each of whom tries to escape those burdens, even though these participants might want to see that others are forced to accept the burdens of the free market.[76] Thus, a crucial idea of neo-liberalism emerges: the free market is a burdensome, fragile human institution. That institution must be supported in order to survive. It is the task of the government to support it.

Typical for the neo-liberals is that the state receives a new function. With the classical economists, the function of the state was restricted to the so-called "minimal state," a state responsible for national defense, internal

---

the economy. For a philosophical essay that reflects on commercial life by means of the history of thought from Plato to Hayek and Baudrillard see Murray (1997): "General Introduction: On Studying Commercial Life."

[75] For an enumeration of the members of the different neo-liberal movements, see Nawroth 1961, 5–6.

[76] The idea of a free market includes the demand that goods be sold at competitive prices. Clearly, that demand is an impediment for maximizing profits for people with power, whether that power be of a military, political or monopolistic nature. The idea of the free market thus implies burdens for some.

justice and maintenance of roads and communication (Smith, 651).[77] With the neo-liberals the state receives the additional task of having to maintain and support the free competitive market. Even more, by this argument, the state will have to take any initiative that improves the value by which they defend the competitive market. Thus, any initiative that brings the actual free market closer to the ideal competitive market will become desirable.

H. Simons, among others, argues against farm subsidies, for consumer information, against advertisement, and for access of consumers to whole-sale markets (Simons 1973, 78–89).[78] Each of these measures is defended as contributing to a more competitive market.

---

[77] In another passage Smith makes the restriction of the government role less absolute. He writes: "In *general*, if any branch of trade, or any division of labour, be advantageous to the public, the freer and more general the competition, it will always be the more so" (Smith, 313) (Italics are mine, WVE). In that same page he provides an interesting exception: "If bankers are restrained from issuing any circulating bank notes or notes payable to the bearer, for less than a certain sum; and if they are subjected to the obligation of an immediate and unconditional payment of such bank notes as soon as presented, their trade may, with safety to the public, be rendered in all other respects perfectly free" (Ibid.).

[78] Farm subsidies are currently still an important problem preventing not only a more efficient global economy but also hurting disproportionately the poorer developing countries. Consider the statement by the President of the World Bank, Paul Wolfowitz: "Let me take a moment to explain how trade barriers are hurting the poor. Trade barriers deprive poor countries of markets to sell their goods. Under current conditions, developing countries are not getting the most out of world trade. Their exports face the most severe restrictions all around the globe. Protection in rich countries is highest in the products that developing countries produce, particularly agriculture and labor-intensive manufactured products and services. Of all of these, agricultural protection is particularly harmful to the world's poor. Three-quarters of the world's poor, remember, live in rural areas; so reducing barriers to agricultural trade in most countries can directly reduce poverty. The sheer size of these barriers is staggering. Rich countries today each year spend approximately US$280 billion-let me repeat that, US$280 billion each year -to support their agricultural producers. That comes out to more than US$5 billion each week. Out of that, the EU accounts for roughly half, US$133 billion; but the United States and Japan spend enormous amounts, as well- roughly the same (US$47 billion for the United States and US$49 billion for Japan). These amounts are particularly disturbing when you compare them with the levels of development assistance. In the national context, if you think about it, it means the United States is spending 2.5 times as much, US$2.50, on its agricultural producers for every US$1 that it spends on development assistance. Japan is spending US$5 on agricultural subsidies for every US$1 it spends on development. This support to agricultural producers is paid by taxpayers, and it is paid by consumers in higher prices. Poor consumers are disproportionately affected by these higher prices. So developed countries, their taxpayers, their consumers, also stand to gain from agricultural liberalization. Reform is fundamentally a matter of long-term self-interest" (Wolfowitz 2005). For research back-up of Wolfowitz's claims see: Anderson & Martin, 2005; Mensbrugghe).

IV. Philosophical Significance of the Neo-Liberal Movement

The most important contribution of the neo-liberals is that they locate the free market in a different ontological space than Adam Smith (Smith, 651).

The neo-liberal movement has presented different kinds of arguments as to why the free market is a value and, thus, ought to be protected and nurtured. Among the most frequently encountered arguments, one finds the following four. First and foremost, neo-liberals defend the free market because it is an arrangement that automatically encourages economic efficiency. Indeed, the free market automatically rewards those who produce most efficiently what others want (Mises 1975, 160).[79] Second, neo-liberals defend the free market because it promotes certain desirable anthropological virtues. The free market is said to promote industriousness, responsibility, reliability, and initiative.[80] Third, neo-liberals defend the free market because of a philosophic predilection for freedom. Indeed, the free market allows everybody to choose constantly in the market place. Even though such freedom of choice is not the highest form of freedom, neo-liberals find that it is a very important instantiation of freedom (Friedman 1962, 8).[81] Finally, neo-liberals defend the free market for political reasons. According to this argument, the political and economic domains are not fully independent. It is said that in the political domain it is possible to have a democratic or a dictatorial government. In the economic domain it is said to be possible to have a free economy, a socialist, or a command economy. The neo-liberal author Hayek in his book, *Road to Serfdom*, defends the thesis that a command economy requires a political dictatorship in order to implement economic plans. He further argues that moderate planning in economic affairs will necessitate more and more planning until it becomes indistinguishable from total planning. Again,

---

[79] Also, "When there is no free market, there is no pricing mechanism; without a pricing mechanism, there is no economic calculation" (111); "for in practice the propertyless manager can only be held morally responsible for losses incurred. And so ethical losses are juxtaposed with opportunities for material gain. The property owner on the other hand himself bears responsibility, as he himself must primarily feel the loss arising from unwisely conducted business" (122) (Additionally: Hayek 1944, 124–25).

[80] The idea that the free market has sublimating potential antedates the neo-liberal movement. That sublimating potential received an appealing formulation in the French expression: "le doux commerce." For a study of the discovery of this kind of potential of the free market, see Hirschman 1977, e.g., 71, 58–63.

[81] This argument is often connected with the argument for stable money, because money is the technical instrument of free choice within the economic domain (Friedman 1962, 27, ch. III; Hayek 1944, 89 ff.; Mises 1975, 98–104).

such total planning will require a dictatorship. Hayek's conclusion is, therefore, that if one wants a democratic government, one has to accept and to defend the free market system (Hayek 1944, ch. V; Friedman 1962, 8–9). The neo-liberal movement defends the free market even though free competition might lead to such undesirable consequences as bankruptcies of certain industries, displacement of labor in unproductive sectors, etc. (Ibid., 100). The neo-liberal theory considers free competition to be so important that it argues that the state should not promote any ends by mechanisms that distort the free competitive market. Among the mechanisms attacked by the neo-liberal doctrine are restrictions of production or provision of subsidies for the purpose of achieving an incomes policy. The neo-liberal doctrine could thus be said to treat the free competitive market as a quasi ultimate or absolute value.

My task now will be to test whether any of the four arguments presented by the neo-liberals for the importance of the free market can be used as a valid argument for the thesis that the free market is an ultimate or absolute value.

Let me start by analyzing the subsidiary arguments. The first subsidiary argument favoring of the free market states that political democracy can survive only if one has a free economy. Such an argument presupposes that political freedom cannot be guaranteed by political institutions or arrangements such as a constitution, separation of powers, independence of the judiciary, life-time or fixed term appointments of crucial functions in society (supreme court, federal reserve boards, professorial appointments). Such an argument refuses to accept the autonomy of different domains (i.e., the economic and the political ones). It fears an overwhelming influence of one domain over another. Such a strategy of argumentation is called reductionism. This reductionist argument had some plausibility prior to World War II with the emergence of fascistic regimes, yet it has lost its practical plausibility since World War II. Indeed, the mixed economies of Western Europe and Scandinavia have not destroyed democracy.

The second subsidiary argument puts forth the belief that the free market promotes desirable anthropological virtues. It is clear that it is nice to have a population that is industrious, responsible, reliable, and has initiative. Is it the case, however, that those are the highest moral virtues?

The moral literature provides a hierarchy of virtues with such virtues as courage, generosity, magnanimity, compassion and friendship situated on a higher moral plane than the virtues extolled by the neo-liberals (Sokolowski). It is not clear how the competitive market could automatically promote this latter series of virtues. The neo-liberal argument amounts to selective appreciation of some virtues. These selectively appreciated virtues are commercially valuable. They are, therefore, instrumental virtues. They are not virtues that directly promote the highest moral good.

The third subsidiary argument states that the free market allows for the exercise of freedom. The free market is, indeed, a system that allows any one individual to make hundreds of choices everyday. However, being able to choose between eggs and bacon or bread and cereal in the morning is one thing. It is another thing to become a free individual in the sense of being able to guide the direction of one's life. Compared with this deeper form of freedom, freedom of choice is but a surface phenomenon.

Besides subsidiary arguments for the free market, the neo-liberal movement presents a main argument in favor of the free market. The neo-liberals argue that the free market promotes economic efficiency. The free market allows soft market arise It gives persons a claim to the social product based on their marginal contribution to that social product. It thereby ties the self-interest of individuals directly to efficiency.

The question which now arises naturally is, why is efficiency valuable? Why is it so valuable, in the opinion of neo-liberals, that it can justify such drastic government interventions as antitrust laws, laws against unfair trade, etc., while at the same time justifying in-action when it comes to bankruptcies caused by lack of competitive efficiency?

The answer to this question can make use of common sense insights. Efficiency is important because human beings are faced with scarcity. It is the scarcity of resources that imposes restraints on human beings' wishes, initiatives and choices. In some cases, it is the scarcity of resources that imposes hardship on people. In as much as efficiency diminishes that scarcity it contributes to all those desirable goals that are thwarted by scarcity of resources.

The argument of common sense locates efficiency as an instrumental value. But if the argument in favor of the free market is based on an instrumental value, then it is the case that the justification of the free market is not absolute but only conditional. It is this conditional validity of the free market that I wish to explore further.

V. The Free Market as a Subsidiary or as an Absolute Value

One way to approach this problem is by means of Hegel's *Philosophy of Right*. Hegel puts forth freedom as an absolute value. Hegel, however, points out that an individual is not capable of reaching freedom alone. He is not capable of doing so because the human will is such that, on the one hand, it aims at the total good (in Hegelian language, the universal) while, on the other hand, in order to will something, human beings have to will a particular (*PR*, ## 5–7). But, a particular is the opposite of the universal.

Hegel sees the solution to this paradox in the creation of social institutions which promote the freedom of all. Participating in such institutions is at the same time promoting such institutions. In this way, a particular deed has universal validity. Thus, accepting a legal contract is, at the same time, enjoying the personal advantages of such a contract and promoting the legal order. In promoting the legal order rather than undermining it, a person increases the trust of others in the legal order. One's personal act thereby has universal significance.

Hegel, however, hastens to add that legal freedom is but a limited form of freedom. Indeed, the legal order does not actually guarantee one's legal rights. Criminals can actually violate them. All the legal order can do is punish a criminal who violated a legal right, after the fact. The legal order cannot always guarantee restitution. Clearly, promotion of legality is not the highest form of freedom (*PR*, ## 73–74).

Similarly, the free market is an institution which promotes the freedom of all. Indeed, the free market is an arrangement which allows individuals a form of freedom that society could not give to its members in the political domain. It allows all individuals to do what they want. In the political domain, that would mean direct democracy and would require unanimity for all decisions. In his analysis of the French Revolution, Hegel argues, as we saw in Chapter 2, that the terror of Robespierre was unavoidable and that its occurrence destroyed a human illusion: the search for a political system without alienation. The economic domain, though, allows for an arrangement where, according to Adam Smith, "Every man... is left perfectly free to pursue his own interest in his own way, and to bring both his industry and capital into competition with those of any other man, or order of men"(Smith, 651). Contrary to what happens in the political domain, giving such a freedom to people in the economic domain does not result in chaos (chapter 2 and chapter 3, Section II of this book).

The discovery of these aspects of the economic domain was one of the achievements of the British, in particular, the Scottish economists. It is on those writings that Hegel's philosophical reflections are based.[82]

Hegel observes that chaos does not occur in the economic domain, when every individual is left free to pursue her own interests, from a th because

---

[82] For a discussion of Hegel's relationship with the British, in particular the Scottish, economists, see Chamley 1963; Denis 1984; Waszek 1988. Particularly influential on Hegel was James Steuart.

it is to some extent a domain subject to determinism.[83] Determinism in the economic domain results from a threat inherent in the free market, combined with a motive in individuals to pay heed to that threat (*PR*, # 186). The threat comes from the free market giving claims to part of the social product only in so far as one has participated in the creation of a product demanded by others; thus, if one does not participate in the social product, the free market has the automatically executed threat of not providing part of the social product.

Given this automatically executed threat and the fact that individuals *must* pay heed to this threat because of their needs, it is the case that the free market is an important instrument for increasing human productivity. The free market, furthermore, allows the human community as a group to produce a diversity of goods that each individual cannot produce for herself.[84]

The free market is thus an institution that provides all participating individuals a claim to part of the social product which is more diversified and bigger than individuals could produce for themselves. The free market is therefore an institution that promotes people's independence from the threat and the pressure of needs. By participating in and willing the free market, the individual thus wills something that benefits all. In that sense, his or her participation in the free market has universal significance.

This Hegelian argument is already present in Adam Smith's theory and is further elaborated by the neo-liberals. There is in Hegel a second and novel argument as to what kind of freedom the free market is providing. According to Hegel, freedom involves the capability of the individual to acknowledge his dependence upon others. Hegel considers this to be a dif-

---

[83] Chaos can have at least three different meanings which it is useful to distinguish. It can mean that a system shows such great disturbance that the underlaying principles of the system are best given up. This was Hegel's opinion about the political philosophy of Rousseau, which inspired the French revolution, which in turn led to the terror of Robespierre. Chaos can also mean that a system shows serious disturbances but that the principles underlying the system are still considered valid and thus only in need of correction. Hegel wrote before 1831 and thus before the great crises of the capitalist system, such as the superinflation of the Weimar Republic, and the 1929 crash of the New York Stock Exchange. One can thus not consult Hegel about their meaning. It is my opinion that it would be in line with Hegel's thought to argue that these crises were not able to undo the truth of Adam Smith's insights in the free market economy. They can be addressed, as Adam Smith addressed some credit problems in his own time, by proper government regulations (Smith, 313). Finally, chaos can also refer to a mathematical concept used to study the disturbances in the financial markets in the capitalist system (Deboeck., 263–314).

[84] This was even recognized by such a sharp critic of the free market system as Karl Marx (Marx 1948, 12). The classic argument has been given in A. Smith's example of pinmaking, resulting in his claims that: "The greatest improvement in the productive power of labour... seem[s] to have been the effects of the division of labour"(Smith, 3 ff.).

ficult task. He believes that an individual prefers to will his independence rather than his dependence. It is precisely at this point that the free market provides help. What an individual is not willing or not able to will by himself, the free market entices him or even forces him to do. Indeed, the free market forces individuals to pay attention to the needs of others, because it is only in so far as one produces goods and services wanted by others that one receives a claim to a share of the social product through which one can satisfy personal needs (*PR*, # 187).

One can thus find in Hegel at least two very different arguments in favor of the free market, because it is an institution which promotes freedom, the ultimate value of human beings, in two ways. First, the free market provides collectively the goods and services to satisfy the needs of its members and it does so in a more efficient way than if everybody were to produce for him or herself. Second, it entices or forces people to pay attention to others, and thus it helps individuals towards their social destiny.

This summary of the main justification of the free market makes it clear, however, that the free market cannot be the highest social institution. Indeed, the two forms of freedom provided by the free market are provided by means of a threat. It is therefore not by means of a voluntary decision that freedom is augmented in the free market. Clearly, this must have consequences. It is to these consequences that I now turn.

VI. Beyond Internal Restrictions of the Free Market

My remaining task is now to see what the consequences are of the presence of a threat or of the lack of voluntary participation in the free market and how these consequences can be remedied.

The main consequence of the fact of guiding production by means of a threat is that the optimum reached by the free market is an optimum responding to that threat. The optimum that the free market strives for is therefore not the optimum optimorum.

At least two major problems emerge when one compares the optimum that the free market aims at with the theoretical optimum optimorum. The first major problem is that of the provision of public (collective) goods.[85]

As is well known in economic literature, one problem with (pure) public goods is that, often, no individual has an incentive to buy or provide these

---

[85] For an excellent summary of Samuelson's views on this problem and a discussion of the whole issue of public goods see Head 1974, 68 ff. The significance of the concept of public good is further defended and elaborated in chapter 6 of this book. I there analyze in detail both the Samuelson and the Olson approach.

goods, and even less to buy or provide them in the optimal amount. This problem of public goods provision is addressed by Samuelson, who gives the government the task of making cost-benefit analyses about public goods and use the power of taxation and the legal power of pre-eminent domain to implement the supposedly economically justified public goods.

Olson addresses a second problem with public goods: the fact that a public good (called by Olson a collective good) can be enjoyed by different people without the owner of the collective good being able to exclude these others from enjoying the benefits of the collective good (Olson 1968, 14–15). Because other people can so easily become "free riders" by enjoying the collective good might not be bought or might not be bought in optimal amounts. Olson sees the solution in the mobilization of the group individual in the public good such that they are willing to make contributions to the organized group which promises the provision of the public good. Olson points out that if mobilization succeeds there is the likelihood of over-provision (there is a feast). If the mobilization does not succeed there is under-provision (there is famine). Olson suggests that if there is under-provision of an important public (collective) good the government might create laws which provide the necessary incentives for the interested group to mobilize itself (union shop or closed shop legislation) (Ibid., 68).

Both Samuelson and Olson concede that the provision of public goods is not necessarily optimal. Hence, there is room for a prudent government role in the provision of public goods, which we will discuss in more detail in chapter 6 of this book.

The second major problem with the free market derives from the fact that the threat inherent in the free market operates only at the micro-level. Thus, macro-events are not controlled by the threat of the free market. It is as if the market turns a blind eye to these events. The most important such macro-phenomenon is the business cycle which creates unemployment and idleness of productive resources.

The purpose of the economic order is to liberate individuals from the fact that resources are scarce. In order to promote this form of liberation for the whole community, the neo-liberal doctrine accepts the burden of free competition including its inherent threat, e.g., the threat of starvation or bankruptcy if one does not pay attention to the demands of others. But now we hit upon an argument that shows us that the threat of the free market is in some sense blind, as in dealing with business cycles. Accepting the argument of the neo-liberal doctrine that efficiency justifies the imposition of an institutional mechanism (the free market) on individuals, do we not have to argue that the government must look for a corrective mechanism in order to curtail the inefficiencies created by the business cycle?

Such an argument brings us from neo-liberalism to Keynesianism.[86] The difficult question in that transition, though, is to know whether Keynesianism can be successfully welded to a free market economy without destroying a vital mechanism of the free market itself, i.e., price stability (Ver Eecke 1975 b, esp. 444).[87]

VII. Freedom and the Free Market

One more point needs to be considered. There are individuals who, because of mental or physical disabilities, are unable to participate competitively in the free market. Just as other individuals, they have a potential freedom that requests realization. The relationship between freedom and economic goods and services is such that, in general, family capital is insufficient to guarantee the freedom of disabled or handicapped persons in contemporary society.

Must the freedom of disabled or handicapped persons be sacrificed in order to satisfy the impersonal requirements of the free market, whose purpose is to increase the possible freedom of all?

In order to approach this problem, I would like to make use of an analogy. First, let us recall that we accepted the neo-liberal doctrine that the justifying ground for the free market is efficiency. Let us further recall that the burdens imposed in the name of efficiency cannot be justified by efficiency itself but need a deeper form of justification. We found such a justification in the concept of freedom. Let me now compare the relationship of the free market to the concept of freedom with a tree and its roots. As for the relationship between a tree and its roots, one can accept the proposition that in order for us to protect and nurture the tree, one needs to feed and nurture the roots of the tree. One cannot hope to have a healthy tree if one allows its roots to be damaged or to be poisoned. Analogously, one has to say about the relation between the free market and the concept of freedom that one cannot hope to promote the free market without nurturing its foundation, i.e., freedom.

---

[86] Keynes argues that the free market can have several points of equilibrium, only one of which includes full employment. Thus, unemployment is a distinct possibility within the free market (Keynes 1965, 26).

[87] Since I wrote these ideas the economic profession and policy makers have become more convinced of the importance of price stability and have found ways to combine the approach advocated by Keynesian theories with methods for keeping inflation better in check, as reflected in substantially lower average global inflation rates than two decades ago without crimping economic growth.

When the promotion of the free market and the promotion of freedom come into conflict, it is, therefore, short-sighted to promote the free market at the expense of freedom. On the contrary, the impersonal requirements of the free market should not be promoted at the expense of freedom.

In order to help us see clearly how one should understand a conflict between the free market and the concept of freedom, I would like to look to a similar conflict, the conflict between the legal system and freedom. Let us restrict ourselves to the problem of property in the legal system. In the first section of this chapter, I appealed to Hegel to demonstrate the relation between property and freedom. Property was demonstrated to be a requirement of freedom that needs to be external in order to be real.

It is now possible that within a society with property rights, there is, from time to time, a person threatened with starvation. Such a threat is an ultimate threat to the freedom of that person. The situation presents us with a conflict between life and property. When the conflict is seen in those terms, one does not have the means to solve the conflict. One, first, needs to relate life and property to another concept that can be presented as the foundation of both. Freedom is such a concept. Indeed, property is seen as a first embodiment of freedom, whereas life is the source of freedom. Thus, in a conflict between life and property, there is a situation in which "there is on the one hand an infinite injury to a man's existence and the consequent loss of rights altogether, and, on the other hand, only an injury to a single restricted embodiment of freedom." Thus Hegel concludes that property rights cease if the enforcement of such a right threatens the life of another (*PR*, # 127).

Can one now argue on the basis of analogy that the requirements of the free market cease when they threaten the viability of the life of mentally or physically handicapped persons?[88]

At first sight, it looks as if the analogy with the tree and the legal system holds. Indeed, the tree, the legal system, and the free market do not have a life of their own. Reference must be made to the roots of the tree or the concept of freedom for the legal system and the free market. Our argument thus takes the following form: just as one cannot destroy life for the

---

[88] Sen makes a similar argument when he says that property rights cease in the face of mass starvation (Sen 1985, 5–6). The general argument that property rights cease in the face of something foundational to property (in Hegel's view: freedom) has affinities with the "functionings and capabilities" approach developed later by Sen and further elaborated by Nussbaum. According to this view, a just society must provide all individuals with the means to reach and develop certain important functions and capabilities. Financing this goal can only occur by some form of taxation which means taking away from some what otherwise would have been their property. A summary of the "functionings and capabilities" approach can be found in the review, by a moral philosopher, of Nussbaum's book *Women and Human Development* (Hausman 2001).

sake of maintaining one objective embodiment of freedom in the legal system, so one cannot make the realization of freedom of the handicapped impossible for the purpose of realizing a system created to further freedom. This reasoning parallels the original analogy: one cannot hope to maintain a healthy tree if one destroys the roots of the tree.

Upon further reflection, the relation between the claims of the free market and the claims of the handicapped seems to be more complicated. Hegel gives at least two further arguments that must be considered when studying the conflict between the principle of the free market and the claims for support of underprivileged persons.

The first additional argument concerns the idea that giving underprivileged persons support deprives those persons of the self-respect and self-esteem that are the reward of earning one's own living (*PR*, # 245).

The second additional argument to be considered is the fact that giving support to anybody without such support being the payment for a contribution to the social product is a violation of the principle of the free market. This violation is all the more troublesome because the principle of the free market (*PR*, # 245) is not freely accepted by the members of society. Indeed, the neo-liberal doctrine teaches us that everybody has a selfish interest in trying to escape the burden of the free market, while advocating that such a burden be imposed on others. Supporting the underprivileged can thus be experienced as a form of betrayal which the state imposes upon its members.[89]

Do these two arguments nullify the original argument in favor of the claim for support of the underprivileged? One must accept, at least, that these two arguments build a solid case for limiting the open-ended claim for support. The two arguments teach us something more: a society cannot hope that support for the underprivileged within a free market system will necessarily lead to an increased spirit of belonging or of community. Indeed, those who receive support are deprived of the self-respect typical of successful participation in the free market. Those who are asked to support the underprivileged may feel betrayed because the state does not apply the threat of the free market to all. Thus, people can become resentful. A welfare state therefore has seeds of destruction in its own soil. Still, these two arguments do no more than limit the claims and point to an inherent

---

[89] The experience of betrayal can easily lead to resentment for either one of the following subjective reasons: 1. a feeling of unjustified deprivation of some pleasures one could have gotten from the money that was taxed away to support the needy. 2. a sense of having been unjustifiably denied the rights to one's own resources. 3. the experience of imposed unfairness because one is excluded from the protection from the harshness of economic life that others receive. I am grateful to George G. Brenkert for suggesting the different mechanisms that can create resentment to welfare measures.

danger of the welfare state. These two arguments do not undermine the basic connection established between freedom and the free market. As such, I wish to affirm that the ontology of the free market discovered by the neo-liberal school lays the foundation for a justification of some actions of the welfare state (Winfield 1990, 183).

Conclusion

The neo-liberal doctrine helped us to see, correctly, that the economic domain is not to be understood as a natural system. This insight led us to the argument that economics has an inherent connection with ethics. That connection was demonstrated most clearly in the analysis of property and in the analysis of the problem of public goods. The force used by the state to transform possession into property was justified by means of the concept of freedom. Similarly, the Samuelsonian and Olsonian approaches to the provision of public goods leave an opening for a legitimate role of the government for any society trying to approach a theoretically proven economic optimum.

Property and public goods are two concepts that are crucial in economic theory. In as much as these concepts are tied to the use of force by the state, economics cannot be separated from ethics. This insight led us then to explore the transition of the neo-liberal doctrine into the justification of the welfare state. Our exploration led to the conclusion that the justification of the free market implies the acceptance of some form of welfare state. At the same time, I hit upon an argument that demonstrates that the welfare state violates the basic principle of the free market.

I would like to end this chapter by explicitly formulating this uneasy paradox: the free market philosophically implies the welfare state even though this welfare state is a violation of the free market principle.

Section III

Tightening the Argument
A Philosophical Dialogue with Economists

5. The Concept of "Merit Good" and the History of Economic Thought

Abstract

The purpose of this chapter is to defend the concept of "merit good" and to expand its application. This is achieved by using a Kantian argument applied to the writings of foundational economists such as Adam Smith and Henry Simons as well as Walter Eucken in the German literature. As a result, the concept of "merit good" is used to classify and to argue for a number of governmental tasks such as the institutional arrangements needed to make a free market economy work efficiently and in a humane way. Methodologically, this paper connects economic theory, the history of economic thought, and institutional economics, thereby demonstrating that economics is unavoidably intertwined with politics.

The necessity of politically imposed institutional arrangements for the economy to function well and humanely demonstrates the validity of Hegel's claim that the economic domain is an ethical arrangement.

I. The Problem

Fifty eight years ago, Richard A. Musgrave introduced the concept of "merit wants" (1956, 333–4).[90] A decade and a half ago, in a talk for an international conference on the problem of "merit goods," John Head complained that:

> it might perhaps have been expected that the merit wants concept would, by 1987, be showing all the usual signs of maturity in the evolution of an economic concept. Simple questions of definition or interpretation should on this reckoning long since have been resolved, and a broad consensus would

---

[90] One can find most of the references to the concept of merit good in one anthology: Ver Eecke 2007.

typically have been reached on fundamental analytical issues relating to normative status and policy relevance. The treatment of the concept in the standard textbooks would by now be routine and highly uniform. In the case of its more celebrated twin, the social want or public good, this familiar process has indeed occurred and has long since appeared substantially complete.

As compared with social wants, however, the merit wants concept raises methodologically much more difficult and controversial issues symbolizing as it does, for the public finance literature, many of the doubts and reservations which have been expressed over generations by economists of varying political persuasions regarding the ultimate normative authority of the consumer sovereignty principle. On these issues the views of economists have traditionally seemed poles apart. (1999, 211)

The main purpose of this chapter is to restart the discussion of the concept of "merit good" by demonstrating not only that Musgrave's original intuition was correct, but by also demonstrating that the concept is much more broadly applicable than Musgrave himself envisioned. The acceptance of my broader interpretation of the concept of "merit good" involves a paradigm shift that Musgrave did not fully realize. It requires a shift from an exclusive individualistic view of economics to a socio-economic viewpoint, in which political and institutional arrangements are understood to have a crucial impact on economic performance. If my thesis is accepted, it will be evident that it is unfortunate that the introductory textbooks in economics largely omit the concept of "merit good." It will also be evident that it is deplorable that the discussion of the merit good problem has become sparse in the literature, more sparse in the English economic literature than in the German one. Much still needs to be discussed about the methods of economically analyzing problems of merit goods. But let us start from the beginning.

While writing an article in 1956 about the theory of governmental budgets, Musgrave discovered an argument for ethical concepts in economic thinking by introducing the concepts of "merit want" or "merit good" – i.e., areas in the economy where the government is justified in interfering with the preferences of individuals (1956, 333–4).[91] In that arti-

---

[91] In a recent autobiographical essay, Musgrave writes that his early training in German public finance and in German theory of the state made him sensitive to a domain in economics that could not be handled by the two concepts based on individualistic assumptions: private and public goods. Musgrave there conceptually acknowledges that economics should be socio-economics, and must include reflections on political and institutional arrangements. Consider this quotation: "Admittedly difficult to define and dangerous to entertain, communal concerns have been part of the scene from Plato on, and my concept of merit goods (applicable to private and social goods alike) was to provide a limited opening

cle, Musgrave starts by arguing that the government has three roles to play: a service role, a distribution role, and a stabilization role.

In its service role, the government has to undertake the production of public goods in an optimal way, and it has to find a means of financing that is equally optimal. The financing method takes the form of a tax system. The difficulties which have to be surmounted to accomplish this double task are well known.[92]

In its distribution role, the government has to ensure that the incomes of citizens are allocated in an optimal way. Taxation and monetary transfers are a technically efficient manner of doing this. The main question for the distribution role concerns, however, not the method, but the amount of redistributing that is to be done. Musgrave calls this a problem of social choice. Together with many contemporary economists, he considers this a non-economic problem, i.e., a problem that cannot properly be addressed by economic methods of analysis. The stabilization role consists in the government creating the correct aggregate demand for the creation of full employment without inflation. This role is also known as the government's duty to avoid the negative consequences of the business cycle, particularly those of economic recession and depression.

As a pedagogical device, Musgrave imagines that these three tasks are performed by three separate departments of the government. He also imagines that the three tasks are performed simultaneously. He further supposes that the funds credited and debited to each of these three departments are sent to a computing department, which ensures that each person receives a credit (in the form of a check, for instance), or a debit (an obligation to pay a certain amount of taxes).

But at the end of his article, Musgrave admits that the government performs certain economic activities that cannot be classified neatly in terms

---

for their role" (Musgrave 1959 and 1987). "Dutiful performance of civil service remains a constructive concept, as does that of responsible public leadership. Though they now tend to be ridiculed, both these alternative modes are essential to make democracy work. Nor are issues of entitlement and distributive justice reducible to principles of exchange, issues which have to be resolved before that mode can be given its role. The broad-based roots of the German tradition, its linkage to the theory of state and to fiscal sociology (Musgrave 1980) helped to provide awareness of these issues" (Musgrave 1993, 66–7). Still, Musgrave often tried to limit the applicability of the concept of "merit goods" in his economic writings (Musgrave 1987).

[92] Economically optimal pricing for public goods requires that the same good have a different price for different consumers who value the same item differently. Thus, toll booths charge trucks and regular cars differently. Theoretically, the differentiation should not stop at groups. If the individuals within these groups have a different evaluation of the item, then these individuals should be charged a different price. The problem is that it is difficult to know the true evaluation of items by individuals. For a more detailed analysis of the problem, see chapter 6 in this book.

of these three functions. He names two such activities: free medical treatment for the poor and subsidies for low-priced housing (1956, 341). These two examples belong, on the one hand, to the service role because they produce a public good. But this service represents, at the same time, a form of redistribution, because not everyone is entitled to free medical treatment, and not everybody can receive grants for housing. Only a certain class of people is entitled to them. The two cited examples seem, therefore, to be economic activities that belong simultaneously to two government departments: the service and the distribution departments.

Musgrave tries to solve this problem by entertaining the idea that these two examples are cases of pure redistribution. Considered as forms of redistribution, the supplying of free medical treatment and grants for low-cost housing become comparable to monetary transfers, combined with an additional limitation imposed on the free choice of the recipients as to what can be done with this money. This kind of redistribution thus does not respect the sovereignty of the consumer's wishes (in this case the wishes of the poor, the ones receiving subsidies); on the contrary, it imposes limitations on their choices. Musgrave's solution, however, creates a new problem: thus classified, these economic activities seem to disregard the normative economic maxim of consumer sovereignty. He tries to soften this new problem by asking whether or not such a limitation upon consumers should, as a matter of course, be condemned. Musgrave does not believe it should because consumers sometimes make irrational choices. They purchase a second car or a second refrigerator before ensuring that they have adequately prepared for the education of their children. Goods for which the government justifiably restricts the choice of consumers deserve a special name. Musgrave calls them "merit wants (goods)" (Ibid.).

In his later publications Musgrave often comes back to the problem of merit goods. Further examples of merit goods are free education and free school lunches (Musgrave 1959, 13; 1987, 453). The examples of compulsory inoculation and all subsidies in kind could be added. In like manner, we could take as examples of demerit goods sumptuary or "penalty" taxes on liquor (1959, 13) and tobacco.

Beginning in 1959 with the publication of *The Theory of Public Finance*, Musgrave takes an important step by providing a definition of the concept "merit goods" that is independent of his own theory of public finance. A merit good is defined as a good which is so important that when the competent authorities are dissatisfied with the level of consumption in the free market, they can intervene, even against the wishes of consumers (Ibid.).

Musgrave does not feel very comfortable with this new concept. He tries to find different kinds of justifications for the concept of merit good, but he admits that the term remains problematic.[93]

Charles McLure, on the other hand, has no such ambiguous attitude towards the concept of merit good. He states plainly that the concept has *no* place in a normative theory of public finance (1968, 474, 482) and that our Western economic theory knows only one norm: the wishes or preferences of individual consumers. One of the tasks of economic theory, for McLure, is to point out what has to be done to satisfy these wishes as much as possible. This is normative thinking. When economists create normative theories about government finance, they have to remain faithful to this goal, i.e., the goal that government should spend money in order to satisfy the wishes of individual consumers as efficiently as possible. However, when economists introduce the concept of merit good, he says, they try to find out how they can get around the wishes of consumers. They try to find ways of violating the fundamental axiom of free-market economics. Such thinking – i.e., thinking about merit goods – has, therefore, no place in normative economic thinking, according to McLure. He further states that the government often denies the legitimacy of consumer wishes. Economists are allowed to describe this, but they are not allowed to include it in their normative thinking.[94]

---

[93] I do not address here the difficulties that Musgrave encounters in trying to differentiate merit goods from public and private goods. Sometimes, he seems to think that merit goods are only applicable to public goods. At other times, he seems to think that merit goods are private goods only. His final position is that merit goods can be both private and public goods (1993, 66–7). I do not address here the problem of the multiple definitions that Musgrave seems to have entertained, which is discussed in Allan G. Pulsipher (1971/72, 278–9). My position is that Musgrave has always rejected a pure authoritarian provision of merit goods, and that he always thought that merit goods were more than a correction of consumer wishes. I understand Musgrave to say that "correction of consumer wishes" covers but a subclass of the merit goods, the total class being better defined as "intervention in consumer wishes." For a documentation of these two problems in Musgrave's texts, see Andel 1984, 631–7). Head claims that Musgrave defines merit goods as "the need to correct individual preferences" (1966, 216). This claim is disputed by, among others, McLure: "Thus by asserting imperfect knowledge to be the heart of merit wants, *Head* seriously misinterprets *Musgrave*" (1968, 477).

[94] In an international conference on the problem of merit goods McLure took a more flexible position (1990, 185). In that same conference, a whole section was devoted to "Irreducibly Social Goods." This paper by Charles Taylor and the comments by Robert E. Goodin, John Broome, Frank Jackson and Peter Gärdenfors are published as part of a book on the conference (Brennan and Walsh, 1990, 45–96). Some of the authors defend irreducibly social goods (merit goods), others reject it, still others believe that it is more important to see the multiple ways in which a good can be social. Clearly, this conference did not produce agreement on the question of the legitimacy of the concept of merit good.

The contrast between Musgrave's and McLure's ideas provides an excellent opportunity to situate ethical thinking in the context of economic thought and to demonstrate anew that economics is in fact socio-economics, requiring explicit reflections about political and institutional arrangements.. Musgrave discovers governmental activities which ignore the wishes of consumers in connection with some goods. McLure argues that the concept of merit good has no place in normative economic thinking. Musgrave admits that he does not have sufficient justification for his new concept but refuses to argue that all intervention by the government which fails to satisfy individual wishes is illicit.

If we agree with McLure, we admit that ethics involves a kind of thinking which is not immediately relevant to economic thinking.[95] If we follow Musgrave, we implicitly accept the thesis that ethics can play a role in economic thinking, although we may momentarily lack sufficient arguments.

Clearly, we are here confronted with a major difficulty. As we are dealing with a normative problem, it would be appropriate to consult philosophical thought (Ver Eecke 1984, 198–202). But first, I wish to sketch the broader context of the problem.

Economic theory speaks about private goods (sugar, bread, oranges) and public goods (national defense, pure air, bridges, roads) (for a good synopsis of the problem of public goods, see Head 1974, chapter 3). Musgrave adds a third concept: merit goods. Economic thinking, per Musgrave's view, thus embraces three kinds of goods. Western economic thinking gives priority to the concept of private good, because this concept is directly connected to the wishes of consumers. The free market is the institution through which private goods are produced and (hopefully) distributed in an optimal way. The two other kinds of goods (public goods and merit goods) are exceptions to the idea of private goods. Therefore, we can call them non-private goods. Since these non-private goods are usually supplied by means of the political system, we can give them another name: political economic goods.[96]

It is important to clearly understand the difference between the two kinds of goods provided by the political system. Public goods are political

---

[95] Based on the work of Hausman and McPherson one could make an ad hominem argument against McLure's position. Hausman and McPherson argue that giving absolute authority to individual preferences in order to legitimate economic outcomes is an ethical position itself. Furthermore, it is not defensible neither theoretically, nor politically nor for the forum of common sense. Indeed, a position like McLure's implies that one cannot differentiate between "expensive, anti-social [preferences], or [preferences that are] the result of false beliefs, manipulation, or problematic psychological processes" (Hausman and McPherson 1966, 83). They must all be considered equally valid.

[96] This name was suggested by H. Briefs.

economic goods provided by the government with the intention of respecting the wishes of consumers. The consumers need help because public goods have technical (factual) characteristics that make it difficult for individuals to acquire them in an optimal way. Merit goods, on the other hand, are political economic goods which the government provides by a method, or at a level, which *dis*regards the wishes of consumers.[97]

The above argument allows us to assert that economic theory needs three, and only three, concepts to be complete. Indeed, there is the normative concept of private goods, and in my view, two reasons, and two only, why a good might be non-private: a factual constraint and a value judgment.[98] The factual exception relates to the fact that some goods can be consumed by different consumers simultaneously. These goods are conceptualized as public goods (e.g., a light increasing safety in an alley). The other exception is that some goods are judged to have special moral value: they are judged to be very beneficial or they are judged to be obnoxious. These judgments give rise to the concept of merit good (e.g., education, which is made obligatory) or its opposite demerit goods (e.g., liquor on whose consumption sin taxes are imposed).

Let us further clarify the difference between goods that are non-private because of reasons of fact and those that are non-private because of reasons of value. Economic theory argues, with respect to public goods, both that factual characteristics are the reason why individuals need help and that this help can be given while respecting the wishes of consumers. There are two factual reasons a good might not be a private good: non-rivalness in consumption and impossibility of exclusion.[99] The factual properties of these goods are, therefore, the reason they cannot be considered private goods and, as a consequence, it is not optimal to provide them through the free market.

A completely different exception to private goods occurs when a value judgment is passed that stipulates that the free market does not ensure a desirable level of consumption. This is the case of Musgrave's concept of (de)merit goods. Because value judgments about merit goods are not made

---

[97] Economists are aware that some preferences are problematic. Thus, John Head points to lack of reliable knowledge (lack of information or presence of persuasive and misleading information) or the presence of irrationality in the consumer as leading causes for problematic preference choices (Head 1974, 217–220).

[98] The above argument implies that economic theory needs at least three sub-concepts for the main concept of economic good. For a study demonstrating the practical importance of using and distinguishing these three concepts see: Godwin (1991, 415–29). An alternative way of introducing value judgments (commitments) in economic theory is Sen's proposal for a hierarchy of preference orderings (Sen 1977, 326–44).

[99] For a further discussion of these characteristics of public goods see chapter 6 in this book.

by individual consumers but by representatives of society (government officials), McLure claims that they should not be part of normative economic thinking, which is itself based on respect of the sovereignty of individual consumers.

The problem, therefore, is: should the concept of merit good belong to normative economic theory? If it should, what are the arguments in favor of its inclusion?

II. Justification of the Term "Merit Good"

McLure accepts the proposition that only one method exists for justifying something economically, namely, compliance with the wishes of individual consumers. When we look at the history of philosophy, we see that one of the major philosophers, Immanuel Kant, built his philosophy on a totally different method of thinking; namely, the transcendental method, which involves the search for conditions of possibility.

Kant's method of thinking consists of focusing on two important facts, and then looking for the conditions of the possibility of these facts. The two facts he was concerned with are the existence of scientific laws and the existence of a feeling of moral obligation (Kant 1956, 166). He deals with the first in the *Critique of Pure Reason* and the second in the *Critique of Practical Reason*. In the *Critique of Pure Reason*, Kant argues against the British empiricists, who assert that knowledge of the world is based solely on sensory perception. Kant asserts that when we look at a table from three different points of view and thus produce three sensory observations, but we claim that there is only one table. Kant asks what the conditions of possibility are for asserting that we only see one table even when we have three sensory impressions. He answers that it is because we live in a world of objects and not in a world of sensory impressions. For Kant, an object is the combination of observed impressions together with the categories of the mind. For example, the table is an object, because we consider it to consist of its observed front together with its postulated back. Or again, due to the category of causality, any material object is the observed phenomenon, together with the postulated continued existence of this observed phenomenon over time.

Kant's argumentation allows us to affirm that if one accepts the idea that there is only one table, then one *must* accept the idea that even though we possess three sense impressions, the real, true perception is the result of the combination of these sense impressions with the categories of the mind. Hence, one must abandon empiricism as a theoretical explanation.

Kant gives us here a new type of method of justification: to look for possibility conditions by means of logical reasoning (Ibid.). This is the same reasoning used in daily life. When my children are thirsty I tell them that they can find drinks in the refrigerator. Whether they feel like it or not, the possibility condition for ending their thirst is for them to get the drinks out of the refrigerator themselves.

In a similar way, one can assert that there are at least two ways to prove that something possesses economic justification. The first way is the familiar way of arguing: that which fulfills, in the best manner, the wishes of the consumers, as they see it, is economically justified. The second way follows the Kantian method of thinking: if citizens and consumers want something, they also have to accept its possibility conditions. They have to accept them whether they want to or not. This second kind of reasoning rests on the insight that there are logical relations in reality. These logical relations have validity, even if consumers do not like them.

We shall call merit goods those goods which are the conditions of possibility of something that is desired by the consumers, even and especially if these merit goods or services themselves are not preferred by consumers.[100] This method of arguing has the advantage that we can set limits to merit goods. The government cannot thwart the wishes of the consumers whenever it feels like it: the government needs arguments. And these arguments set limits to government actions. The government might be annoyed with corporations and might want to punish them. The government cannot punish them because it is annoyed with them. It can punish them if the courts establish that they violated, for instance, anti-trust laws, which I interpret as laws promoting efficient production, which in turn I consider a merit good.

If my philosophical reasoning is correct, it means that economic thinking necessarily has to propose that the government should perform economic activities which interfere with the wishes of some consumers. Let me restate my thoughts in a different way. If my philosophical reasoning is correct, we can assume that economic thinking will propose economic activities to the government which will respect neither the Pareto principle nor the consumer sovereignty principle (examples are banking regulations and anti-trust laws). This means that economists will recommend to the

---

[100] Such a defense of merit goods leads to the distinction between a potential and an actual merit good. A potential merit good is a good which is a possibility condition for something that consumers want, but which is under current circumstances also desired by the consumers. A potential merit good becomes an actual merit good if it is not wanted itself. This distinction is similar to the one used by Folkers when he distinguishes between merit need and merit good (1974, 23). McLure's definition of merit goods, on the other hand, is restricted to actual interference with consumer preferences (1968, 479).

government some economic activities which might cause disadvantage to some citizens, and might favor others. Economics must therefore necessarily become political economy or socio-economics, where the first label stresses more the political dimension and the second the social dimension involved in providing (de)merit goods (Smith, 1937, 247–50, 651-2, 767–8; Schumpeter, 1954).

Someone might argue here that the provision of public goods sometimes has the same consequence of interfering with consumer wishes, as in the case of the expropriation of land for the creation of highways. But, this comparison between public and merit goods is unwarranted. In the case of public goods, economic theory of optimal allocation requires that those who experience negative utility from its provision must be compensated. Where compensation is not given, because it is impractical or because the consumer is assumed to exaggerate the amount of disutility (strategic behavior), the theory still requires us to regret the inconvenience of the disutilities, because the provision of public goods intends to improve the situation of everybody. Merit goods are another matter. The theory of (de)merit goods does not include the idea that disutilities have to be compensated. Thus, policies aimed at lowering the rate of smoking need not include compensation for the inconvenience imposed on smokers. Similarly, antitrust legislation does not include compensation for the restrictions imposed on monopolists. Disutilities for some are intended in the very concept of merit good (Musgrave & Musgrave, 1973, 80–81). That an economic concept includes the intention of imposing disutilities on some gives us an opportunity to situate, systematically, ethical problems within an economic framework.

In the second part of this chapter, I wish to articulate what the different kinds of merit goods are. It is interesting to discover that these different kinds of merit goods are already present in the history of economic theory. We will discover these different types of merit goods defended by Adam Smith, the neo-liberals, Keynes, and the contemporary theories of the welfare state.

III. Justification of the Different Kinds of Merit Goods

The sole method of justification that we will use is implied in the question: what are the conditions of possibility of a given thing that the citizens, as economic actors, wish?

Western citizens as economic actors wish first for a free market.[101] A free market cannot exist as a factual arrangement if certain conditions are not fulfilled. Adam Smith thought about this intensively in Part V of his *Wealth of Nations.* As conditions for the possibility of the free market Adam Smith names the following: (i) national defense; (ii) a legal system which protects property, enforces contracts, and is executed by judges and politicians; and (iii) bridges, roads, etc., to enhance commerce (653–716, especially 659, 670, 681–2, 690).

The two first tasks are sometimes mentioned as tasks for the minimal state.[102] These tasks cannot be defended by the public goods argument alone, because the provision of these goods does not respect, and does not even intend to respect, the wishes of all consumers. Smith seems to know this very well when he makes the following statement concerning property rights:

> Civil government, so far as it is instituted for the security of property, is in reality instituted for the defense of the rich against the poor, or of those who have some property against those who have none at all. (674)

Furthermore, Smith invokes value judgments for the justification of these governmental activities, a move which would be superfluous or out of place if one used the argument of public goods. Consider Smith's statement:

> Even though the martial spirit of the people were of no use towards the defence of the society, yet to prevent that sort of mental mutilation, deformity, and wretchedness, which cowardice necessarily involves in it, from spreading themselves through the great body of the people, would still deserve the most serious attention of government. (739)

Smith also makes an appeal to a second value judgment when he writes:

---

[101] One could argue that the free market is not a good per se, but that it is an institutional or legal arrangement. Still, I want to maintain that institutional arrangements are produced. They involve the use of some resources. They result in something that is desired. In as much as institutional arrangements result in something desirable, they are a good or a service. In as much as they require resources they must be called economic goods. Given the necessity of institutional arrangements, which themselves are economic goods, economics is thus necessarily socio-economics. This was clearly understood by Schumpeter (1954). This is also an accepted premise in a recent technical publication (World Bank, 1997) and in a moral analysis of the different economic systems (John Paul II, 1991, ## 24, 29, 34, 35, 36, 40, 42, 48).

[102] The German term is *Rechtsstaat.*

That degree of liberty which approaches to licentiousness can be tolerated only in countries where the sovereign is secured by a well-regulated standing army (668).

With reference to merit goods, as I have been using the term, Smith not only realizes that the wishes of some consumers are harmed by the minimal state, and that an appeal can be made to value judgments; he also proposes that these goods be financed differently than public goods. Ideally, public goods should be financed through taxation of the individuals who benefit from the use of these goods. Furthermore, the amount of the taxation should be directly linked to the usefulness enjoyed by each consumer. When a consumer derives more use from a bridge because he drives a truck, he should pay more taxes than another consumer who derives much less use from this bridge because he only uses it to ride a bike to his job. For the goods of the minimal state, however, Smith recommends that another method of financing be used. He proposes a financing method which breaks the connection between the amount of taxation and the subjective utility experienced from the provision of the good. Smith proposes that the goods from the minimal state be financed by general revenue to which each contributes according to his ability to pay, independently of the utility he derives from its provision. Appropriately, this method of financing is called the "ability-to-pay-method" (767).

For me, the violation of the wishes of some consumers, the use of value judgments, and the recommendation of a different financing method are three reasons why I do not want to subsume the tasks of the minimal state (national defense, enforcement of justice) under the concept of public good. According to my reasoning, I can classify them as merit goods, since they are the condition for the possibility of the free market as a factual arrangement. Thus, contrary to most economists, I would not consider national defense or police protection as examples of *pure* public goods.

In my analysis of Adam Smith's thought, I implicitly encountered a significant ethical problem: the right of ownership. Adam Smith admits that the protection of the right of ownership is a governmental action taken for the advantage of the rich and to the detriment of the poor, or for the advantage of those who have property and to the detriment of those who do not (674). The question now becomes whether this economically necessary protection of property is ethically justifiable. Marxists answer that the right of ownership must be limited, more exactly, that the ownership of the means of production in the hands of private persons must be prohibited. Western democracies answer by giving non-owners other forms of security such as unemployment benefits, work accident insurance, the right of unionized protection of wages, and so on.[103]

We learned about a first kind of merit good from Adam Smith: the goods and services connected with the idea of the minimal state and justified by the fact that they are the conditions for the possibility of the free market.

The free market is not, as Adam Smith says, a natural phenomenon that would flourish if greedy and unenlightened kings did not interfere. The neo-liberals[104] draw attention to the fact that the free market is a vulnerable human institution. Many (if not most) participants wish to escape the rules of the free market because it theoretically prevents the use of power to increase the benefit from economic transactions (e.g., monopolistic practices). The endeavor to escape from the free market took a serious turn in the nineteenth century with the creation of cartels, trusts, and unions.[105]

The neo-liberals tend to look at the free market, not as a natural fact, but as a valuable human institution that succeeds in guaranteeing almost automatically the value of economic efficiency. The neo-liberals claim that the free market is worthwhile, because it promotes that efficiency. They are also prepared to claim that the government has to do whatever it can to make economic reality approach the efficiency that the theory of the ideal free market demonstrates to be possible.

In order to prevent individuals from escaping the discipline of the competitive free market, the state will have to impose measures that violate the Pareto principle. I call these measures the possibility conditions for implementing the ideal efficiency of the free competitive market. An important representative of the neo-liberals is Henry C. Simons, founder of the Chicago school and author of *Economic Policy for a Free Society*. In that

---

[103] Hegel argued that property is a first and necessary objectification or embodiment of freedom. He thereby defends jointly the right to property *and* the philosophical necessity of overcoming poverty and destitution. I developed these ideas more extensively in chapter 3, Section III "The Proper Relation Between State and Economy" and in chapter 4, Section I "The Function of Property."

[104] The term "Neo-liberal" is a translation of the German term *Neoliberalismus*, and covers such diverse groups as the Vienna marginalists, the economists centered around the *Ordo* group in Freiburg/iBr, and the Chicago School of Economics. Egon Edgar Nawroth provides a splendid overview of the doctrines of different German neo-liberal authors (Nawroth 1961).

[105] Guilds, mercantilism or physiocratic policies all violated the laws of the free market. These violations occurred, however, before the defense and glorification of the free market by Adam Smith. The nineteenth century's practices, on the other hand, can be seen as a direct challenge to the presentation of the free market as normatively desirable.

work he assigns the government five groups of tasks, of which four are significant for us.[106]

First, Simons recommends two measures in connection with the monetary system. He suggests that the banking system should be based on an obligatory 100 percent reserve requirement instead of the fractional one presently in place. He also proposes that banks should lose the right to convert short-term debts into long-term ones. Both measures would limit the power of banks to create credit. Simons argues that this is necessary, because the creation of credit is a major cause of inflation, which deforms economic activity and leads to inefficiency (1973, 62-3, 78–9).[107]

Second, Simons argues that monopolies should be opposed by the government. Natural monopolies such as electricity, water supply, and so on have to be controlled by public authorities. Artificial monopolies have to be broken up. Production limitations and the creation of artificially high prices have to be legally treated as crimes. Buyouts of industries need to be legally limited. The creation of connections between related industries also has to be prohibited. Thus, the possession of stocks in other companies has to be limited, as does the possibility of becoming a member of the board of directors of another company (81–3).

Third, Simons attacks tariffs and subsidies, especially in foreign trade and agriculture. Only in the case of an "infant industry" does Simons accept the argument that a temporary subsidy is justified (69–70, 84).

Fourth, Simons recommends that a series of measures be taken to improve the efficiency of commerce. He claims that advertising is useless, and therefore he recommends that high taxes should be placed on it.[108]

---

[106] Roughly the same governmental activities were argued for by a group of authors centered around the German journal *Ordo*, in Freiburg/iBr. The main theoretical representative of that school was Walter Eucken (1982, 115-31). The best known public figure of that group is Ludwig Ehrhard, who was credited with engineering the German economic miracle after the second world war.

[107] I am not alone in calling stable monetary policy a merit good. B. Molitor does so too, even though he calls it a different kind of merit good, i.e., security (1988). I classify security concerns (a social safety net) as a fifth kind of merit good and would also put there Molitor's other examples of protection against work related accidents and obligatory retirement savings. I believe that one needs different arguments to justify the government's role in monetary policy and in providing a social safety net. Therefore, I believe that I am justified in separating monetary policy and the provision of social security in putting them into different categories of merit goods. Finally, let us point out that Schumpeter, without using the word "merit good," stressed the great importance of money by making the banker together with the entrepreneur responsible for economic development (1969, 95–127).

[108] Currently the argument is made that advertisement provides economically useful services: it provides information and it helps new products find a quicker acceptance in the market. It is my opinion that it is within the spirit of Simons's argument that advertising that is economically useful should be allowed. On the other hand, I also believe that legis-

Furthermore, Simons sees no advantage in the protection of wholesale prices. He proposes that wholesale prices should be legally accessible to everyone. Finally, it appears to be important for Simons that consumers should be better informed. He advocates easily comparable price indications, and easy quality comparisons between different goods (72, 85 ff.).

Clearly, the neo-liberal program cannot be defended on the grounds of the public goods argument. Indeed, Simons does not respect the Pareto principle. He, in fact, makes it clear that he does not even intend to respect the wishes of those who through their activities diminish or distort the efficiency of economic activities. We are again confronted with a series of merit goods.

The neo-liberals defend their program with the argument that the competitive free market improves efficiency. A new question now arises: Is efficiency a value that one should pursue unconditionally? In other words, can one argue that efficiency is so important that it entitles the government to use its power to execute the neo-liberal program against the wishes of individual citizens?

What arguments are there available to defend the proposition that the government can *justly* impose the measures defended by the neo-liberals? In other words, what are the possibility conditions for the neo-liberal program to be just?

Here we can call on Kant again. Kantian ethics looks for the basis of ethical prescriptions, not in a religious faith in God, but in human reason. As maintained by Kant, living a moral life is living according to the moral law, in conformity with the demands of reason and out of respect for reason. Both Simons and his German counterpart, Walter Eucken, have presented their program as rational. Whether their proposals are defensible in their details is a matter of continuing debate. What is no longer debated by the majority of academic authors is that the government has a positive role to play in promoting economic efficiency by fighting inflation, regulating banking, and fighting monopolistic practices.[109] But academic authors are not the major group of economic actors who are affected by government regulations that promote fair business practices. Ideally, for Kant, restric-

---

lation requiring truth in adverting is similarly in agreement with the spirit of Simons's writings on advertisement.

[109] Of course, there is still a debate over the role of the government in economic matters. The debate now centers around the thesis that market failure is not enough to justify a role for the government. The "Public Choice" economists have argued that one must still prove that government intervention will not create bigger failures than the failures created by the market. However, arguing for a restriction in government tasks is, in effect, agreeing that there is room for legitimate government tasks even though some authors argue that the government should have no function at all in some areas, such as patent law.

tions on one's freedom should appear rational to those on whom the restrictions are imposed.

We are now ready to give an argument for the third kind of merit good. Rationality of the citizens is a precondition for the government being able to impose the measures advocated by the neo-liberals with the intention of reaching the efficiency promised by the free competitive market and having these measures accepted by their citizen-voters. How can we hope that the burdens required for the efficiency of the free market will be accepted if the citizens' rationality is defective? In Kant's opinion, rationality is the condition for the possibility of having binding values. But, this provides an argument for the support of education in as much as it improves the rationality of the citizens-consumers. Improvement of educational instruction for the whole population is therefore a third kind of merit good. This theoretically postulated third group of merit goods is not without its empirical confirmation. Christian Scheer has argued that the expansion of the public budget in the latter part of the 19th century in all Western societies was the result of the expansion of subsidies for education (1975).

Conclusion

The concept "merit good" refers to those economic activities of the government that cannot be justified by the idea that these activities help consumers achieve the satisfaction of their wishes. Such activities are captured by the concept of public good. Merit goods can be justified, though, by a Kantian method of reasoning. They can be justified as the necessary conditions for the possibility of what the citizens of a free market wish.

I have defended three kinds of merit goods: those that are connected with the minimal state, those which are connected with the neo-liberal program, and those merit goods that are connected with the improvement of the exercise of reason, namely education.

These three types of merit goods are not the complete series. Reason requires more than micro-economic efficiency. It requires macroeconomic efficiency across the business cycle, justice, and human dignity. This is precisely what the contemporary welfare state tries to do with its economic stabilization programs, its redistribution efforts, and its social programs such as unemployment compensation measures and social security arrangements.[110] For these measures I do not give arguments here.[111]

I believe, however, that I have given ethical thinking an essential place in economic theory by providing a method for the justification of the concept of merit good, which was first introduced by the public finance economist Musgrave. By maintaining the validity of the concept of merit good, I thus distinguish myself from economists who have tried to reduce the concept of merit good to characteristics belonging to the concept of public good.[112] My theory is also different from the theory of sociologists who use social habits as a category to explain the difference in the provi-

---

[110] Many of the examples given by Musgrave are cases of redistribution in kind or categorial redistribution (obligatory education, free school lunches, subsidized housing, subsidized or free inoculation) and would thus have been treated in that part of the argument.

[111] I do that in an unpublished book-length manuscript on merit goods with the tentative title: *Private, Public and Merit Goods*.

[112] John G. Head wrote three magnificent articles on the merit good problematic. He is ultimately not able to maintain the difference between public and merit goods because he emphasizes preference correction as opposed to preference interference as the defining characteristic of merit goods (1966; 1969; 1988). In the latter article, we find the following: "This whole line of argument clearly suggests, however, that all social wants problems can in a fundamental sense be characterized as generalized merit wants problems involving a hierarchy of 'higher' and 'lower' preference orderings in combination with impulsiveness or weakness of will" (30). For me, public and merit goods need to be justified in a totally different way. The idea of interpersonal utility interdependence, too, is used by some to connect public and merit goods (Culyer 1971; Brennan and Lomasky 1983; Brennan 1990). My thought is that the merit good idea would require, for instance, more redistribution than interpersonal utility interdependence can justify. Interpersonal utility interdependence can only justify part of what the merit good idea intends to justify. It therefore remains important to continue to distinguish merit and public goods.

Another way to defend the usefulness of the distinction between public and merit goods is by means of contemporary epistemology. Contemporary epistemology argues that all human insights are limited. One author captures that insight very pictorially by calling all human insights "angular truths" (Desan 1972, ch. 3). Some economists reduce or hope to reduce the problem of merit goods to matters of lack of information, wrong information, or irrational decisions. Such a view overlooks the angularity of all human insights. When I make decisions about buying computer software, it is not possible to hope that I as an individual could consider the monopolistic aspects of software sales techniques. It is for others who are better placed to make such analyses, e.g., the anti-trust division of the Justice Department. In my view, as in the view of Desan, it is irrational to expect from human insights more than is reasonable. This opens the door for epistemologically justified conflicts between individuals and supra-individual organizations. This does not mean that when there is a conflict the supra-individual organization is always right. It means that one needs to recognize the existence of real conflicts. The concept of merit good captures such conflicts.

An author who understands very well the difference between the concepts of public and merit good and who, furthermore, understands the ethical dimension of the concept of merit good is Birger P. Priddat (1992; 1994).

sion of merit goods in different societies.[113] Finally, my theory is different from the theory of those economists and political scientists who are looking to a proper political process (democratic constitutional policies) as the justifying mechanism for the imposition of merit goods (Mackscheidt, 1974; Brennan & Lomasky, 1983; Brennan, 1990).

A positive result of my view of merit goods is that I am able to create a conceptual space for the writings of economists who deal with fairness, subsidies, and financing methods of morally worthwhile projects (Buchanan, 1983). A further positive result is that I am able to distinguish between public goods and goods defended in the political arena by value arguments. Values provide arguments that justify overruling the wishes of individuals and must therefore be located elsewhere than in the public good discussion. If value arguments, stripped of the impact of public goods, have a kernel of validity, it is as merit good arguments (e.g., hardened criminals must be executed; public education must be done by vouchers).[114] A further positive result of my view of the concept of merit good is that institutional economic arrangements can be seen as economic activities for which there is a conceptual home in pure economic theory. Institutional arrangements violate the wishes of some economic actors (e.g., in antitrust legislation) and thus exhibit the characteristic that defines the category of merit good. No economic activity should be without a conceptual home. However, my view of merit goods is that it houses many more economic activities than Musgrave imagined.[115]

---

[113] Cay Folkers very properly stresses the societal preferences at work in merit goods (1974). That societal preferences are not always congruent with individual preferences indicates the presence of claims on resources that do not fit into the consumer sovereignty tradition. Still, for me, the question remains whether or not Folkers's claim might not have a more solid justification than the simple statement that merit goods are the expression of social habits.

[114] Malkin and Wildavsky argue that the traditional distinction between public and private goods should be abandoned (1991). The authors write: "We have seen that it is impossible to develop a definition of public goods that rests on the technical properties of the thing itself. We have also seen that it is impossible to justify government financing of public goods in a value-free manner. The flaws in public goods theory allow economists to promote their personal values under the guise of economic 'science'" (372). By maintaining both the concept of public and merit good, one can refute the objection of these authors against the concept of public good, because the presence of value judgments overruling personal preferences is by definition a merit good.

[115] In his interpretation of the concept of merit good, which includes a partial redefinition, Klaus Mackscheidt observes that the concept of merit good is applicable to domains not envisioned by Musgrave (1981, 264). Bruno Molitor makes use of a characteristic of German language to systematically broaden the applicability of the concept of merit good. German language allows for the creation of a verb *meritorisieren* (making meritorious) and a noun from that verb *Meritorisierung* (the fact of declaring something meritorious). Molitor thus argues for making the whole area of security a merit good concern for the gov-

Finally, my view of merit goods provides the opportunity to explain certain anomalies. Take the case of education. Many economists call education a public good. The paradox is that the local tax contribution for public elementary and secondary schools in the United States is financed for 96% by property taxes.[116] Typically, young couples with children do not possess the largest, most expensive homes. These are sometimes owned by childless couples or couples whose children are grown. Labeling education a public good means that the government has an opportunity to help consumers achieve the fulfillment of their wishes by collecting from everyone what they want to pay for the service in return for the provision of that service. Providing education as a public good therefore requires that the government only collect what individuals feel the service is worth to them. (The government is allowed to disregard strategic bargaining and free-rider strategies.) The provision of education as a public good thus requires that the government make individuals pay in proportion to their benefit. However, the actual financing method of education, violates this rule. Couples without children but with expensive homes are forced to pay more than couples with children and less expensive homes. If education can only be justified as a public good then, conceptually speaking, some people are forced to pay more than they should, while others are allowed to pay less than they should. Using force in order to make someone pay more than he should could be called theft. But, the government uses its taxation power to force some people to pay more than is conceptually justified. Calling education a public good exposes its current financing methods as theft.[117]

---

ernment (1988). Molitor's approach allows for two generalizations not present in Musgrave's texts. Molitor can ask the question: what are the conceivable subfields for providing the merit good category "social security?" Molitor can also ask the question: what are the conceivable techniques that the government can use to promote a whole category of merit goods? In a later publication (1989, 59) he creates the concept "Meritorisierungsinstrument" (means for approaching a good as a merit good). Thus Mackscheidt and Molitor develop a problem that is much broader than the one addressed by Musgrave when he asks the question of how one can defend single cases of merit goods such as free school lunches, subsidized housing, subsidized medical care etc. I therefore feel that both Mackscheidt's and Molitor's writings vindicate my approach of expanding the concept of merit good according to its inherent philosophical dimension.

[116] Figure is for 2001–02. See publication by US Census Bureau: *Public Education Finances: 2002.* http://ftp2.census.gov/govs/school/02f33pub.pdf, Table 4, p. 4.

[117] David Schmidtz (1991, XVI,159) makes a similar point when he argues that the public goods argument does not entail the right of the government to use coercion. If coercion is to be justified additional arguments need to be given such as survival of society or equality. Schmidtz seems to be sympathetic to the argument of survival and grants that others might want to make the argument of equality. In both cases a solid value argument is needed for justifying coercion. Schmidtz therefore argues, as I do, that the use of coercion in the provision of public goods can only be justified as a merit good. That requires a different kind of argumentation than the public goods argument.

In my view, education is partially a public good and partially a merit good. As a public good, it is proper that the ones having the most immediate benefit pay the most. This is the case where public colleges request tuition from students. The citizens of the state all benefit from a literate and educated population. (In a literate population my medical prescriptions will not be easily misread and I will not have to pay exorbitant fees for my pharmacy to hire a literate clerk who can read my prescriptions. In a literate population the chances of having an illiterate son- or daughter-in-law are slim, which I assume to be a desirable state-of-affairs for all parents.) Thus, all citizens may be asked to contribute to financing education. Still, this argument does not allow the state to charge some individuals out of proportion to the benefits they receive. Using property taxes to finance education does tax some individuals out of proportion to the benefits they receive. Since the concept of public good does not justify such a method of financing, the government should either abandon that method or look for another justification. Calling education partially a merit good would justify such a financing method. Indeed, ability to pay has been a financing method defended for merit goods. Property taxes can be considered taxes levied according to the ability to pay method.

The example of education illustrates one last important aspect of my theory of private, public, and merit goods. In my view these three concepts are all ideal concepts.[118] They are more or less realized in all goods. Thus, in my view, it is incorrect to ask whether a particular good is a private, public, or merit good. The proper question to ask is which *aspects* of a particular good exhibit characteristics typical of the concept of private good, of the concept of public good, and of the concept of merit good.[119]

---

[118] Paul Samuelson introduces the idea of an ideal concept for public goods in defining it as "*consumption goods* . . . which all enjoy in common in the sense that each individual's consumption of such a good leads to no subtraction from any other individual's consumption of that good" (1954, 387). In a subsequent paper Samuelson defends what I take to be an ideal concept interpretation of the term "private good," while presumably retracting his ideal concept interpretation of the term "public good." Consider: "What are we left with? Two poles [the ideal concepts of public and private goods] and a continuum in between? No. With a knife-edge pole of the private-good case, and with *all* the rest of the world in the public-good domain by virtue of involving some 'consumption-externality'" (1969, 108, including footnote 2). Musgrave clearly sees the ideal type argument in Samuelson's concept of public good (1969, 124, 126–34, 142). I do not see Musgrave as explicitly conceiving his own concept of merit good as an ideal concept.

[119] Birger P. Priddat argues that every public good voted for by a majority against the will of a minority must be considered as having a merit good aspect for the minority. This merit good aspect often relates to the financing system disliked by the defeated minority. He thus implicitly holds two of the theses that I hold: first, a good can be both a public and a merit good and second, the concepts of public and merit good are ideal concepts that apply to aspects of concrete goods (Priddat 1992, 246).

Take the example of bread. Most economic textbooks take bread to be a private good. I would say that the governmental requirement of providing printed information about the nutritional content is an interference with the choices of producers.[120] That requirement must therefore be justified as a merit good aspect in the provision of bread. Similarly, the governmental prohibition against using sawdust to increase fiber content is again a governmental interference. That I now have bread without sawdust or bread with content labels printed on the package is not the result of market forces mediating the wishes of consumers and producers. It is the result of governmental interference. Bread is thus not a 100 percent private good. It has private good aspects as well as merit good aspects. Calling the concepts of private, public, and merit good ideal concepts is not just a matter of philosophical sophistication (of course it is that, too). Seeing these three concepts as ideal concepts will allow economists to correctly describe the

---

Norbert Andel gives a different interpretation of the facts that Priddat and I observe. He sees an interference in both merit and public goods and thus prefers to conceptually group public and merit goods into one theoretical group: those goods where there is market failure (Andel 1968/69, 212–3). But Andel provides the observation necessary to maintain the difference between public and merit goods when he writes: "What can be said with reference to merit wants is also true for some public goods." But if something is true for *all* merit goods while it is true only for *some* public goods, then there must be a conceptual difference between public and merit goods. This is what I maintain, while allowing for the fact that concrete goods may be both public and merit goods.

Klaus Mackscheidt, also, observed that public goods sometimes have characteristics typical of merit goods. In order to limit the cases of goods that are both public and merit goods, Mackscheidt restricts his definition of the concept of merit good by excluding interferences with individual preferences resulting from a democratic majority imposing its will on a minority for purposes of providing a public good. Still, Mackscheidt explicitly preserves the two concepts of public and merit (1981, 262–4). In a recent letter, Mackscheidt discusses situations where a public good (successful inoculation against infectious diseases) cannot be provided without meritorisation of the public good (provision of subsidies). He thus reaffirms the idea that the concepts of public and merit good are different. However, he differentiates the two concepts not purely on the basis of the ideas they capture, but also on the basis of their extension. Thus Mackscheidt demands from a merit good that it be a good that is not just a public good, but a private good as well (1997). My view is that the concepts of public and merit good (and the one of private good as well) can be defined by their ideational content. The question of how many of the concepts apply to one concrete economic event is not immediately part of the conceptual problem. This is the state of affairs not only for the concepts of private, public, and merit good but also for those of a beautiful, just, and good person. In this latter case, philosophers are not bothered by the fact that a human being can be labeled either beautiful, good, or just or a combination of them. If it is acceptable that a person can be beautiful, good, and/or just, why is it problematic if concrete economic events are called simultaneously private, public, and/or merit goods?

[120] The positive justification for such government imposed information is to make informed consumer choice more possible and also to diminish, what common sense would consider, fraudulent practices.

facts (what kind of a good is bread?) and will allow economists to provide a justification for methods of taxation which, like current methods of financing education, would otherwise have to be rejected as disguised theft.

6. Objecting to a Libertarian Attack on Governmental Functions in the Economy: The Concept of "Public Good"

Abstract

Some authors see the concept of public good as nothing but a social construct for two reasons. First, different economists seem to create different definitions of the concept. Second, different countries treat different services as public goods.

I collected and analyzed eighteen different terms used by economists in order to point to public good aspects. I reduced the eighteen terms to two crucial ones that allow me to affirm that the ideal concept of public good points to an opportunity for collective gain, but that the non-exclusion possibility makes optimal financing difficult. The lack of optimal financing introduces the problem of whether or not the use of coercion (forced payment by means of government-imposed taxes) is justified. Alternatively, it raises the question of whether or not injustices created by the private provision of public goods (discrimination in club goods) demand governmental supervision of private initiatives with public goods. These questions introduce value judgments captured by the concept of merit good. Therefore, the problem of realizing the potential for gain present in public goods has no unique solution and requires ethical and political judgments. However, the presence of socio-political considerations in the realization of public goods does not invalidate the concept of public good itself, which consists of pointing to opportunities for gains by collective action, whether that collective action is privately or governmentally organized.

This chapter supports Hegel's claims about the desirability and the possibility of fruitfully mobilizing the government in order to deal with public goods or externalities.

I. The Thesis in a Nutshell

I see the technical economic concept of "public good" as a mental construct that is epistemologically valid because it captures an idea derived from two different characteristics that are undeniably present in the objective world. This concept is an ideal concept in as much as its central idea is derived from several characteristics that are more or less present in real situations (Adams & McCormick 1993, 109). This will have, among others, the consequence that a concrete economic event can be both a public and a non-public good (i.e., a private and/or even a merit good) because, in real life, economic events are more or less public goods rather than strictly pure public goods.[121] The idea captured by the technical concept of public good is defined as an opportunity for gain for a collectivity because of non-rivalnessness in consumption, where the opportunity for gain is difficult to finance because of the non-exclusion possibility. Notice that the two characteristics of non-rivalness in consumption and non-exclusion possibility can be present in degrees. Exclusion might be practically impossible (breathing the clean air that is provided) or it might be technically possible at greater or lesser costs (toll booths for highways, scrambling-unscrambling of TV signals) and, thus, economically more or less desirable. Furthermore, the non-rivalness in consumption might extend to the whole of mankind (ozone depletion), to a nation (national defense), to a metropolitan area (pollution), or to one single family (the heating of a home). In other words, the public, for a particular public good, is the population "N," where "N" can vary from all human beings to only the members of a household. The non-rivalness in consumption, too, may be more or less present. Thus several people can use a bridge without one person diminishing the enjoyment of the bridge by the other as long as there are not too many users. When there is congestion then non-rivalness is not complete. There is partial rivalness. Thus, the more congestion the less non-rivalness applies. To make matters even more complicated, some

---

[121] Thus, inoculation is a private good. It also has externalities (prevention of an epidemic) and is thus also a public good. It can also be declared a merit good and be made obligatory. The theoretical position that the concept of public good is not an absolute and exclusive tag for an economic event is also taken by others when they point out that the nutritional value of bread is rival in consumption (only one person can consume the bread) and thus a private good, whereas the visibility of eating bread is non-rival in consumption (many people can enjoy simultaneously seeing a poor person eat bread) and is thus a public good. Bread is thus partially a private and partially a public good (Adams & McCormick 1993, 111). The concept of public good is, therefore, not like the concept of being pregnant, but rather like the concept of being just. One is either pregnant or not. However, one is always more or less just and also more or less greedy or shrewd.

authors have given special names to what I see to be only subcategories of the concept of public good. Thus, some authors call public goods that have feasible low-cost exclusion possibilities "toll goods" (theaters, toll roads, libraries). They call public goods where the sub-parts are rival goods "common-pool resources" (fish taken from an ocean) (Ostrom & Ostrom 1991, 168). Others defend the use of a new label for public goods that have congestion and technical possibilities for exclusion, i.e., "club goods" (Head 1974, 85–86; Cornes & Sandler 1994, 382–384; Adams & McCormick 1993, 110–111). I maintain that it is useful to introduce these subcategories when one discusses different methods of addressing the problem posed by the presence of public goods. According to my claim, it is not necessary to introduce these distinctions in order to demonstrate the validity of the concept of public good and the challenge connected with the concept. The validity of the concept consists in pointing to an opportunity for gain by a collectivity whereas the challenge consists in the fact that there is no general method of financing available to efficiently realize (i.e., workable and obeying the Pareto principle) the opportunity for gain.[122]

---

[122] Some authors succinctly describe the market's failure to provide public goods when they argue that the Nash non-cooperative equilibrium is not a Pareto optimal provision (Cornes & Sandler 1994, 372–3), whereas Samuelson describes the government's difficulty in providing public goods when he writes, "it is in the selfish interest of each person to give false signals" to the government about one's interest in a public good if that information will also be used to determine one's tax share (Samuelson 1954, 388). Different authors have reacted differently to the lack of a perfect solution for financing the opportunity for collective gain present in public goods. Samuelson reacts with despair when he writes, "If the experts remain nihilistic about algorithms to allocate public goods, and if all but a knife-edge of reality falls in that domain, nihilism about most of economics, rather than merely public finance, seems to be implied" (Samuelson 1969, 109). Others point out that in most, if not all, provisions of public good, the government interferes with some wishes of some consumers such as the confiscation of land for the provision of highways (Andel 1968, 213). Still others, such as Mackscheidt, argue that free rider possibility in the provision of public goods is sometimes very high where the public good is an externality attached to private consumption (avoidance of an epidemic if there is enough private inoculation). Mackscheidt argues that it might be useful to meritorize private goods with important externalities by lowering the threshold of free riding (by subsidizing the good). This, in turn, means that the provision of the public good (avoidance of an epidemic) is achieved by interfering with the level of freely chosen consumption of inoculation as is the practice with the provision of merit goods in general (education, seat belts in cars) (Mackscheidt 1997). Samuelson reacts with despair, to the absence of a perfect financing method for public goods; Andel, by noticing the regretful presence of interference; Mackscheidt, by advocating artful interference. Clearly, the above indicates that the provision of public goods might imply (or necessarily implies) that there is an overlapping of the concepts of public and merit goods. The presence of merit good aspects in the provision of public goods means that considerations other than economic efficiency unavoidably enter the picture. Such considerations include redistribution, in addition to the impact on freedom and on regional autonomy (Adams & McCormick 1993, 114).

Given the difficulty of finding a satisfactory solution, even at the ideal level, it would be surprising if an analysis of concrete instances of public goods were simple. I will show that at least eighteen ways are used in the economic literature to point to economic problems related to public goods. This number is more than the five given by radical opponents of the concept of "public good," Malkin and Wildavsky, which they accuse the economic profession of using.

I will reject the conclusion of Malkin and Wildavsky that the concept of a public good is purely a culturally relative concept. I will concede, nevertheless, that cultural, or social preferences and institutional arrangements play important roles in trying to realize some of the gains presented by goods, having public goods aspects. Economic analysis will unavoidably become again economics. My conclusion, which justifies the validity of the concept "public good," implies that there is potentially a legitimate role for collective action. Such collective action can be undertaken by the government or by non-governmental groups. Samuelson has analyzed the first approach and Olson the second. Each argues that his approach does not automatically guarantee an optimal outcome. Both agree, however, that abstaining from collective action is abandoning an opportunity to realize a potential gain. My paper will argue that the concept of public good is a necessary analytic tool for showing the presence of potential gains from collective action.[123]

II. Problems with the Concept

A. Objections from the Outside. Malkin and Wildavsky: The Concept "Public Good" Has No Epistemological Validity

One of the most radical objections against the concept of "public good" was undertaken in a joint article by Jesse Malkin and Aaron Wildavsky entitled "Why the Traditional Distinction Between Public and Private Goods Should be Abandoned." The article, which sympathetically quotes libertarian writers, was published in a political science journal (Malkin & Wildavsky 1991, 369). Since libertarians object to most governmental func-

---

[123] I will not analyze in what cases governmental collective action is more desirable than private group action. *A fortiori*, it will be clear that the validity of the concept of public good does not imply that the government must *produce* the public good.

tions, the concept of a public good, for them, must be placed under suspicion, because the concept's very existence presumes a legitimation of governmental activity. The fundamental objection of Malkin and Wildavsky seems to be that the concept of a public good itself gives rise to the possibility of justifying governmental functions, which they regard as undesirable, if not, illegitimate.

It is my view that Malkin and Wildavsky are right in pointing out that the concept of a public good is sometimes, maybe most of the time, abused in day-to-day political reality. However, they are mistaken when they try to locate this political abuse in the idea that the concept of "public good" itself has no true content and is actually nothing other than a social construct (Malkin & Wildavsky, 372).[124] For my part, I will use the arguments of Malkin and Wildavsky to articulate the strongest possible objection to the concept of "public good" but then, in opposition to their position, I will argue that the political abuse they observe results from a misapplication of that concept.

The part of Malkin and Wildavsky's thesis, relevant for our study here, is their claim that the concept of a public good is a social construct that can have many meanings.

The first observation made by Malkin and Wildavsky is that the specific signifier "public good" is used for expressing the particular idea under discussion. The choice of this signifier has consequences, they argue, because our language has automatic associations connected with the signifier "public" (as demonstrated, for example, by the definition of this word in Webster's *Third New International Dictionary* (Malkin & Wildavsky, 357)). Malkin and Wildavsky then quote two economists (D. Suits and G. L. Bach) who explicitly espouse what is but a connotation of the signifier "public"; they take for granted that use of this word must indicate that the good or the service has to be provided by the collective or the government if it is to be provided at all. Malkin and Wildavsky then make the further claim that "many economists...are saying that goods they deem to be public ought to be supported by the government" (Ibid.).

I agree that the choice of signifier is important for correctly conveying the meaning of a word. This observation, however, is more relevant for words in everyday language than for technical terms in the sciences, because the meaning of technical terms is specified by their definition. On

---

[124] Philosophically, one describes such an attitude as one which denies the concept epistemological validity but locates its power in voluntarism (i.e., the will; in this case, the political will to decide one way or the other). Other authors, too, distinguish, as I do, between political abuse and epistemological validity of the concept and refuse, also, the claim of Malkin and Wildavsky that political abuse makes the concept epistemologically invalid (Adams & McCormick 1993, 114).

the other hand, alternative signifiers for the idea under consideration, such as collective good (used by Olson) or social wants (used by Musgrave), are at first sight no improvement. For these reasons, I would prefer to concentrate on the task of looking at the scientific definition of the idea (i.e., the signified) behind the term "public good."[125]

Malkin and Wildavsky claim, speaking descriptively, that economists use different definitions for the concept "public good"(358). A first candidate for a definition of public goods is the following: those goods that have the characteristic of *non-rivalness in consumption* (358). Such goods can be enjoyed by many people (e.g., clean air), in contrast to private goods, which are marked by rivalness in consumption (e.g., bread). A second definition labels as public goods those goods that have non-exclusion possibility (Ibid.). This term means that we are confronted with goods that anyone, whether he pays or not, can enjoy (clean air), in contrast to private goods, where property right enforcements prevent consumption if one does not pay (bread). A third strategy for defining public goods uses the two previous characteristics simultaneously (358–59). Economists who use this strategy differ as to which of the two characteristics they consider the more crucial one. Thus, some take non-rivalness in consumption as crucial and non-exclusion possibility as secondary. If one takes this view, television and radio signals would be public goods, even though technology exists that can exclude non-paying citizens. Other economists opt for non-excludability as the crucial characteristic. Thus, clean air, which is non-exclusive but is rival in that a firm cannot pollute while, at the same time, allowing others to have clean air, would be a public good for these economists. Still, other economists argue that both characteristics are essential. These economists give lighthouses and national defense as examples of public goods.

Malkin and Wildavsky next point to a fourth definition of public goods. That definition uses three essential characteristics; in addition to non-rivalness and non-excludability it includes impossibility of rejection (360). This term points to the fact that whether consumers like it or not, they must consume the good – for instance, breathe the air, be it polluted or clean.

Malkin and Wildavsky find a fifth definition in Samuelson's strong polar case of a public good, sometimes called the concept of a pure public good. Besides non-rivalness and non-excludability, Samuelson seems to add equal consumption for all consumers (360).

At this point Malkin and Wildavsky shift their argument. They ask which goods would be classified as public goods under the different defini-

---

[125] Other authors, too, notice the possible misleading nature of the label "public" in the term "public good." They, too, separate the superficial problem of misleading associations from the heart of the matter which is the technical definition (Cornes & Sandler 1994, 370, 375).

tions. Clearly, what concrete goods count as public goods will differ from definition to definition. Malkin and Wildavsky make their strongest theoretical claim by building on a mistake made by Samuelson (361). Samuelson had concluded that his concept of a pure public good made it imperative to say that in concrete cases, we have many goods which more or less embody the idea of a pure public good with a "knife-edge pole of private-good case, and with all the rest in the public-good domain" (Samuelson 1969, 108).[126] Malkin and Wildavsky now point out that bread certainly is a candidate for the knife-edge pole of the private good case. But, they argue, if we assume that some people enjoy seeing others consume private goods, then these private goods automatically become public goods. Thus, under Samuelson's definition of public goods, the distinction between private and public good cannot be maintained. For Malkin and Wildavsky, maintaining the distinction requires drawing a line at some point, a line arbitrarily specified by economists or by the voting public to be at 90 percent, 80 percent or 70 percent "publicness" (Malkin & Wildavsky 1991, 364).

Malkin and Wildavsky conclude that a good is not definable as a public good by any objective criteria, or further, by any criteria inherent in the goods themselves. On the contrary, they argue, a good becomes public because society decides to treat it that way.

B. Mistakes Made by Insiders: The Concept of Public Good Is an Ideal Concept as Are the Concepts of Private and Merit Good

a. Samuelson: Are the Concepts of Private and of Public Goods Equally Polar or Ideal Concepts?

Samuelson wrote three very influential articles on public goods (Samuelson 1954; 1955; 1958). In those articles, he introduces the idea of a *pure* public good, i.e., a good that, if provided to one person, needs to be made available in *equal* amounts to *all* (Samuelson 1955, 350). By introducing the idea of a pure concept, he is able to develop two logically necessary conclusions: that there is an opportunity for collective gain and that individuals are motivated neither to pay for nor to truthfully reveal their interest in the public good to an agency (the government) if that agency intends to use taxation power to force people to pay according to their bene-

---

[126] This is a wrong conclusion, because both the concept of private and of public good are ideal or polar concepts. For a concrete illustration see the first footnote of this chapter.

fits (Samuelson 1955, 350; 1954, 388–89). By reflecting on the applicability of his theory for real policy matters, Samuelson correctly understood the nature of his theoretical effort and thus maintained the ideal at the core of the concept "public good." However, he did not give the concept "private good" the same ideal status. He was therefore forced into maintaining counter-intuitive conclusions.

Let me quote the passage where Samuelson makes the above reflections.

> In my papers I often spoke of 'polar' cases: e.g., the polar case of a 'pure private good'....At the other pole was what I called a 'pure public good'.... I did not demur when critics claimed that most of reality fell between these extreme poles or stools, but instead suggested that these realistic cases could probably be analyzed fruitfully as a 'blend' of the two polar cases.
> I now wonder whether this was optimal semantics....

> Thus, consider what I have given in this paper as the definition of a public good...: 'A public good is one that enters two or more persons' utility'. What are we left with? Two poles and a continuum in between? No. With a knife-edge pole of the private-good case, and with *all* the rest of the world in the public-good domain by virtue of involving some 'consumption externality'...

> So I now think the useful terminology in this field should be: pure private goods in which the market mechanism works optimally, and possibly close approximations to them, versus the whole field of consumption-externalities or public goods.

> This does, however, lead to an uncomfortable situation. If the experts remain nihilistic about algorithms to allocate public goods, and if all but a knife-edge of reality falls in that domain, nihilism about most of economics, rather than merely public finance, seems to be implied. (Samuelson 1969, 108-9)

As Samuelson himself connects the free market with the concept of private good, it seems legitimate to clarify the ideal concept of private good by quoting Adam Smith's understanding of the free market.

> All systems either of preference or of restraint, therefore, being thus completely taken away, the obvious and simple system of natural liberty establishes itself of its own accord. Every man, as long as he does not violate the laws of justice, is left perfectly free to pursue his own interest his own way, and to bring both his industry and capital into competition with those of any other man, or order of man. The sovereign is completely discharged from a duty, in the attempting to perform which he must always be exposed to innumerable delusions, and for the proper performance of which no human

wisdom or knowledge could ever be sufficient; the duty of superintending the industry of private people, and of directing it towards the employments most suitable to the interest of the society. (Smith, 687)

If one accepts the notion that the ideal concept of "private good" requires allowing the market to work completely, then the application of that ideal concept to the real world requires allowing the market to work as much as possible. Thus, even though national defense is considered a public good, there is no a priori demand that the government produce that good. Cannons and rifles can very well be produced by the free market and bought by the government through a bidding system. The government restricts itself to providing national defense; it does not have to take control of the production of arms. Cannons and rifles remain goods that are rival in consumption and subject to exclusion and thus remain private goods. As instruments for providing national defense these arms potentially become public goods.[127] Similarly, if permissible pollution units are specified, then nothing prevents society from letting the free market find the most effective way of preventing pollution. In my view, it follows that if one accepts the thought of ideal concepts then it is wrong to argue that one ideal concept can be applied to a greater or lesser extent (Samuelson's pure public good) and another not (Samuelson's private good).

Furthermore, truth in the deductive method of science is established first of all at the level of the ideal concept. The problem of correctly seeing how ideal concepts apply to reality is a totally different matter from evaluating an ideal theory or an ideal concept. Samuelson saw correctly the consequences of calling his definition of public goods an ideal concept. Unfortunately, he either did not see that the concept of the free market (or the concept of a private good) is also an ideal concept or he did not correctly see the consequences of calling it an ideal concept.[128]

b. Musgrave: The Concept Merit Good Is an Ideal Concept Just as the Concepts of Private and Public Good

Musgrave introduces in his work the concept of "merit good" as a label for a number of economic activities of the government that he did not consider to be proper public goods. His definition of the concept of "merit good" is

---

[127] This conclusion is similar to conclusion from the argument that bread is both a private good (nutritional value) and a public good (the visibility of eating bread, particularly by the poor, is pleasing to many). See also footnote 118.
[128] An illustration of the ideal and thus unreal dimension of the definition of private goods is the requirement that they be infinitely divisible (Arrow & Hahn 1971, 61). This requirement is necessary for another often-used assumption in micro-economics: smooth indifference curves.

as follows: goods or wants "considered so meritorious that their satisfaction is provided for through the public budget, over and above what is provided for through the market and paid for by private consumers" (Musgrave 1959 b, 13). He also writes that a merit good "by its very nature, involves interference with consumer preferences" (Musgrave 1959 b, 13). He gives as examples "free hospitals for the poor or public subsidies to low cost housing" (Musgrave 1956, 341). Musgrave also allows for de-merit goods. He writes, "[T]heir satisfaction may be discouraged through penalty taxation, as in the case of liquor" (Musgrave 1959 b, 13).

Difficulties develop when Musgrave clarifies the relationship between the three theoretical concepts of private, public, and merit good and concrete economic events. In his first writings Musgrave classifies merit goods as public goods ("social wants" in his terminology), because he says, "the benefits derived from such services extend beyond the specific beneficiary" (Musgrave 1957, 111). In later writings he concedes that merit goods could also be private goods. With reference to merit goods he writes, "Wants are satisfied that could be serviced through the market," and "Separate amounts of individual consumption are possible" (Musgrave 1959 b, 9). Nevertheless, Musgrave continues to write that some merit goods have many public good aspects. In the German translation of *The Theory of Public Finance* and in the English original from the third edition on, Musgrave hesitantly introduces the idea that there could be *polar cases of private and public goods*.[129] In order to relate the concepts of private, public, and merit goods, he proposes two vectors, each with three possibilities. The first vector is the degree of externality or percent of benefit that is social. This first vector allows for three possibilities: all, part, or none of the benefits of the good might be social. The second vector addresses the degree to which consumer sovereignty applies. This vector also allows for three possibilities: consumer sovereignty applies either fully, partially, or not at all. The case of a good for which vector one indicates that all benefits are social or are externalities, and for which vector two indicates that there is full consumer sovereignty, Musgrave calls the case of a 100 percent public good (his category, "social want"). The case of full consumer sovereignty in vector two and no degree of externality in vector one is then the case of a 100 percent private want. The case of full consumer sovereignty in vector two and a partial degree of externality in vector one Musgrave calls a mixed situation with both public (social) and private benefits. All the other cases are merit wants. Musgrave adds without explanation

---

[129] (Musgrave 1959 b, 89), [Musgrave at Harvard]. See also (Andel 1984, 634). What Andel refers to as the "third edition" is actually the edition in which the title page refers to Musgrave as being at Harvard. The earlier edition identifies him as a professor at the University of Michigan.

that "the case [merit want situation] at closer inspection *frequently proves to be one of social [i.e. public] want*" (Musgrave 1959 b, 89 [Harvard] my emphasis). It looks to me as if Musgrave understands the concepts of private, public, and merit good as tags that can be attached to concrete cases. The polar nature of the case is introduced only as a surprising result. It is not a permanent feature of Musgrave's thinking on these three concepts. In his publication *Fiscal Systems*, he often, if not exclusively, considers merit goods to be *private goods*. He writes, "they are quite capable of being subjected to the exclusion principle" (Musgrave 1969 a, 12).

Clearly, Musgrave shifts his opinion in considering whether merit goods are private or public goods. It is not that Musgrave does not know the definitions of the concepts of private, public, and merit good, but rather I propose that the weakness of Musgrave's view lies in his conception of the nature of the concepts of private, public and merit good. Musgrave seems to work with the idea that these three concepts are taxonomic and are thus like tags which are able to identify concrete economic goods. The concepts are supposed to separate economic activities which have mutually exclusive characteristics. The difficulty of such a conception of the three economic concepts starts when Musgrave notices that economic activities that must be tagged as public goods (because they are provided for by the government) have a secondary characteristic that does not agree with the definition of public goods (the violation of consumer wishes). A new difficulty arises for Musgrave when he sees that goods provided by the government on meritorious grounds can also be provided efficiently through the market (medical services and housing). Musgrave ends up accepting the position that merit goods are not a subcategory of either the tag public good or the tag private good, because a merit good can be both a private and a public good.

Musgrave has no difficulty in maintaining that the three concepts have different definitions, yet he seems puzzled that several concepts can apply to one and the same economic event. I propose that the three concepts of private, public, and merit good are unambiguously different, but that they can apply to the same economic activities. For this to hold, the concepts must be considered tags, not for real events, but for mental constructs using characteristics of real events. The three concepts are not like tags that answer the question of whether or not an object is made from wood, iron or aluminum. These usually are all or nothing questions and the answers are therefore also mutually exclusive (A table is normally either made from wood, or from iron, or from aluminum.) The three economic concepts under discussion are more accurately tags for answering questions like: is this person just, or friendly, or generous? These concepts all apply in degrees[130] and are also not mutually exclusive. If the three concepts of private, public, and merit good are similar to the concepts of just, friendly, or generous, then a concrete economic activity can be said to possess all three characteristics and to possess them in varying degrees.

Let us take the example of milk. Milk is a prime example of a private good since it is excludable and is marked by rivalness in consumption. However, one could also rightly argue that, in some countries, milk is a merit good because the state subsidizes it in order to *increase its consumption by the poor.* Finally, one could argue further that milk is a public good because many people enjoy the idea that children in their country have milk available to them. In this sense, consumption of milk represents a psychic externality and to this extent is a public good. These three characteristics can be truthfully described simultaneously for milk only if the three concepts of private, public, and merit good point to *aspects* of goods rather than being tags for concrete goods.[131]

The importance of conceptually seeing that one service can be simultaneously a private, a public, and a merit good is demonstrated in Kenneth Godwin's article "Charges for Merit Goods: Third World Family Planning" (Godwin 1991) where the author analyzes the effectiveness of family planning in developing countries by means of the distribution of contraceptives. As family planning is considered desirable by the elites, Godwin claims that they can be considered a merit good (416). However, contraceptives are also "a private good, rival and exclusive" (416). Finally, Godwin argues that "many women would use effective, reliable contraception if it were available and affordable" (416). But, as contraceptive services are neither affordable for many women nor readily available, the market by itself is of little help in reaching the goals of the merit good policy. Looking at the delivery of contraceptives in a third way, some countries consider it a public good, where the elite realizes that different women are willing to pay different prices and where the government can provide help both by making the provision easier and by charging a different price to different people according to the public good's principles.

Godwin now makes the following observations: on the basis of it being a merit good, some want the government to "offer these services at little or no cost" (417). This is the case with Ecuador. However, in an alternative example "the Columbian public health-care system charges for its services" (423). It applies a user fee, the amount of which differs according

---

[130] This has also been observed about the concepts of private and public good by others (Adams & McCormick 1993, 109).

[131] I differ from others who call a public good a category and call excludability and rivalness in consumption characteristics (Ostrom & Ostrom 1991, 165 ff.). I see no difficulty in calling the concept "public good" a characteristic or an aspect of concrete economic events.

to income, which is one method used to deliver and pay for public goods. The first approach leads to a centralized delivery of the contraceptive services. The second approach leads to a decentralized approach. Interestingly, the difference in efficiency between the two countries is dramatic. Columbia has a greater decline in fertility rate and pays four dollars per acceptor, whereas Ecuador spends fifteen dollars (425). I now want to present my own conclusion with reference to this evidence. According to Godwin, Ecuador considers contraceptive services to be solely merit goods and delivers them free of charge. Columbia considers the contraceptive services to be at the same time private, public, and merit goods. Godwin's article demonstrates that Columbia, and other countries following similar policies, is more effective than countries that act as if contraceptive services are only merit goods and not also private or public goods. The merit good aspect is present in the willingness by the government to subsidize the level of provision of contraceptive services beyond the level justified by the public good argument (i.e., the level determined by the willingness to pay by all potential consumers). One advantage of introducing the public good argument is that it allows for a policy that can rely on user fees when there are not enough health dollars in the country's budget to fully finance the delivery of contraceptive services. At the same time, labeling contraceptives a public good does not prevent a governing elite from also declaring it a merit good that justifies looking for means to increase its consumption beyond the level guaranteed by the willingness to pay. In order to avoid the inefficiency of the Ecuador model and to obtain the benefits of the efficiency of the Columbia model one needs to conceptualize contraceptives as merit, public, and private goods *at the same time.*

The three concepts are, in a second way, similar to tags like just, friendly, or generous in that they point to less tangible aspects of economic activities or economic goods. For less tangible characteristics we can expect many different descriptions. And indeed, economists have used many words to describe the characteristics of economic events possessing public good aspects. They have also used many words to describe the special relations human beings have with such economic events. I will assemble both the words pointing to characteristics of economic events and the words describing human relations with such economic events. In the following sections I will argue that all the characteristics of economic events with public good aspects can be reduced to two characteristics that together form the ideal concept "public good."

III. In Search of a Definition

A. An Enumeration of the Characteristics Used to Classify an Economic Activity or an Economic Good as a Public Good

Malkin and Wildavsky claim that, according to their reading, economists do not point to multiple characteristics of economic events that are public goods, but rather, present five different definitions of the concept. If this were the case, then Malkin and Wildavsky would be right in objecting to the economic profession.

I am convinced that a better approach requires looking at the many characteristics that economists have observed in goods with public good aspects and then seeing if a single definition can be developed.

In his *Public Goods and Public Welfare* Head enumerates the following characteristics as features used to define public goods: (1) decreasing costs in production, (Head 1974, 176) (2) externalities, (85) (3) Samuelsonian joint supply, (77 ff.) (4) non-exclusion, (80) (5) non-rejectability, (82) (6) benefit spillovers, (271) (7) unenforceability of compensation, (185) (8) indivisibility, (161) (9) non-appropriability, (28) (10) non-rivalness in consumption, (78) (11) economies of scale, (179) (12) multiple user good, (79) and (13) lumpiness, (168). Head wrongly rejects (14) Marshallian joint supply (78–9). Other authors add: (15) free rider possibility, (Buchanan 1975 b, 207) (16) non-subtractability, (Ostrom & Ostrom 1991, 165–7), (17) the fact of not being packageable, (Ostrom, et al. 1991, 140) and finally (18) the strategy of holding out (Ostrom & Ostrom 1991, 170). There are, therefore, at least eighteen terms referring to characteristics of economic events with public good aspects. However, some of the eighteen characteristics are obviously related to each other in as much as they point to the same aspect, albeit from somewhat different angles. I will therefore group the above-enumerated characteristics with the purpose of arriving at a single definition of the concept "public good," a result that, if achieved, would undermine one of Malkin and Wildavsky's attacks on the concept.

Group I. Not Internalizing the Price of an Aspect into the Price of the Total Good

(2) *Externalities* are costs and/or benefits from consumption or production that are not reflected in market prices (Penguin 1972, 158–59).[132]

(6) *Benefit spillovers*, according to Head, refer to positive externalities resulting from the provision of services by one jurisdiction that are enjoyed by residents of another jurisdiction (Head 1974, 270–78). Clearly, this concept is a subcategory of the concept "externalities." It restricts the beneficiaries to lower level governmental jurisdictions.

(7) *Unenforceability of compensation* is understood by Head as the central characteristic of externalities (Head 1974, 185–86).

(5) *Impossibility of rejection* is defined by Head as an extreme form of external diseconomy (Head 1974, 83).

(14) The term *Marshallian joint supply* refers to a situation where two or more products are necessarily produced by one process, such as meat and wool from sheep (Penguin 1972, 239; Head 1974, 78–79A). Head provides an argument for treating this case as consisting of private goods that can be handled in a Pareto-optimal way by the market and therefore does not belong to the problematic of public goods (Ibid.). If we take another example, that of the bee-keeper, then we have the case of one product or service that is paid for (honey) and another service (pollination of the apple trees leading to increased apple production) that is jointly supplied but where compensation is unenforceable. Marshallian joint supply can therefore present a public goods problem if one jointly supplied service is such that compensation is unenforceable.

---

[132] Some authors warn that externalities cannot be identified with public goods even though there are similarities. Thus, Bohm points out that public policy addressing externalities often aims at curtailing "mainly private activities with negative effects on other[s]...whereas public policy concerning public foods is about increasing – or even creating – something that is suboptimally provided by the private sector" (Bohm 1997, XVII). This difference is conceptually irrelevant, if the purpose is to see possibilities for collective gain. The same author points out that Marshall connected the concept of external economies with some forms of economies of scale (45). The connection between these concepts is taken up when I discuss the concept of "economies of scale".

Group II. Violation of Infinite Divisibility Theoretically Required by the Concept "Private Good"

(8) *Indivisibility*: This concept means that certain goods are not available in all desirable quantities, but only in specific sizes.[133]

(15) *Lumpiness* is a synonym for indivisibility (Head 1974, 168).

Group III. One Good, Many Users; Decreasing Cost Possibilities

(3) *Samuelsonian Joint supply*: In order to avoid confusion, one should distinguish between Samuelsonian and Marshallian joint supply. The term 'Marshallian joint supply' refers to a situation where two or more products are necessarily *produced* by one process, such as meat and wool from sheep (Penguin 1972, 239; Head 1974, 78–79). This concept belongs in the discussion of public goods only if there is unenforceability of compensation of one of the jointly produced services. The term 'Samuelsonian joint supply' refers to a situation where, because one product can be enjoyed by many, it becomes efficient for consumers to join together in the production process. Samuelsonian joint supply is, thus, a production reaction to a characteristic of the consumption condition (Head 1974, 77).

(12) *Multiple user good*: Sharp introduced this term to avoid the confusion that is possible with the term "Samuelsonian joint supply."[134]

(10) The term *non-rivalness in consumption* conveys the same characteristic as Samuelson's concept "joint supply." The only difference is that this term describes the characteristic from the *point of view of consumption* and *not of the solution in production*. This concept also means to convey the same characteristic as the one referred to by Sharp's term "multiple user good." The difference is that Sharp describes the characteristic from the point of view of the economic good under consideration and not from the point of view of consumption of that good.

(1) *Decreasing production costs* simply refers to the fact that there are economies of scale (Penguin 1972, 135–37). Head, however, looks at the possible effects on consumers of decreasing production costs. He points out that a major consequence of economies of scale for consumers is that each additional consumer buys not only a rival good (a car or a PC), but

---

[133] (Penguin 1972, 135). Head accuses Buchanan of using "indivisibility" confusingly as a portmanteau term for two characteristics: joint supply and impossibility of exclusion (Head 1974, 78-79).

[134] (Head 1974, 168; Bird & 1972, 4). Head also draws attention to some unfortunate terms used upon occasion for this characteristic, such as: jointness of demand, joint consumption, consumption externality, non-rivalness in consumption (Head 1974, 78 n. 15).

also provides, at the same time, a positive externality for all other consumers of this good: i.e., a lower unit price for the car or the PC (Head 1974, 28, 176–79). Economists can thus look upon the case of decreasing production costs or economies of scale as a case in which consumers are confronted with a rival good that has also an externality that is non-rival in consumption (i.e., the price at which the rival good can be offered given the quantity of the rival good demanded, which is strongly correlated with the quantity of consumers demanding the rival good). According to Head the cheaper price of a PC resulting from an increase in demand for PC's is similar to the cheaper cost imposed on consumers resulting from an increase in consumers for goods generally recognized as public goods, such as bridges and lights in back alleys. For the study of the concept of public good, the relevant aspect of decreasing cost in production is therefore the positive externality of lowering the price for all consumers by the mere fact of buying an additional unit of the rival good or, in other words, the non-rival consumption gift of a lower price for a rival good resulting from any increase in demand of the rival good.

(11) *Economies of scale* are the cause of decreasing production costs per unit with increase in demand. Economies of scale are relevant for these results in that they produce something for the consumer. I analyze the different aspects of this phenomenon under the term 'decreasing costs in production' in the previous paragraph.

(16) *Non-subtractability* which is defined as the the fact that "consumption by one person precludes its use or consumption by another person" (Ostrom & Ostrom 1991, 165–7). Such a good is thus completely rival in consumption. A completely non-subtractable good is a good where joint consumption takes place without the crowding out effect. It is thus completely non-rival in consumption. If the good is partially subtractable we face partial non-rivalness in consumption where there is partial loss in enjoyment from additional consumers.

Group IV. Payment Problems: The Inability to Prevent Enjoyment without Pay

(7) *Non-exclusion* is a term used to describe the enviable position of a consumer who can enjoy a product without having to pay for it. This situation arises when a producer or a consumer has no economically sensible method of excluding another consumer from enjoying the good or service without the latter paying his/her share in the good or service that s/he co-consumes.

(17) The fact of *not being packageable* is defined as the impossibility "of being differentiated as a commodity or a service" so that "it can be

readily purchased and sold in the private market" and where "those who do not pay for a private good can then be excluded from enjoying its benefits." Political scientists using the term "packageable" identify the idea with the exclusion principle of economists (Ostrom, et al. 1991, 140–1). In my view, the word "packageable" points to a possible strategy to make the exclusion principle work.

(15) A *free rider* is a person who makes use of the advantages of the non-exclusion situation (Buchanan 1975 b, 37, 148). Malkin and Wildavsky claim that individuals "indicate a more honest revelation of preferences than that predicted by free rider theory" (Malkin & 1991, 336). However, they overstate their claim when they conclude that it is a fictitious problem. Other authors counter this claim by pointing to experiments that "offer persuasive evidence that free riding is a real phenomenon" (Williams & McCormick 1993, 113). These other authors also point out that "less-than-total free-riding do[es] not demonstrate that the free-rider problem is not prohibitive" (Ibid.)).

(18) *Holding out* is one strategy that a free rider may use (Ostrom & Ostrom 1991, 170). Holding out can be justified by claiming that one has no interest in the public good, less interest than is actually the case, or by disputing the fairness of one's assigned payment. The crucial factor is that the arguments are used in order to refuse participation in financing the public good. When holding out is possible, one is in the presence of a public good.

(7) *Non-appropriability* is a term used to describe the problem from the point of view of an economic good. Head defines it as "that property of a good which makes it impossible for private economic units, through ordinary private pricing, to appropriate the full social benefits (or be charged the full social costs) arising from their production or consumption of that good."[135]

B. Reduction of the Many Characteristics to a Few Crucial Ones

Let us now reflect more formally on each of the four groups of characteristics of public goods.

Group I includes externalities, benefit spillovers, unenforceability of compensation, impossibility of rejection, and Marshallian joint supply. The relationships among these characteristics can be presented as follows. Externalities can be either positive or negative. In the former case, they

---

[135] (Head 1974, 28) He also explicitly mentions that it is meant to convey the same problem as Musgrave's "impossibility of exclusion." (Head 1974, 28 n. 55, 180)

are often referred to as "external economies" while in the latter they are often called "external diseconomies." An extreme form of external diseconomy is the impossibility of rejection. A particular form of external economy is the benefit spillover of local government actions onto non-residents or people outside of the political locality. Another particular form of external economy is a Marshallian joint supply in which the producer of one service has no way of charging a fee for a second jointly supplied service. Externalities are a problem because the price of an aspect of a good cannot be included in the price of the good itself. Thus, there is a price internalization problem. Until the price internalization problem is solved, there is the problem of unenforceability of compensation. These complex relations are represented in Table I.

Table 1: Group I: Externalities

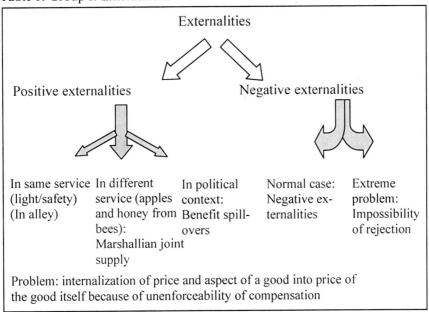

Externalities				
Positive externalities			Negative externalities	
In same service (light/safety) (In alley)	In different service (apples and honey from bees): Marshallian joint supply	In political context: Benefit spillovers	Normal case: Negative externalities	Extreme problem: Impossibility of rejection

Problem: internalization of price and aspect of a good into price of the good itself because of unenforceability of compensation

Group II includes indivisibility and lumpiness. These two terms are essentially synonymous

Group III includes Samuelsonian joint supply, multiple user good, non-rivalness in consumption, non-subtractability, decreasing production costs, and economies of scale. The first four concepts are essentially synonymous, describing a single characteristic seen from four points of view. The term "multiple user good" describes the characteristic under consideration from the point of view of a good which has special features in its consumption possibilities: it can be used by many consumers and, thus, possesses the characteristic of non-rivalness in consumption. This is the case, because enjoyment of the good by one consumer does not subtract from the usefulness of that good for another consumer. The good is therefore said to be non-subtractable. In consuming such a good, consumers are not rivals. Samuelsonian joint supply is an efficient production strategy for goods with the special consumption feature of non-rivalness in consumption.[136] Head proposes the fifth term "decreasing production costs" as the most general term. Decreasing costs can be obtained from the production side and from the consumption side. The former is, in economic literature, called "economies of scale." The latter is labeled with one of the four essentially synonymous terms mentioned above (i.e., Samuelsonian joint supply, multiple user good, non-rivalness in consumption or non-subtractability). I have interpreted decreasing costs in production and economies of scale as creating a possibility of a non-rival gift of cheaper pro unit costs for a good with each increase in demand of the good. The relationships among the items in Group III are represented in Table II.

Table II: Group III: Opportunities given decreasing costs

Opportunities given decreasing costs

| (On production side) Economies of scale or decreasing production costs lead to non-rival gift of cheaper pro unit costs in consumption by increased demand. | (On consumption side) Can be labeled by four synonyms by emphasizing: 1. Reason for problem seen in consumption: non-rivalness in consumption, 2. Reason for problem seen in consumed good: its consumption by one person does not subtract (non-subtractability) from usefulness for another person. 3. Characteristic of the good: multiple user good. 4. Name of author who proposed a production strategy to deal with the problem; Samuelsonian joint supply. |

---

[136] It is very important to see the difference in point of view taken when using these synonyms. Failing to do so easily leads to confusion. See Olson's attempt to relate his concept of exclusive collective good to jointness of supply. (Olson 1968, 38 n. 58)

Group IV includes non-exclusion, free rider possibility, non-appropriability, non-packeagability, and the possibility of holding out. These terms too emphasize a same characteristic from different angles. Non-exclusion possibility focuses on the fact that non-paying consumers cannot be excluded from the enjoyment of a good or service. Non-packageability focuses on a characteristic of goods that make exclusion difficult or impossible (i.e., the good is not neatly packageable so that it can be sold in separable units). Lack of packageability of a good or impossibility of exclusion means that consumers can enjoy a good without paying, in other words, they can be free riders. "Free rider" is, thus, a term for non-paying consumers of goods that are not packageable or that are non-exclusive. A strategy to become a free rider of such goods utilizes holding out voluntary payment by exploiting the fact that one cannot be excluded from enjoying the good anyway.

These four groups can now be further combined. Combination A relates Groups II and III. Combination B relates Groups I and IV.

These four groups can now be further combined. Combination A relates Groups II and III. Combination B relates Groups I and IV.

Combination A: Group II and Group III are related as a cause is related to an effect. Indivisibility or lumpiness is one of the reasons for economies of scale or for the *availability of decreasing costs*, i.e., of an opportunity for gain.

Combination B: Group I and Group IV are related to each other because the problem with externalities is at bottom the *unenforceability of compensation*. This concept is closely related to the concept of non-exclusion or *non-appropriability*.

Head, however, points to two differences between these two seemingly similar concepts. First, unenforceability of compensation in the case of externalities takes place concerning services which are often of a different nature than the ones that are paid for, as when production of apples co-produces flowers, providing free nectar to the honey industry (Head 1974, 185-86). Non-appropriability because of non-exclusion possibilities in the enjoyment of pure public goods, on the other hand, refers by definition, to the same service. Second, externalities may extend to only one or to a few persons; pure public goods extend by definition, to all members of the relevant group (Head 1974, 186).

In my view, the second difference discussed by Head concerns a feature of public goods that does not touch its essence. Indeed, nothing prevents us from extending the use of the concept of the relevant group, used by Head exclusively for the concept of a pure public good, to the phenomenon of externalities. The number of persons who enjoy the externalities could

then be called the relevant group or the relevant public for the externalities.[137]

In my view, the first distinction is also unessential from the point of
view of economic optimalization. I see a pure public good as a good that
is nothing but externality. Thus, the theorem regarding the difficulties that
occur in the search for a social optimum with pure public goods has dramatic generality precisely because these same difficulties arise with all
goods having externalities.

As a consequence, we are left with the idea that the eighteen characteristics can be reduced to two combinations: Combination A and Combination B. Combination A stresses the opportunity for gain resulting from the
existence of goods that can be used by many. This characteristic can then
be elevated to an ideal level. Instead of stressing that a good can be used
by many, we now can say that for that good there is *non-rivalness in consumption*. Combination B stresses the *problem related to the realization of
the opportunity for gain*: unenforceability of compensation because of non-
exclusion possibility. This non-exclusion possibility can be treated as a
technical problem; namely, the problem of finding barriers for non-paid
consumption (such barriers include toll-booths, TV signals that are usable
only with a descrambler, and taxation schemes). The non-exclusion possibility can, however, also be elevated into an absolute problem. This is the
case when barriers can not be found or when implementing barriers is too
expensive. Thinking of non-exclusion possibility as being without a perfect solution is equivalent to elevating it into an absolute and, thus, an ideal
level.

Thus, the eighteen characteristics by which public goods aspects or
problems are described can be reduced to a related pair:

1) Decreasing costs from multiple users, thereby offering an opportunity
for gain.

2) Unenforceability of compensation because of non-exclusion possibility. This makes financing the opportunity for gain difficult, if not impossible.[138]

---

[137] This move is, in fact, made by Samuelson when he changes his verbal definition of public goods without changing his mathematical model. Thus, in the Biarritz conference, he
writes, "A public good is one that enters two or more persons' utility" (Samuelson 1969,
108). Other authors, too, make this move when they recommend that the public affected by
a public good should ideally be equal to the political community that makes the decision
(Ostrom, et al. 1991, 147).

[138] This conclusion is different from those of some other authors who are satisfied to notice
that different approaches stress one or the other feature as important for the breakdown of
the basic theorems of welfare economics (Cornes & Sandler 1994, 375). These authors
look for empirical cases where the theory of public goods makes a contribution. My ap-

IV. Implementation Problems

The concept "public good" is a multidimensional concept because it captures two characteristics. Authors looking for solutions for the potential, but unrealized, gain present in public goods can address either one of the two characteristics. Samuelson addressed the non-rivalness in consumption. Olson addressed the non-exclusion possibility. Both concluded that a general optimal economic solution does not exist. In my view, this conclusion also gives non-economic factors a role in the choice of solution and makes the solution of the public goods problem a socio-economic problem. I will therefore conclude that valid economic reasoning about the concept of public good both establishes that there is a pure economic challenge and that all kinds of payoffs (social, political, legal) are at work in finding a solution. That solutions will have to be artful does not mean that the problems for which they are solutions are not valid problems. The latitude that might exist with solutions does not mean that the problem is a fiction as Malkin and Wildavsky's article suggests.

A. Samuelson: The Non-Rivalness in Consumption

As the primary characteristic for his analysis, Samuelson selects decreasing cost resulting from the fact that there are multiple users.[139] From this he is able to derive, with the assumption of self-interested behavior,[140] an

---

proach intends to theoretically capture the *necessary* features for the breakdown of private goods analysis or market performance.

[139] "Collective consumption of goods…which all enjoy in common in the sense that each individual's contribution of such a good leads to no subtraction from any other individual's consumption of that good" (Samuelson 1954, 387). Even more explicit is the following: "The possibility or impossibility to apply an exclusion principle is less crucial than consumption externality, since often exclusion would be wrong where possible" (Samuelson 1969, 105). Other authors have observed the above-mentioned choice made by Samuelson (Cornes & Sandler 1994, 371). They do not point out, as I do, that Olson chooses non-exclusion as the crucial characteristic for his reflections.

[140] Stretton and Orchard strongly attack this assumption. They point to a multiplicity of motives at work in the provision of public goods and then claim that the economist's model is unrealistic and, thus, useless (Stretton & Orchard 1994, 78–9, 277). In my view, economic analysis of public goods can be used to demonstrate the presence of a challenge: an opportunity for collective gain and the difficulty of financing that opportunity. In my paper I do not choose between advocating for the creation of private incentives (merit increases in salaries; increase in insurance premium after an accident) or advocating societal support for responsible behavior (medals for heroic behavior in war or outstanding achievements; public praise for altruistic efforts).

optimal level of provision.[141] In the case of a positive economic good, the optimal level of provision is bigger than the sum of quantities that the consumers would individually buy. Left to the free market, public goods will, in that model, be under-provided.[142] There thus exists an opportunity for economic gain. According to Head – and I agree with him – Samuelson's statement provides a benchmark for the assessment of market performance.

Samuelson includes the second characteristic (unenforceability of compensation) in his analysis when he looks for a method to realize the opportunity for gain. Samuelson's proposal consists of two steps (Samuelson 1954, 387–8 "Optimal Conditions"). First, he asks that the government inquire about how much each citizen is willing to pay for a particular public good (e.g., a bridge). If an entrepreneur is willing to provide the public good at a price that is less than what the citizens are willing to pay, then there is an opportunity for gain for all in the provision of that good.

Second, the government must use its tax power to force people to pay what they declared they were willing to pay. Samuelson uses the government to overcome the unenforceability of compensation.[143] He then points out that citizens will realize that their declared willingness to pay for a public good will be used twice by the government: once to decide whether or not to provide the good and once to decide how much to tax citizens for a particular good. Thus, claims Samuelson, citizens will have a selfish incentive not to reveal their true preferences. Consequently, he concludes, an ideal solution exists, but it cannot be realized by the government.[144]

Samuelson thus argues that the government is technically capable of dealing with the unenforceability of compensation for public goods by using its power of taxation. However, says Samuelson, one can not hope,

---

[141] The mathematical proof is given in Samuelson 1969. The geometric proof is given in Samuelson 1955.

[142] This is the conclusion popularized in Galbraith, 1958. Conversely, others point out that there are theoretical cases (empirically extremely rare) where the Nash non-cooperative equilibrium is identical with the Pareto-optimal solution (Cornes & Sandler 1994, 374).

[143] Up to this point Samuelson's ideas were already captured by Adam Smith when he writes that the government has three duties to perform in the economy, the third being "the duty of erecting and maintaining certain public works and certain public institutions, which it can never be for the interest of any individual or small number of individuals, to erect and maintain; because the profit could never repay the expence to any individual or small number of individuals, though it may frequently do much more than repay it to a great society" (651).

[144] Thus Samuelson writes that there is an "Impossibility of decentralized spontaneous solution" (Samuelson 1954, 388–9) and "Although the optimum is definable, rational people will not, if left to themselves, be led by an invisible hand to the bliss point. On the contrary, it will pay for each rational man to dissemble, trying to mask his preference for the public goods and to engage in other game strategy maneuvers which, when all do them, will necessarily involve deadweight loss to society" (Samuelson 1958, 334).

even at the level of the ideal concept, that the government will succeed in using its tax power in such a way that the opportunity for gain is *fully and optimally realized*.[145]

Even at the ideal level, the concept of public good represents a difficult-to-realize opportunity for gain. It is difficult to get the information about the desirability of the public good. Or, in economic jargon, there is a problem of true preference revelation.

Nevertheless, even without perfect knowledge, the government must decide whether or not to provide the public good. It also must decide how much of the public good it should provide. Finally, the government must decide, all without guaranteed information, on a tax schema. Under such circumstances, it is not possible for the government to reach an optimal solution and a Pareto distribution of taxes for the public good.

Some authors have introduced sophisticated demand-revealing processes consisting of a two-step taxation system. First, there is a tax levied on each citizen which, added together, covers the total cost of the public good. In order to guarantee Pareto optimality, the tax on each individual is not to exceed the declared willingness to pay of each citizen. Second, an additional tax, the Clarke tax, is imposed in order to guarantee that the citizens are economically motivated to reveal their true preferences.[146] If the Clarke tax succeeds in eliciting true preferences, then the first tax satisfies the Samuelsonian conditions for Pareto optimal provision of the public good.

Several problems emerge with the use of Clarke taxes. First, Clarke taxes are taxes beyond the cost of the public good. They can be substantial for small groups. Happily, they decrease as a proportion of the total tax when the group of citizens increases. Still, charging more than the cost is not an optimal solution (Mueller 1979, 74 ff.).

The second problem with the Clarke taxes is that the outcome can be manipulated if individuals come together and coordinate their responses (Stevens 1993, 162).

---

[145] "[My theory] is in fact an attempt to demonstrate how right Wicksell was to worry about the inherent political difficulty of ever getting men to reveal their tastes so as to attain the definable optimum." (Samuelson 1955, 355)

[146] A Clarke tax is a tax used to encourage true preference revelation for public good projects. A Clarke tax is imposed on person A if A's preferred option wins because of A's declared monetary interest in one particular approach to a public good. The amount of Clarke tax is equal to the amount that A's preferred option would loose without A's declared monetary interest. Take the case of Dutch elm disease, which can be approached by experts' removal of sick elms or by doing nothing. If A declare that it is worth $40 to him to have nothing done and that option wins by $30 then the Clarke tax for A is $10 ($40-$30=$10) (Stevens 1993, 160–161).

Thirdly, and theoretically extremely interesting, Clarke taxes aim at a voting mechanism that allows the expression of the intensity of one's vote. Take the following case. Citizen A prefers outcome Y over X with $30.00 and citizens B and C each prefer outcome X over Y with $10.00. Democratically, the vote is 2 to 1 in favor of outcome X. Using a democratic procedure X should be realized. If efficiency is to prevail, then the money value of outcome Y is $30.00 and of outcome X $20.00. Thus Y prevails. Clarke taxes that aim at efficiency can easily require that majority vote be overruled (Stevens 1993, 160–2). Efficiency, democratic procedure and fair taxation cannot always be jointly achieved.

Where does the Samuelson's impossibility theorem and the critical evaluation of the Clarke tax proposal leave us with regard to governmental provision of public goods? Three remarks need to be made, in addition this question.

First, even if Clarke taxes encourage true preference revelation, citizens are charged more than the cost of the public good. The governmental provision of public goods using Clarke taxes is therefore not economically optimal. If Clarke taxes are not used to encourage true preference revelation, then the government decides in partial ignorance of true preferences and its decision can easily be inefficient. Thus, it is important to analyze the lack of efficiency involved in governmental delivery of public goods.

Second, the governmental provision of public goods almost always involves the use of coercion in one of its many forms (compulsory payment by means of assessed taxes; confiscation of property (e.g., land); majority rule imposing the interests of the majorty on the minority) (Priddat 1992, 246). The pure economic justification of governmental provision of public goods is that nobody needs to be made worse off and some can be made better off.[147] Coercion allows for some people to be made worse off. It also permits violation of freedom and of property rights. The use of coercion in the governmental provision of public goods points to a dimension that is not pure economics. It requires reflecting on whether the use of coercion that violates the freedom and the property rights of some is a price one wants to pay for the provision of the public good. Such a reflection requires comparing the merits of the provision of a public good with the demerits of the use of coercion.[148] If the provision of the public good has

---

[147] Technically this can be achieved when there is a benefit-based tax system. For a discussion of the difficulties to implement such a tax principle see Kiesling (1992, 201 ff.). In the case in which all taxes would be Pareto-efficient payments for public goods one could argue that we have a voluntary exchange theory of taxation (Head 1974, 152 ff.).

[148] On the other hand, if the public good is very meritorious, as with inoculations to prevent an epidemic, then, argues Mackscheidt, the government should use techniques appropriate for merit good provision in order to diminish the attractiveness of free-riding. Thus, the government should provide inoculation so much below cost that enough previous free-

little or no merit, then the use of coercion might not be justifiable. Samuelson's approach to the provision of public goods requires us to not only consider the public good's aspect of public goods but the merit good aspect as well, given that coercion is involved.[149]

Third, it is possible that unavoidable governmental ignorance in providing public goods, combined with the use of coercion, can lead to very undesirable results. This is because special interest groups could be able to make use of the government's power of coercion for their own benefit without the government having the necessary knowledge to understand what is happening. A case in point is the 1911 compulsory national insurance in Great Britain. The public good of affordable health was coercively provided by the government but with some important negative consequences. Based on the research of David Green (1993), Schmidtz and Goodin write:

> medical associations...joined forces with for-profit insurance companies (which also viewed friendly societies as an obstacle to higher profits)...they played a major role in amending early drafts of the 1911 National Insurance Act so that the final legislation would do maximum harm to friendly societies.

> Two features of the Act are crucial. First, the Act established price floors that made it illegal for friendly societies to offer health care at lower prices. Second, the Act compelled male workers earning less than a certain income to purchase government medical insurance, thereby making it more difficult if not pointless to pay friendly societies dues. (Schmidtz and Goodin 1998, 68)

The case of the 1911 compulsory national health insurance in Great Britain can be seen as an example of interest groups (ab)using the government's power of coercion in the provision of a public good in order to im-

---

riders consider it in their own self-interest to buy inoculation at the reduced cost in order to prevent an epidemic (Mackscheidt 1997). Mackscheidt explicitly recognizes the connection between the concept of public and merit good for dealing with the free rider problem inherent in the provision of public goods. He also recognizes that "meritorisation" of a public good can only be done for sufficiently meritorious public goods.

[149] David Schmidtz does not use the concept merit good, but he develops a similar argument when he writes that the use of governmental coercion requires additional arguments beyond the public good's argument of efficiency (Schmidtz 1991, XVI). For Schmidtz, the fact that coercive production of public goods would involve the survival of society would be an acceptable argument (159). He mentions that others might use the argument of equality (XVI). He also demands that the government use "sufficiently delicate way[s]" to provide public goods (ibid.). See also footnote 112.

prove their gains at the expense of another group.[150] It is a serious warning, but potential abuses in the implementation of public goods should not blind us to the real presence of potential gains for a collectivity captured in the concept of public good. In short, the demerits of coercion must be compared with the merits of the public good. This is truly a matter of socio-economics or political economy.[151]

From the Samuelson theorem and the analysis of the Clarke tax proposal, one could draw the conclusion that government involvement in the provision of public goods should be abandoned. This might be too pessimistic a conclusion. Rather, based on my conclusion one must accept the idea that the provision of public goods will not always be Pareto optimal and that there sometimes will be regrettable interference with the prefer-ences of some consumers. A farmer's land might be expropriated for building a highway. An airport might be built notwithstanding objections to the noise by nearby home owners. It might be possible to recompense the farmer at estimated market value, and it might be possible to impose limits on the noise of airplanes. The first solution tries to approximate Pareto optimality. The second solution tries to balance the nuisance in a way that many, if not all, parties involved can accept, even if they all protest. The realization of the gains promised by the public good concept also involves an analysis of the social and political aspects of society. Samuelson's public good's theorem is pure economics. The realization of

---

[150] Sandler, expanding the ideas of Olson, gives an argument on why such abuses might be unavoidable or might even be pursued consciously. He writes, "To foster collective action...institutional design may have to engineer a sufficient skewness of benefits to promote participation among agents who are best positioned to make a difference" (Sandler 1992, 197). Thus, if the medical associations and insurance companies were best positioned to make a difference in creating a national health insurance, then the argument demands that these agents be given exaggerated benefits in order to ensure their participation. However politically effective this advice might be, it is a frightening argument in as much as it advices the state to be unjust in the name of effectiveness!

[151] If the government finances public goods by means of general revenue and not by user fees, then a new argument emerges demonstrating the socio-political dimension in the implementation of public goods. Indeed, any time that the government has limited revenues, it encounters an additional constraint when trying to realize public goods. Besides the economic constraint of selecting only those projects where the willingness to pay is greater than the cost, the government faces the additional constraint that it lacks revenue to pay for the realization of all economically justifiable public goods. The question arises as to which of those economically justified public goods will be realized. It will be those that the socio-political process considers most meritorious. As merit criterion one could choose a purely economic criterion (greatest percentage surplus of willingness to pay over cost of the project), a political criterion (which projects will provide most votes?), or a moral criterion (which project will help the least well of the most?). The choice between these different criteria is not a purely economic matter (Stretton & Orchard 1994).

the gains connected with public goods requires a broader form of reflection: it requires socio-economics.

B. Olson: Impossibility of Exclusion

Olson is an author who does not look for the government to realize the opportunity for gain present in public goods. He studies the conditions under which individuals acting out of self-interest will provide a public good. The crucial characteristic of public goods that will act as a disincentive for paying voluntarily is the non-exclusion possibility (i.e., even if one does not pay one cannot be excluded from enjoying the public good once it is provided). Notwithstanding this disincentive, public goods are sometimes provided voluntarily by collective action financed by dues or fees. The solutions for overcoming the disincentive of non-exclusion possibility are different in small, medium and large groups.

Olson mentions three methods to overcome the problem of providing a public good in a small group. One person might have enough interest in the public good to alone finance the good, as in the case of a family with teen-age daughters wanting the safety of a light in the back alley. If the most interested person is not willing to pay alone, he might create social pressure by organizing a social gathering and proposing a burden-sharing where the holdout's are socially embarrassed. Finally, the person most interested in the public good might demonstrate to all the participants that a minimum contribution of each is required to collect enough for the provision of the public good. The most interested person, the leader, makes the members of the small group aware of the undeniable connection between their contribution and the provision of the good. The non-exclusion possibility is dealt with in this last case by demonstrating that the non-exclusion possibility will not apply since the good itself will not be provided if everybody does not contribute or does not contribute enough. Bargaining is still a possibility, but it is diminished by the logically demonstrated possibility of non-provision in case of lack of payment.

For medium groups, it is unlikely that the first strategy, that of one person paying the total cost of the public good, will occur often. The other two strategies can still be used: social pressure (a list of contributors to the church organ is published) and demonstration of connection between payment and provision (a publication of total cost, payments received and assigned payments to reach the goal of, say, building a new parish center). Holding out and underpayment remain possible strategies, but the potential gains created by the non-exlusion possibility are made less attractive by the creation of social pressure and individual guilt.

With large groups (workers interested in safety in the workplace or citizens interested in preserving the ozone level) the two remaining strategies that could be used in groups of medium size lose much of their importance. Indeed, the connection between the payment of one individual and the provision of the public good is almost non-existent (the payment or non-payment of union dues by one worker will not change the prospect of better safety laws; similarly, the contribution of one citizen will not measurably change the ozone level). The paradox with public goods for large groups is that the payment of dues or fees for the public good by any one person is both personally significant (union dues are substantial) while it is insignificant with reference to the total cost of the public good and, thus, to the level of additional provision and additional enjoyment. It is, therefore, not economically rational for members of large groups to pay for their public good. But, if all members of the group follow their private economic rationality, then the public good for the group will not be provided. Paradoxically, private rationality leads to collective irrationality. Adam Smith said it well when he wrote:

> ...it can never be for the interest of any individual, or small number of individuals, to erect and maintain [certain public works and certain public institutions]; because the profit could never repay the expence to any individual or small number of individuals, though it may frequently do much more than repay it to a great society. (Smith, 651)

Olson observes that some groups are able to provide their public good notwithstanding the logical difficulties just described. Olson then asks the question: How do they do it? Olson argues that the successful provision of a public good for large groups consists of a two-step process. First, the potential beneficiaries of the public good must be mobilized. The latent group must become an active group. Second, the active group can then pursue its public goods (unions may seek legislation promoting work safety). In order for a latent group to become mobilized into an active group, there needs to be a leadership that articulates the goals of the group. Articulating the goals of the group is not sufficient for overcoming the disincentive created by the non-exclusion possibility for public goods benefiting large groups. Individuals simply do not have the personal incentive to voluntarily contribute to public goods that benefit large groups (Olson 1968, 44). The leadership, thus, needs to create private incentives associated with the membership in the large group (Olson 1968, 132). The leadership of some groups have natural incentives available (decrease in malpractice insurance for physicians becoming members of the AMA) while leaders of other groups must rely on more artificial incentives (Christmas parties, picnics, credit unions). In both cases, the mobilization of the latent group into an active group requires that the selective incentives for joining the group are large enough to motivate the individual members to pay their dues or fees to the group. The dues or fees can then be used to provide the public good for the group.

Several critical remarks can be made about the voluntary provision of public goods by the mobilization of latent groups using private incentives. First, the solution is not optimal because the provision of the public good is not determined by its usefulness but, instead, by the success or failure to mobilize the latent group. If the mobilization fails, then the good will not be provided.[152] If the mobilization succeeds, then the public good will tend to be overprovided because the willingness to pay dues is not limited by the usefulness of the public good, but also, if not mainly, by the attractiveness of the selective incentives which are often unrelated to the primary public good targeted. If the mobilization of the latent group succeeds, there is overabundance. If it fails, there is famine.

A second critical remark concerns a suggestion of Olson about large groups that fail to mobilize themselves. Olson suggests that it might be the case that the mobilization of a group is the easiest, if not the only, way to realize the provision of a public good (work safety laws promulgated under the pressure of unions). Might it not be justified for the government, so Olson asks, to create artificial incentives for the relevant latent group so that they can mobilize themselves, and thus, become the engine for the provision of a desirable public good? Through legislation – authorizing union shops or closed shops – the government can create a legal situation that provides workers who want work, with private incentive to join unions. Olson understands that his suggestion involves the use of the government's coercive power as part of the strategy to promote the provision of certain public goods. Accepting coercive power for the provision of a public good rests on the meritorious judgment that the public good is worth the loss of some degree of freedom. This is not a purely economic analysis whose recommendation is justified because it is Pareto optimal. Instead, it is a recommendation based upon the declaration that a good—in this case a public good—is also a merit good. Declaring that a good is a merit good means that economic opportunities may be evaluated against the loss of some freedom. Certain societies are more willing than others to declare goods merit goods (e.g., railroads, banking, clean rivers). Furthermore, different states and countries have different political methods for validly declaring that some goods are merit goods (voting along party lines might or might not be possible to impose; two third majorities might be required

---

[152] "The existence of larger unorganized groups with common interests is therefore quite consistent with the basic argument of this study...they also suffer if it is true" (Olson 1968, 167).

for some laws; courts might be able to routinely overrule legislative votes on constitutional grounds or they might almost never have that opportunity). Introducing a judgment based on merit about methods for providing public goods radically transforms pure economic analysis into questions of socio-economics.

Conclusions

1. Conceiving the idea of a public good as an ideal concept allows us to show that there is an opportunity for gain.[153] Samuelson's analysis shows us that the government is not capable of fully realizing that opportunity.[154] Olson's study demonstrates that voluntary provision through group formation also does not guarantee an ideal provision of the good. In short, the ideal concept "public good" points to the presence of an opportunity for collective gain, but at this level of analysis, the realization of that opportunity remains a problem.[155]

2. Samuelson's approach can be used to partially justify the claim of Malkin and Wildavsky that the government cannot be counted on to optimally provide a public good. Olson's approach can be used to justify further the claim of Malkin and Wildavsky that private initiatives can provide some public goods.[156]

3. It is wrong, however, to hope that private initiatives will provide public goods at *optimal levels*. That is the insight provided by Olson. It is, again, wrong to suggest that demonstrated difficulties in realizing the op-

---

[153] Because of the development of technology, the growth in population, and increased resource needs, Sandler, among others, argues that the relevance of the problem of collective action connected with public goods will increase (Sandler 1992, 200).

[154] The first of these two ideas–opportunity for gain–is proven mathematically within a general equilibrium model for m public goods, k private goods and n consumers by D.K. Foley (1967, 1970) and is labeled "a generalization of Lindahl's equilibrium solution" (1967, 66). The second idea is verbally conceded when the author writes: "There is ...no reason to think that Lindahl equilibrium can be embodied by any working political process because it requires that individuals reveal information about their preferences under circumstances in which such a revelation would be to their disadvantage" (72).

[155] Other authors ask themselves what kind of institutional arrangement (or incentive structure) would provide the equilibrium that best approaches the optimal allocation (Cornes & Sandler, 1994, 377 ff.) But such an approach presupposes the validity of the concept of public good, which is what I tried to establish in this paper.

[156] This conclusion is similar to the position of others who also separate the two questions of, on the one hand, the potential gain from collective action and, on the other hand, the question of who needs to organize the collective action: the government or the private sector?(Adams & McCormick 1993, 113)

portunities present in public goods justify saying that the very concept "public good" is nothing but a social construct. Sometimes, there are opportunities for gain beyond atomistic economic activities.

4. It is a legitimate question whether private or governmental initiatives are better at realizing those opportunities. Most likely, private initiatives will be better in some cases, while government initiatives will be better in other cases.[157] But to accept that conclusion is to agree that the concept "public good" is a valid, even though problematic, concept for analyzing certain economic problems. If the solutions for realizing the opportunities demonstrated by the concept "public good" have culturally and socially determined components, it is wrong to claim that the concept of "public good" itself is merely a cultural construct, whose sole validity consists of an act of political will. In my view, the concept of public good has a clearly defined ideal content, where – unfortunately – that ideal content is empirically present only in varying degrees and has no agreed upon implementation strategy .

5. The successful defense of the validity of the technical economic concept of public goods provides us with a more precise way to articulate one of the governmental functions vaguely pointed to by Hegel when he writes:

> ...factors which are a common interest, and when one man occupies himself with these his work is at the same time done for all. The situation is productive too of contrivances and organizations which may be of use to the community as a whole. These universal activities and organizations of general utility call for the oversight and care of the public authority. (*PR*, # 235)

---

[157] It might also be the case that a delicate cooperation between private and governmental initiatives takes place as when clubs are allowed to privately provide public goods to their members but where the government stipulates that discrimination on the basis of sex or race is not acceptable. Another example, borrowed from Hegel, is the provision of great public works by means of monetary taxation instead of forced participation as in the building of Egyptian pyramids. Monetary taxation allows each individual to chose by what work one will earn the money to contribute to the cost of the public good instead of being forced to help directly in the provision of the public good (Hegel 1967 a, # 236 remark; Priddat 1990, 95–107; also Chapter 3, Section III of this book) . The substitution of taxes for direct participation has only recently been extended to military service and seems reversed in cases where prisoners are forced to work on public works as a means to pay for the cost of the public good of imprisoning them. Clearly, these last examples remind us that values are involved in the choice of method of payment of a public good. Indeed, changing to a volunteer army where combatants are paid leads to an increase, percentage-wise, in the poor who serve in the army. This raises value judgments which cannot be handled solely by the economic arguments of the concept of public good. It raises (de)meritorious questions of an ethical and political nature and brings us again into socio-economics.

In more precise language we can now say that the government may have a role to play whenever there are important public goods.[158] In some cases, the government may be called to provide the public goods by itself (bridges, highways), in other cases, the government may be called to an oversight role when private groups try to realize the public good (clubs with discriminating membership rules). It was these potential governmental roles that Malkin and Wildavsky hoped to deprive of legitimacy by questioning the validity of the concept of public good.

---

[158] I therefore agree with the main thesis of a book by Levine that the correct starting point of economic science must be "political economy" (Levine 1977, IX). My defense for the concept of merit good in the previous chapter was a contribution in the same direction.

Part II

Applications

Section I

Reflections on the Political Economy in the US

7. Structural Deficiencies in the American System

Abstract

Hegel reflected upon the desirable connections between the economic and the political domain. He saw a number of structural difficulties that had to be addressed. Some of the solutions that he himself advocated are now unacceptable. Still, the new approach developed by the United States does not seem to be satisfactory either.

The work of Goetz Briefs teaches us how the structural difficulties, pointed to by Hegel, develop into specific anomalies in all Western countries. The work of Mancur Olson, Jr. teaches us that countries blessed with uninterrupted democracies are burdened with an economic growth retardant. The work of Theodore Lowi points to the specific anomalies generated by the deficient American approach to those structural difficulties. All three authors see the emergence of interest groups, which dominate the political scene, as the concrete form of the structural difficulties inherent in combining the free market with democracy.

A public religious document – Catholic Social Teaching and the U.S. Economy (U.S. Bishops' Pastoral, 1984) – both praises and criticizes the American situation. The descriptive criticism by the religious document supports the theoretical criticism of Briefs and Lowi and could be called an illustration of Hegel's claim that in all its richness, a society based on the free market is not rich enough to deal with poverty.

I. After Nozick and Rawls

In the 1970's two important books in political philosophy were published: Rawls' *A Theory of Justice* and Nozick's *Anarchy, State, and Utopia*. These two books give a crucial importance to the concept of freedom in terpreted as liberty – that is, the possibility of an individual to choose without undue restrictions by the government.

Of the two, Nozick goes the farthest in defending the principle of liberty as the basis of societal organization. Indeed, Nozick restricts the functions of the state to those normally associated with the "minimal state": protection of "all citizens against violence, theft, and fraud and...the enforcement of contracts."[159]

Nozick eloquently states the reasons for so restricting the functions of the state in the last paragraph of his book:

> The minimal state treats us as inviolate individuals, who may not be used in certain ways by others as means or tools or instruments or resources; it treats us as persons having individual rights with the dignity this constitutes. Treating us with respect by respecting our rights, it allows us, individually or with whom we choose, to choose our life and to realize our ends and our conception of ourselves, insofar as we can, aided by the voluntary cooperation of other individuals possessing the same dignity. How *dare* any state or group of individuals do more. Or less. (333-334)

By jealously stressing the principle of liberty, Nozick affirms a noble aspiration in American political practice and theory. However, as John Langan writes, such an affirmation "is likely to strike most readers as referring to a different order of things than we find in the grandeur and misery of human endeavor" (1977, 256). More specifically, many an author has stressed the fact that the power of the state has to be used to restrain economic power in order to maintain free competition and to generate a distribution of goods and services that is morally acceptable.

One can think of Rawls' *A Theory of Justice* as a work that can be used to give to the state a redistributive task. Still, Rawls maintains the principle of liberty as the first principle of a just society (1971, 244). However, Rawls adds a second principle which deals with "social and economic inequalities" or with "the distribution of income and wealth and...the design of organizations that make use of differences in authority and responsibility, or chains of command" (60–61).

This principle goes under the name of the "difference principle." Rawls deduces his two principles by creating a fictitious situation in which participants, under a veil of ignorance concerning their own particular situation, choose the principles by which the just society is to be organized. But as Langan has remarked, such a technique

> involves a dualism between the noemenal selves who choose in the original position, and the phenomenal selves who suffer not merely from the biases of interest but also from the urgings of need. Adopting the standpoint of the

---

[159] Nozick 1974, 26. The minimal state is also called the "night watchman" state or the "protective state." see also footnote 99.

noemenal selves of the original position and maintaining it in such a way that the principles of justice can be applied in our present sublunary world of conflicting interests may well be a more difficult task and may require a more fundamental conversion than trying to instill and maintain an attitude of benevolence. (1977, 350)

Clearly, the criticism of Nozick and Rawls by Langan opens the way for further philosophical reflection on the *concrete conditions* for the good society in our contemporary world. This is precisely what I propose to do in this chapter. In section II, I will analyze how American capitalism or late capitalism in general has been transformed, under the motivation of the liberty granted to the citizens of Western democracies, into a new economico-political order known as interest-group liberalism or laissez-faire-pluralism. I will use the writings of Lowi, Briefs and Olson to demonstrate that in this new order, the pursuit of justice or of the common good is so absent that there is cause for alarm. In section III, I will return to Hegel who, at the dawn of capitalism tried to stipulate the institutional conditions for combining justice and liberty in such a way that real freedom would be available for all citizens. Unfortunately, I will have to argue that some of these institutional requirements are absent in American capitalism. In section IV, I will evaluate the analysis of the American economy made by the Bishops' Pastoral on *Catholic Social Teaching and the U.S. Economy* and demonstrate that the criticism presented in this religious document is consonant with the criticism extracted from the writings of Hegel, Briefs, and Lowi.

II. Justice. Concern for the Common Good: The U.S. System and "Interest Group Liberalism" or "Laissez-Faire Pluralism"

The American economic system started to dominate the world scene in the second phase of capitalism. That second phase has been described aptly by Theodore Lowi as "interest group liberalism," by Goetz Briefs as "laissez-faire-pluralism," and by Olson as the period of "collective action" (Lowi 1979; Briefs 1957 b; Olson 1968, 1982, 1983).

In his book, *The End of Liberalism*, Theodore Lowi analyzes the American scene from 1930 onward. He argues that a new kind of relationship developed between the free market and the state. He sees interest groups as the moving forces. He does not focus on the history of ethics and ethos patterns as we will see that Briefs does. Lowi concentrates, instead, upon the formal changes that have occurred in the United States.

According to Lowi, the changes in the relationship between the state and the economic order are of such a magnitude that he calls the new state of affairs "the second republic." The first republic (which lasted, depending upon the criteria used, until about either 1930 or 1960)[160] was a federation in which most of the governing was done by the states. The little governing done by the federal government was done by congressional legislation. The second republic is characterized by the fact that the functions of the government and the size of its bureaucracies have increased. In particular, the federal government has accepted the functions of *regulation* and *distribution*. The first function leads to a kind of national police power; its accompanying animal, the second to a fiscal and monetary policy. This extension of governmental tasks leads to a government centered around the executive; it also leads to Congress delegating its legislative powers to agencies which are supposed to fill out the details of legislation, based on Congress' intent. There is, in effect, a shift in legislative power away from Congress and towards administrative agencies.

Lowi mentions three presidents who contributed in important ways to building this new republic. The first was Franklin D. Roosevelt with his New Deal. The second was John F. Kennedy, who defined the problems of the United States as non-ideological, but complex. These problems could be addressed, he claimed, by the President and a professional bureaucracy. He therefore requested, in his 1962 Economic Report, for instance, vast discretionary powers. The third was Richard M. Nixon. He requested from Congress the authority for revenue-sharing, which gave the President even more discretionary power.

But clearly, if governmental decisions are not made by Congress, they do not undergo the mediating process of public debate and modification. In order to have some mediation, the executive substituted for the public debate in Congress (Lowi 1979, 278) a bargaining process with the affected interest groups. Lowi calls this state of affairs socialism for the organized interest groups (279). He also calls it the state of permanent receivership, in as much as it is a state of affairs that protects industries, corporations, or economic activities that cannot stand on their own, provided that they are organized and can bring political pressure to bear. The state achieves this goal by means of regulatory or fiscal policies.

Lowi does not object to all government regulations or all fiscal policies. He objects to the discretionary method of applying these policies. Thus, he favors the unconditional guarantee of all deposits of up to, say, $40,000 (it

---

[160] It is 1930 if one starts a new period with the emergence of the "new republic"; it is 1960 if one starts the new period with the maturation of the "new republic."

was later increased to $100,000) in all banks that are members of the Federal Reserve System. He objects to the discretionary power to guarantee loans that was enjoyed by the Emergency Loan Board. Such a discretionary power invites bargaining. It thus becomes tremendously pro-organization and pro-establishment. It is also inefficient and prevents innovation. More importantly, it bypasses the requirement of public debate over the purpose and the morality of such public decisions. Having bypassed public debate, the second republic, or interest group liberalism, cannot, according to Lowi, achieve justice. Indeed, a minimal requirement for justice is that decisions be made according to a just rule because "Without the rule, the whole idea of justice is absurd" (296). Bargaining democracy is putting its faith in the process, not in the rule.

Lowi sees the solution to the problem in what he calls juridical democracy. Lowi likes to see the government restrict its scope and return the legislative duty to Congress. He wants specific legislation from Congress. He wants, from federal agencies, administration by rule, not a case-by-case approach. His hope is that Congress would then be forced to debate the *legitimacy* of governmental actions.

Furthermore, Lowi believes that the need to publicly debate the legitimacy of governmental acts before they are implemented will automatically give a place to moral concerns. Thus, he argues, "the powerful would be immobilized if they had to articulate what they were going to do before they did it" (298) or that "it would simply not be possible to support segregation in any form, because a [juridical] democracy cannot abide two systems of law, two criteria for the provisions of government services – in brief, unequal protection of the laws" (299).

Briefs presents a critique similar to Lowi's critique of contemporary democratic capitalism. Briefs's specific contribution, though, is the fact that he presents an analysis which allows us to locate the American economic order within the context of the whole capitalist system. Indeed, Briefs's writings include reflections upon the rise and development of capitalism from its beginnings. His writings also cover more than the economic, political, and juridical aspects of capitalism; indeed, Briefs's writings also analyze the cultural components of the capitalist system, such as its philosophical traditions, its religious movements, and its ethical convictions and practices. Briefs's oeuvre can therefore usefully broaden the knife-sharp critical analysis of the American economic order made by Lowi.

Briefs rejects the belief that commercial society combined with a constitutional state is the embodiment of the good society, because the advent of the commercial society was promoted by forces which have now given rise to a new, questionable social order. Among the circumstances that make the commercial society (capitalism) possible are, according to Briefs, those which undermine the existing ethics and ethos pattern. Instead of a communal, religiously-bound ethic, modern times saw the emergence of a new ethic, an ethic that defines human relations according to the model of relations existing between alien classes, for instance, the relations between traders, merchants, and colonized people. This new ethic, then, will defend the right of individuals to act according to their own personal interest.

However, the excitement about commercial society was tied to the belief that individuals would act according to enlightened self-interest, not short-sighted, or purely egoistic self-interest; to the belief that the possibility of self-interest leading to harmful actions would be checked by economic competition; and finally, to the belief that individuals would adhere to traditional standards of human behavior.[161]

The rising middle class made commercial society a reality. It resulted in major "social disruption and swift decline of marginal standards" of ethics (Briefs 1957 a, 53). As Briefs notes, these social disruptions are well documented in the social and economic literature of the nineteenth century, in the Committee Reports of the British House of Parliament and in the Reports of the factory inspectors (54).

One of the reactions to these social disruptions which had long-term consequences was the organization of individual economic players to make concerted action possible. The first to organize themselves successfully formed the *Amalgamated Society of Engineers* in 1851. This self-organization of workers was followed in Europe by the organization of peasants. In the depression of 1873 to 1898, business organized itself into cartels. The last to be organized were the professions and government employees (55–56). The transformation of the free market economy from a competitive order between individuals to a competitive order between groups became generally accepted. Promoting that transformation became part of public policy after World War I in Europe and after the Great Depression in the United States.[162] The war, particularly in Europe, had led to the belief that the economy could be directed. It was felt, further, that the task of directing the economy would be easier if the economic subjects were themselves organized. Finally, social Darwinism was replaced by a "desire for security, for stability, for the good things in life, for the rights of the common (person), and a sense of belonging to a sheltering collectivity" (56). Thus was created the favorable environment for the maturation of interest-groups. This same environment promoted the misunderstanding of those interest groups, and there were valid reasons for misinterpreting

---

[161] For a report on the different interpretations on what actually happened, see Hirschman 1982.

[162] Though cartels were mostly prohibited in the United States.

them. Indeed, the unions, farm associations, and cartels "were formed to secure some degree of justice in these respective markets, a degree of justice which the 'blind forces' of the supply and demand apparently failed to produce" (58). Furthermore, these interest groups claimed to represent large social strata such as labor, the farming community, business, etc. Finally, the interest groups appeared to be instruments for the reform of the old order.

Briefs's thesis, however, is that the emergence of interest groups is a second phase of liberalism. It is a second phase because the principal actors are different. In the first phase there were, or were supposed to be, only individuals and small firms. The first phase of the free market was supposed to be atomistic competition. In the second phase of capitalism, group-formation is tolerated, encouraged and legitimated. Briefs calls it a second phase of liberalism, because it adopts the same ethics of behavior between aliens as exists in the first phase. Indeed, interest groups replace individual interests. Interest groups defend the proposition that their interests can be maximized without too much concern for the consequences of their actions upon other groups or upon the society as a whole. Furthermore, just as in the first phase of capitalism, competition (now between groups) is hailed as the regulating mechanism. And just as in the first phase, the new economic agents (the interest groups) strongly oppose state interference even though they may welcome the help of the state to pursue their interests.

Thus, the erosion of ethical standards and ethos patterns unavoidably continues. This submarginal ethical behavior creates new burdens. Organized groups will be able to carry their burdens by shifting them upon the anonymous unorganized masses. In the recent past, a major technique to achieve this has been inflation. Since the distributive effects of inflation hit different groups in different ways, inflation is basically unjust—as Keynes has already argued (Keynes 1963, 82, 103).

Briefs gives five reasons for the erosion of ethical standards in a society organized around interest groups (62–63). First, interest groups have adopted pleonexic policies. This is expressed very well in the statement by Sam Gompers: "More and more and ever more." Second, power searches for ever-widening horizons for group competence and jurisdiction. Third, our secularized civilization produces a universal urge for security, a security which must be foolproof. Fourth, the principle of subsidiarity is being undercut.[163] This principle requires that a lower social organization be allowed to perform the tasks it can perform. However, for this principle to work, the lower social organizations need to be willing to take responsibil-

---

[163] The subsidiarity principle is a crucial principle in contemporary Catholic social teaching. One finds a good short description of this principle in Rahner 1968/1970, vol. II, 356–357.

ity. Typical of interest groups is that they do not accept responsibility for their own actions, but appeal to the state to do so in their place, for instance, by requiring import restrictions or loan guarantees in order to remedy negative consequences of their own decisions. Finally, a secular government does not acknowledge a God-ordained natural law and will therefore inevitably borrow its own ethics from the existing social order.

This leads Briefs to draw the conclusion that under the pressure of interest groups and because of the lack of a metaphysical view of humanity and society, democracy itself has changed. The first transformation occurred when, during the Enlightenment, rationalism undermined the need for a metaphysical foundation for the state through its contractarian, utilitarian, or popular sovereignty arguments. The second transformation occurred when rationalism was unable to define the common good. Democracy then became expediency in the form of bargaining democracy. In such a democracy, the state bargains with the interest groups involved. Neither the bargaining interest groups nor the government are willing or able to guide their decisions in light of a common good. Briefs calls this unhappy situation "the meeting of the secondary phase of liberalism with the tertiary phase of democracy."[164]

Still, this pessimism is not Briefs's last word. He does not present a detailed plan of action as Lowi has done. Instead, he points to the limits and the possibilities which the new situation has created. It is Briefs's conviction that the emerging awareness of these limits and possibilities creates the opportunity to search and to affirm ethical principles explicitly. Let us quote the eloquent words by which Briefs introduces the conclusion:

> A degree of freedom exists, and there are functions of the state that are vital. But we realize now as never before the existence both of a realm of necessity ruled by economic laws and of a variable zone of freedom. Because of this freedom, ethics again has a place in economic life and hence, going even further than Max Weber's admission of "value relations," a place in economics proper. The era of determinism accommodated by silent and implicit ethical assumptions is over. (Briefs 1957 a, 75)

Whereas Briefs' conclusion that interest groups have pernicious influences is based upon a socio-economic analysis of the history of Western civilization, Olson comes to the same conclusion on the basis of a very focused study. Indeed, Olson asks two questions. First, why is it that England has such a low growth rate now when during the industrial revolution

---

[164] Briefs 1957 a, 67; see also Briefs 1966, 48, 77, 264, 281, 286. Here Briefs calls it the third phase of liberalism. That third phase he defines as the period in which the interest groups are independent variables; they are a state in the state (Id., 48–49).

it used to have the highest. Second, why have Germany, Japan and France all much higher growth rates (Olson 1982, 3 ff.; 1983, 8–9).

In order to answer this question, Olson starts by rejecting a number of explanations such as the claim that there must be a difference in industriousness between the English and the Germans, Japanese and French; or that the British have an anti-commercial attitude that keeps the ablest and best educated away from business pursuits; or that the British ruling elite is inclined to embark on un-economic prestige projects such as the building of the Concorde. Olson rejects these arguments because they cannot explain why England once had the fastest growth rate while it now has the slowest (Olson 1983, 9–13).

Olson proposes as his explanation the idea that a growth retardant becomes over time more burdensome (Id, 12). Such an explanation needs to show why the growth retardant has become more burdensome in Great Britain than in Germany, Japan and France.

Olson uses as growth retardant the creation of interest groups to promote public goods that are of special benefit to the members of the group. He uses three steps in his argument. First, he relies on a previous publication to remind the readers that the provision of public goods benefitinglarge groups requires the creation of an organization whose main purpose is looking after the interests of the individuals linked by a joint concern for the same public goods (Olson 1968, 9–16, 132–167; Olson 1983, 13–16). Thus, according to Olson's argument, safety in the work place requires the presence of unions pressing for work safety laws. In a second step, Olson points to the historically known fact that groups will not be organized until some time after their common interests have emerged (Olson 1983, 16) and that once organized they are not likely to disappear (Id., 18). As a consequence, developed democracies accumulate more special interest organizations as time goes on (Id., 17). Although, sometimes, interest groups pursue goals that improve economic efficiency (construction lobbies opposing usury laws; farm organizations opposing tariffs on farm equipment) (Id., 19), they more often lobby for policies that diminish economic efficiency (labor-unions trying to block labor-saving innovations; sugar beet producers lobbying for tariffs on imported cane-sugar) (Id., 19). In a dynamic economy, interest groups tend to oppose changes that would threaten relative advantages of their members (Id., 19 ff). Economic growth is to a large extent the result of the introduction of appropriate changes (adjustments to new circumstances; introduction of new and better technologies). In as much as interest groups are motivated to resist many changes, they are behaving as a growth retardant. In the third step of his argument, Olson compares the vicissitude of this growth retardant in England, the country with low economic growth, and Germany, Japan, and

France, countries with a high economic growth. Olson sees as main difference between these two categories of countries, the fact that Great Britain has experienced centuries of uninterrupted normal functioning of democracy (Id., 26), whereas the group of other countries have not. Indeed, Germany and Japan have been defeated in the second world war and the occupational forces abolished the privileges that the special interest groups had in those countries (Id., 25). Although France has not been defeated and occupied by a foreign country since 1870, it has not experienced political stability. Since 1789, France has introduced several new constitutions which undid the advantages of favored interest groups of the previous regime (Id., 26).

Olson's theory, created to explain the slow growth of England and the fast growth of Germany, Japan and France, thus leads to the conclusion that a country with a longer history of stability and freedom of association will have accumulated more interest groups.[165] Their activity creates a growth retardant because these groups do not aim, in the language of Briefs, at the common good but aim at policies that benefit narrow group interests, even if these policies are harming society as a whole.

From the studies of Lowi, Briefs, and Olson, it is clear that the combination of democracy and the interest-group phase of capitalism has negative consequences. These consequences are of such proportion that Lowi argues that such a society is not just, Briefs argues that the common good cannot be guaranteed, and Olson argues that uninterrupted democracies are burdened by an economic growth retardant.

It is curious that democratic capitalism ends up in this situation, for it had been conceived of as a new societal organization that would replace one dominated by the ideals of chivalry. This chivalric ideal had been discredited in the 16th and 17th century by such authors as Hobbes, La Rochefoucauld, Pascal, Racine, and Cervantes (Hirschman 1982, 11). Instead, the image of a commercial society emerged as an attractive alternative to the chivalric society with its passionate and savage exploits of the aristocracy and the experience of looting armies and murderous pirates (Id., 63). Hirschman sums it up well when he concludes his survey of the history of the arguments for capitalism before its arrival:

> Capitalism is...hailed...because it would activate some benign human proclivities at the expense of some malignant ones—because of the expectation

---

[165] Olson describes a study, by a graduate student of his, which compares the length of time a state is part of the federal state and their economic growth. The study finds an inverse relation between the time a non-confederate state is part of the federal state and growth rate. In the states of the Confederate South, where an occupation destroyed existing privileges of interest groups, economic growth was faster than in the Union states (Id., 33 ff.).

that, in this way, it would repress and perhaps atrophy the more destructive and disastrous components of human nature (Id., 66).

If we want to understand the transformation from the optimistic hopes projected into democratic capitalism in the 18th century to the critical disappointment we notice in 20th century authors such as Lowi and Briefs, we will need to analyze the basic structures of democratic capitalism. I intend to do so in the third part of this chapter by means of Hegel's analysis. Both Lowi and Briefs connect their critical appraisals of contemporary democratic capitalism to the absence of or the ineffectiveness of the political control of the economic order. It is precisely this problem that is central to Hegel's reflection.

III. Freedom. Hegel's Good Society

Hegel drew upon Adam Smith and other British economists for his understanding of modern society. It is true that Hegel's ideal society combines a capitalist free market system with a constitutional monarchy. It is equally true that the United States is not and will not become a constitutional monarchy. Nonetheless, Hegel is an important witness here because he shares with us a sense of the goals of the economy but he deliberately chose a monarchy and a different legislative structure over the democratic system of the United States; and his reasons for doing so are very instructive.

I will first analyze the demands Hegel makes upon the political system. Second, I will analyze how Hegel believes that the free market as corrected and guided by a proper political order can guarantee freedom in the post-industrial society.

A. The Government

Crucial for the good society, as Hegel sees it, are a number of institutional arrangements which must guarantee that the state will reflect the interests of the individual while allowing the state to effectively promote the common good.[166] Such an arrangement will, Hegel hopes, elicit the emotional respect of the individuals for the state in the form of patriotism.

As institutional arrangements are a prerequisite for the good society, they must be firmly guaranteed. Such a guarantee occurs in the constitution. It is possible to interpret Hegel's view of a constitution in such a way that it looks very much like the American political practice. Hegel stresses the need for a head of state because only an individual – not a group or a committee – is able to represent the unity of the state (*PR*, # 320). Hegel also stresses the need for separation of executive, legislative, and judicial branches of government. Furthermore, Hegel argues for two legislative houses. One is supposed to be more closely in touch with the individual interests of society – the lower house or, in the United States, the House of Representatives, the other is supposed to be more concerned with the common good of the state – the upper house or, in the United States, the Senate. Finally, Hegel gives important consideration to civil servants and the bureaucracy.

There is another way of interpreting Hegel's view of the good society though, which highlights the differences between Hegel's ideal view of a free state and the practical realization of freedom in the political system of the United States. For that interpretation, one can draw attention to the fact that Hegel argues against an elected head of state but for a hereditary monarchy. He also argues that membership in the upper house of the legislation should be determined by birthright and not by elections. Even though the lower house was to represent the individual interests in society, Hegel rejects general elections as a means to select the representatives. Furthermore, Hegel assigns an educative function to the civil servant and to the bureaucracy that is in sharp contrast with the United States' admiration of the individual entrepreneur and its condescending attitude towards civil servants and bureaucrats. Finally, Hegel argues that the major economic organizations have such an important public function that the state should play a role in the appointment of chief executives of such organizations.

Let us analyze each of these differences. A major difference between Hegel's view of the state and the American political practice comes from

---

[166] Adam Smith formulated sharply a general threat to the common good in a free market society coming from selfish political actions. He writes that the landlord and the worker do not acquire the knowledge of the economic system in their daily tasks. The third class, the employers do. But their interests are often different form those of the whole society and they are screwed. Hence, he warns sternly, "The proposal of any new law or regulation of commerce which comes from this order [the employers], ought always to be listened to with great precaution, and ought never to be adopted till after having been long and carefully examined, not only with the most scrupulous, but with the most suspicious attention" (250). Hegel's proposals can be seen as addressing this warning.

Hegel's rejection of an elected head of state. Hegel wants a head of state and not a committee because only an individual can represent the unity of the state (Ibid.). But, Hegel also expects the head of state to represent the common good. One can count on both the conscience of the head of state and on the constitution to promote and defend the common good.

There is one major factor by which the head of state might be enticed to give in to individual demands at the expense of the common good. That factor is the need to be (re)appointed or (re)elected as head of state. Besides military coups, there are three main methods available to select a head of state: inheritance, general popular elections, and restricted elections. Communist parties, or military regimes us restricted elections. They were also used in the selection of an Emperor in the Holy Roman Empire. The restricted elections of the Holy Roman Empire were an anachronism in Hegel's time, and he does not even give an argument against them. Whereas the United States has chosen a modified form of general elections for the choice of a head of state, Hegel opts for a hereditary monarch.[167] Hegel argues that a hereditary monarchy saves the state "from the risk of being drawn into the sphere of particularity and its caprices, ends, and opinions, and...from the war of factions around the throne"(Ibid., # 281). Hegel rejects the method of directly electing a head of state because this would imply "that the ultimate decision is left with the particular will (the vote of individuals), and hence the constitution becomes a Compact of Election, i.e., a surrender of the power of the state at the discretion of the particular will" (Ibid.). Now the economic order is the domain where the particular will is allowed to flourish. Thus, Hegel's argument implies that accepting a political system where the head of state is elected, as is the case in the US, means that one accepts the risk of such an undue interference of interest groups in the political process itself that the unity of one state, of one nation, is threatened.

A second major difference is Hegel's rejection of general elections for the selection of the two legislative houses. Hegel sees the legislative branch of the government as the place where the mediation between individuals as they have integrated themselves in classes, associations, and corporations on the one hand, and, on the other hand, the state as it is represented by the head of state, takes place.

To guarantee this mediating role structurally, Hegel proposes that the upper house consist of the landed gentry and that the lower house consist of deputies representing the important branches of the economic order rather than individual citizens. By requiring that the upper house consist of the landed gentry, Hegel hopes that the upper house will necessarily

---

[167] For an article analyzing the crucial function of a monarch in Hegel's political theory see Cristi 1983.

mediate between the head of state and the economic order, without being unduly influenced by personal gain. The landed gentry, Hegel thought, had something in common with both the head of state and the economic order. Indeed, the landed nobility participated in the economic order as do all other economic subjects; on the other hand, the landed nobility obtained its position not by means of its participation in the economic order, but by inheritance. The landed aristocracy thus, just as the king, acquired its political rights by birth and not by virtue of its successful participation in the economic order. Both are therefore structurally free to promote the common good. They need not fight structures or risk their political future to promote the common good.

The lower house is also assigned a mediating role. They are to repre-
ᵃⁿᵗ ᵗʰᵉ "ᵉˢˢᵉⁿᵗⁱᵃˡ ˢᵖʰᵉʳᵉˢ ᵒᶠ ˢᵒᶜⁱᵉᵗʸ," (Ibid., # 311) ᵗʰᵉ ᵇᵘˢⁱⁿᵉˢˢᵐᵉⁿ, ᵗʳᵃᵈᵉʳˢ ᵃⁿᵈ
manufacturers. They are not to represent individuals, for Hegel believes that it is an illusion to think that people participate in the political process as atomistic individuals. This belief is also the reason that Hegel objects to general popular suffrage:

> In large states it leads inevitably to electoral indifference, since the casting of a single vote is of no significance where there is a multitude of electors. Even if a voting qualification is highly valued and esteemed by those who are entitled to it, they still do not enter the polling booth. Thus the result of an institution of this kind is more likely to be the opposite of what was intended; election actually falls into the power of a few, of a caucus, and so of the particular and contingent interest which is precisely what was to have been neutralized. (Ibid.; Buchanan 1974, 99–101)

Thus, the lower house should have some form of proportional representation that guarantees the presence in the legislative debates of the important social groups. Its function would be precisely the public mediation between the common good and the conflicting interests of these groups. Hegel even hopes that the legislative debates, because of their public character, will educate public opinion so that the population better understands the rationality of the affairs of the state (*PR*, ## 314–315).

A third difference is Hegel's understanding of the role of the civil servant and the bureaucrat. Hegel thinks that the civil servants and the members of the state bureaucracies make a direct and indirect contribution to the good society. The direct contribution they make is the fact that in modern states, members of government bureaucracies are able to act according to universal principles rather than according to subjective interests or motivations (e.g., hatred, revenge) (Ibid., # 296), and thus, one can come to expect that the transactions between the state and its citizens will be conducted in a dispassionate, upright and polite demeanor. Hegel believes that this fortunate manner of conduct of the bureaucrats is the result of the long education of civil servants and of the ethical attitudes that they develop because of their unique position in a constitutional free market system. This prolonged education makes the civil servants capable of grasping universal principles and makes them interested in pursuing the common good. Hegel believes that the position of the civil servant in a constitutional free market system gives a structural guarantee that the civil servants will *in fact* act according to universal principles and pursue the common good. Indeed, the civil servant in Hegel's ideal society mediates the monarch's concern with the common good and the private sector which is allowed to pursue private interests (Ibid., ## 295, 297, 297 addition). Thus, the monarch educates the civil servants to see the common good. But the private sector, with the right to pursue its private interests, will fight "against the intrusion of subjective caprice into the power entrusted to a civil servant" (Ibid., # 295). It therefore will pay off for a civil servant, Hegel believes, to be "dispassionate, upright and polite" (Ibid., # 296).

The indirect contribution made by members of government bureaucracies to the good society, according to Hegel, is that by their numbers they increase the middle class and by their influence they improve the characteristics of the middle class. Indeed, Hegel believes that the interaction (outside their working hours) of civil servants with other members of society raises the thoughtfulness and the consciousness of what is right among the middle class (Ibid., # 297 and addition). But, let me quote Hegel directly:

> The middle class, to which civil servants belong, is politically conscious and the one in which education is most prominent. For this reason it is also the pillar of the state so far as honesty and intelligence are concerned. A state without a middle class must therefore remain on a low level.... It is a prime concern of the state that a middle class should be developed, but this can be done only if the state is an organic unity like the one described here, i.e., it can be done only by giving authority to spheres of particular interests, which are relatively independent, and by appointing an army of officials whose personal arbitrariness is broken against such authorized bodies. Action in accordance with everyone's rights, and the habits of such actions, is a consequence of the counterpoise to officialdom which independent and self-subsistent bodies create. (Ibid., # 297 addition)

Clearly such a laudatory appraisal of members of government bureaucracies is most uncommon in the United States where a pragmatic philosophy joins hands with a common resentment of bureaucrats. The popular image of the bureaucrat in the contemporary United States is not that of the one who implements justice and fairness, but that of the one, who by his "red tape," hinders progress and impedes normal day-to-day exchanges and transactions.

A fourth and final difference between Hegel's ideal view of a free state and the practical realization of freedom in the American political system is the fact that Hegel believes that the major economic organizations have such an important public function that the state should play a role in the appointment of chief executives of such organizations (Ibid., # 288). Hegel does not advocate a communist theory of the state, where the legitimacy of private and particular interests is very much restricted. Indeed, Hegel starts paragraph 288 of his *Philosophy of Right* by claiming that "Particular interests which are common to everyone fall within civil society and lie outside the absolute universal interest of the state proper." However, Hegel does not accept the idea that the economic order should exist as a more or less fully autonomous domain. Indeed, he explicitly claims that "these circles of particular interests must be subordinated to the higher interests of the state" (Ibid.). In the United States, the political order has the right to regulate the free market because the constitution claims to have as its purpose the promotion of the general welfare.[168] The promotion of the general welfare, though, is pursued very rarely by appointment of the chief of a corporation – as is the case with the Postal Service. The general welfare is more often promoted by regulation, e.g., fair-trade laws, anti-trust legislation, rules for public utilities. Clearly subordination of the free market by means of control of appointments (as advocated by Hegel) provides a deeper form of subordination of the free market to the political order than the prevailing method in the United States, where political or legal regulation of business activity is the preferred method (e.g., rules of the Food and Drug Administration, decisions by the Federal Trade Commission).

If a modern society has a hereditary monarch and a constitution which provides for an upper house where members are landed aristocracy, and which provides for a lower house where the major interest groups have a guaranteed proportional representation; if a modern society can further count on the educating influence of the civil servants; and if finally, the major economic organizations are made politically responsible, then, Hegel believes, the free market can make a fundamental contribution to the good society. It is now time to examine this claim.

---

[168] The Constitution of the United States of America, p. 1.

B. Free Market

In Hegel's good society, there is no need, as there was in Plato's *Republic*, to force individuals to take jobs that they are best qualified to perform (Plato 1979, 423 d). It is also not necessary to share wives and children so as to assure a feeling of unity, nor is it necessary to prohibit private property to make adherence to the common good possible (Id., 457 b–466 d).

Based on a reading of the British economists, Adam Smith and Sir James Steuart, Hegel was able to invest the emerging free market with the hope of enabling the good society to develop without an appeal to some of the authoritarian or paternalistic methods thought necessary in Plato's *Republic*.[169] This was all the more important as this intellectual appreciation of the free market matches well with Hegel's own affirmation of the central function of free work in human consciousness.

Within his architectonic, Hegel expects that the free market will be able to deliver three desirable goals. The first goal is that of providing, in a guaranteed way, the goods and services needed for the members of society. The second goal is that of integrating the individual in a preliminary way into his or her community. The third goal is that the free market will allow people to reconcile themselves with nature and, in the process, allow them to develop self-esteem.

Hegel has a typical philosophic way of assigning these different functions to the free market.[170] Indeed, he calls the free market one of the three ethical institutions. The other two are the family and the state. These three institutions are ethical because they embody and give institutional form to the moral principle. Typical for the moral principle is the fact that the individual has the right and the duty to do the good as he or she sees it. Morality is thus, first, the free choice or free commitment to something; and second, the choice of and the commitment to a good.

These two aspects of morality are more easily perceived in the family and in the state than in the economic order. Hegel describes the moral aspect of the family as follows:

> Hence in a family, one's frame of mind is to have self-consciousness of one's individuality within this unity as the absolute essence of oneself, with the result that one is in it not as an independent person but as a member. (*PR*, # 158)

---

[169] For two book-length treatments of Hegel's dependence upon the British (Scottish) economists, Adam Smith and James Steuart, see Chamley 1963 and Waszek 1988.

[170] The relation between the free market and Hegel's view of freedom and thus of the moral-ethical aspects of the free market were systematically explored in Chapters 3 and 4.

He summarizes the two elements as follows:

> [the essence of marriage consists] in the free consent of the persons, especially in their consent to make themselves one person, to renounce their natural and individual personality to this unity of one with the other. (Ibid., # 162)

The moral aspect in the family requires a free consent and a commitment to a goal, a common good, the unity of two wills.

Similarly, Hegel sees a moral dimension in the state: free consent to the common good, which in this case is the discussion, selection, and enforcement of the rules by which the life of the community is to be governed.

As far as the economic order is concerned, there is a problem. It is clear that one of the two moral components is present; there is free choice. Adam Smith says it well when he writes, "Every [one], as long as he [or she] does not violate the laws of justice, is left perfectly free to pursue [their] industry and capital into competition with those of any other [person], or order of [persons]"(Smith, 423). We are not amazed therefore that Hegel characterizes the free market as "the system of *atomistic* by which the substance is reduced to a general system of adjustments to connect self-subsisting existences and their particular interests" (*PR*, # 523).

It is difficult to see how the other component, the commitment to a good, is realized in the economic order. Again, Adam Smith is worth quoting: Every individual "generally, indeed, neither intends to promote the public interest, nor knows how much he is promoting it...he intends only his own aim" (Smith, 423). Hegel, too, understands this aspect of the free market; he even saw its politically disastrous consequences. He writes:

> Particularity by itself, given free rein in every direction to satisfy its needs, accidental caprices, and subjective desires, destroys itself and its substantive concept in this process of gratification. (*PR*, # 185)

Hegel therefore confirms that one can look upon the free market as the "disappearance of ethical life" (Ibid., # 181). In less philosophical terms he writes: "Civil society [the economic order] affords a spectacle of extravagance and want as well as of the physical and ethical degeneration common to them both."[171]

---

[171] Ibid., # 185; See also Briefs 1983. The basic thesis of this article is that there is marginal pressure to undermine legal and moral norms in the capitalist system, because economic doctrine expects too much of competition as the regulator of self-interest.

However, these negative remarks are not Hegel's final judgment concerning the ethical relevance of the free market. Hegel, informed by the British economists, accepts the proposition that there is an invisible hand at work which in a quasi-deterministic way guarantees a common good. That good is the fact that the free market provides more and better products and services (as they are desired by the consumers) than any other system. The argument advanced is that individuals need products and services in order to satisfy their needs. The free market is a system that does not give anybody a right to a share in the social product unless one has contributed to that product. More technically, the free market guarantees that one gets a claim to a share of the social product of goods and services, in direct proportion to the marginal value of one's own product.

This means that if one does not, or cannot, produce something, or if one produces something that nobody is asking for, then one does not receive a claim to the goods and services available in society. The free market thus becomes a system that automatically rewards or punishes individuals according to whether they contribute to the useful products of society. The free market thus has the power to reward or punish, and it does so automatically. The domain in which the free market can reward or punish is a domain to which no one can be indifferent. Indeed, in as much as human beings are bodily subjects, they cannot afford not to be sensitive to what the free market system can award or punish them with; if they do, they will suffer bankruptcy or starvation. Individuals, in as much as they are tied to the necessary requirements of their own existence, are forced to accept the laws of the free market. It is in this specific sense that one can say that the free market makes use of a threat or uses compulsion and thus that there is determinism at work. The consequences of this mechanism are important. It guarantees that even self-interest and selfishness can be mobilized for productive purposes. It also guarantees that individuals will pay attention to each other.

Let us elaborate upon these two points. The fact that the free market is based upon self-interest has long been heralded. It is supposed to guarantee a more productive society; it is also supposed to guarantee a more steady supply of goods (Smith, 14).

The fact that it forces individuals to pay attention to others is a rather important anthropological feature. Indeed, a long tradition of philosophy and of Christian thought has affirmed that human beings are social beings. This social dimension has frustrating aspects,[172] and it is therefore not surprising that individuals prefer to will their independence rather than their social dependence. The free market, thereby, helps individuals to accept

---

[172] Sartre said: "Hell is just--other people" (Sartre 1958, 52).

what they might not be willing or able to accept freely; that is, the fact that they have a social destiny.

This brings us naturally to the second goal assigned by Hegel to the free market. The free market is supposed to provide preliminary integration of the individual into society. This integration is then completed in the state. However, Hegel stresses the idea that the integration of the individual into the state does not have to start from scratch. The good citizen is not a magically transformed chameleon of the self-interested "homo economicus." Even though Hegel points out that the free market educates the "homo economicus" towards a social being or towards an individual integrated in social groups, and even though Hegel points out that the state must promote the legitimate self-interest of the citizen, he nevertheless maintains that there is a radical difference between the "homo economicus" and the citizen. Indeed, the emotional attachment of the citizen to the state (patriotism) means that the individual is willing and able to recognize that the value of his life lies in something other than himself. He is therefore, in principle, willing to *freely* accept the subordination of his self-interest to the interest of the community as it is organized in the state. His willingness to pay his fair share of taxes and his willingness to serve in a just war are the two instances in which the citizen transcends the "homo economicus."

We have already seen that the free market entices and forces the individual to pay attention to the needs of others. The free market, thus, automatically makes the "homo economicus" a socially oriented individual. Clearly the "homo economicus" remains self-interested even in the attention paid to the neighbor's needs. The "homo economicus" does not become altruistic. She does not transcend the self. She remains selfish, but not solipsistic. Hegel sees further integration: the integration in a class (*PR*, # 207), or in an association (Ibid., # 251), or in a corporation, in the process of integrating oneself into the economic order. In order to become a member of the free market, one has to develop a skill; one has to choose one of the many professions available. One, therefore, automatically becomes a member of a class; one can even decide to become a member of a professional association. In becoming a member of a professional class, one also becomes *somebody* for the economic order and one is recognized by others and in one's own eyes as being somebody worthwhile (Ibid., ## 252–256). Furthermore, the rewards specific to that profession specify the kinds of wishes that are realistically satisfiable. Where desires are infinite, one's acceptance of a specific profession provides the individual with a bundle of attainable goods that others accept as satisfactory for a decent human existence. Inserting oneself into a particular economic class thus provides help in accepting one's finitude.

The insertion into a corporation has the further advantage that a person is partially liberated from the threat which forced him to enter in the economic order in the first place. Indeed, the corporation provides a stable basis for the livelihood of the family. It furthermore allows the sublimation of the self-interest motive, that is, the motive which is minimally required to set the free market in motion. The insertion into a corporation allows the individual to be assured of his self-interest while being free to work for the interests of the corporation. The insertion into a corporation thus allows the person to transcend individual self-interest and become concerned about a common good: the good of the corporation.[173]

The third goal assigned by Hegel to the free market is that it can allow for a reconciliation of the person with nature and with his or her own bodily aspect. Avineri is right in quoting Marx when he says, "He (Hegel) conceives labor as the essence, the self-confirming essence" of a human being (Avineri 1964, 90, n. 25). Hegel did, indeed, develop labor as the solution to the problem of self-consciousness which had the paradoxical task of affirming that it is not something objective, whereas it needs objectivity. Hegel develops the solution in his famous analysis of the master-slave dialectic. However, Hegel also argues that labor does not come about automatically. Because labor requires restraint of desire, it comes about only under a double threat: the fear of death which teaches consciousness the value of life and the threat of the master which imposes on the subordinate (the slave) the burden of service and labor. We are ultimately called upon to discover that work is *our* essence (Hegel 1967 c, 118–119). Thus, we reconcile ourselves with a situation in life that has its negative aspects. The free market economy sanctions this insight by giving a moral significance to the ability of earning a living and by interpreting its failure in a moral sense as well, the easiest one being that poverty is explained by laziness.

Hegel nevertheless goes beyond this optimistic view of the free market. He notices that there are a number of problems in the free market system for which he hoped that the state would provide adequate help. Hegel also notices a number of problems for which he saw no solution.

For the problems for which Hegel finds that there were solutions, he enumerates the administration of justice and what is called, in modern terminology, public goods or externalities.

a) The administration of justice is connected with the idea of the protection of property. It not only requires a legal system but also police as protection against thieves and an army as protection against foreign occupation. Hegel, however, does not reduce the problem of poverty to a

---

[173] Ibid., # 251. This aspect is stressed very much in "Theology of the Corporation" (Novak 1981, 210–211).

utilitarian argument or a formal entitlement theory. For Hegel, "property is the first embodiment of freedom and so is in itself a substantive end" (*PR*, # 45).

As property has this intrinsic connection with freedom, Hegel sees correctly that the task of the state cannot be restricted to the protection of existing property rights. The administration of justice needs to be combined with an attempt to remedy the problem of excessive poverty, i.e. the lack of property by some.[174]

b) The problem of public goods is that of goods which might benefit a large number of people without the producer being able to receive payment for his or her services. One special form of public goods is that of government regulation of goods offered to the public.[175]

Th gr I srrs thrmm ininroonnoolod problems for which did not see a solution. They are: 1) The fact that the problem of luxury might result in cynicism; 2) The fact that the division of labor leads to meaningless jobs or, more generally, that work is not work for oneself, but for the anonymous market; 3) The fact that poverty is widespread and results from accidental phenomena outside the control of individuals. Hegel suggests that it might even be system-generated.

Hegel sees that the mobilization of productive forces in the free market is liberating. In previous times a family might have been concerned about whether or not its budget would permit it to buy enough potatoes—Ireland in the mid-nineteenth century – or enough bread – France in the eighteenth century. If the problem of a contemporary family is whether it can afford to go twice or only once a week to a restaurant, that is a liberation from the previous situation in which the demands of natural needs were more pressing. However, the new possibilities create their own enslavement. One feels the need to emulate – keep up with the Jones – and to assert oneself in some distinctive way. Thus, the road is open for infinite refinement of one's desires. These refinements, though, require the possession of resources; the needy, however, do not have them at their disposal. On the contrary, they remain threatened by the pressing demands of their natural needs. Cultural and natural enslavement thus coexist. Referring to the cynical mode of life adopted by Diogenes, Hegel then argues that when "luxury is at its height, distress and depravity are equally extreme, and in such circumstances Cynicism is the outcome of opposition to refinement" (*PR*, # 195 addition).

---

[174] This argument was developed in more detail in chapter 4.

[175] The problem of public goods is discussed in standard economic textbooks on "Public Finance." A survey essay of considerable depth is "The Theory of Public Goods" (Head 1974, 68–92). Hegel discusses public goods problems in his *Philosophy of Right*, ## 231–236. In my view regulation of products is often a problem of (de)merit goods.

A second permanent deficiency of the free market is that the division of labor does not allow the free market to perform its educative function. Work not only keeps a person busy, ideally, it also teaches one to master the material with which one works. It invites one to cooperate with others. It ends up helping one to acquire habitually executed skills recognized by others as worthwhile (Ibid., # 197). The division of labor, though, "makes work more and more mechanical" (Ibid., # 198). This in turn results in the "distress of the class tied to work of that sort," so much so that they will be unable "to feel and enjoy the broader freedoms and especially the intellectual benefits of civil society" (Ibid., # 243).

A third critique of the free market is the creation of poverty. Success or failure in the free market depends not only upon skill and hard labor but also upon luck. Thus, all kinds of contingencies play a role in the creation of poverty. Hegel already points to the fact that the existence of a rabble of paupers "greatly facilitates the concentration of disproportionate wealth in a few hands" (Ibid., # 244).[176] Furthermore, Hegel thought that unemployment was the result of overproduction and he therefore believed that the free market was inherently unable to eliminate poverty (Ibid., # 245).

Indeed, the poor can either be supported without being required to work or the state can give them work and pay them accordingly. The latter method Hegel believes to be self-defeating. Giving work to the unemployed would add to the productive activities of society. The unemployment problem was created by overproduction. It is not rational to try to solve the problem of overproduction by producing even more. The first method of supporting the unemployed or the poor without them having to work also produces serious problems, according to Hegel. First, it deprives the unemployed or the poor of the means to acquire self-esteem and social respect which are the result of successfully earning a living. Second, if the support for the poor is based on private charitable donations, then the poor and the unemployed are never certain of what to expect. This uncertainty can be removed if the state uses its power of taxation to guarantee a steady stream of income to the poor and the unemployed. However, this method violates a basic principle of the free market, where one has a claim to the social product *only* if one contributes to that product. Hegel thought that such a violation of the free market principle would lead to resentment. The state still might get away with some form of welfare program, but Hegel foresaw that resentment would limit its scope.

Hegel was the first great systematic philosopher to have understood the contribution that a free market organization of the economic domain makes

---

[176] In modern economic theory, the existence of a rabble of paupers could be conceptualized by the existence of high level of unemployment. In turn this fact pushes down wages and thus makes the use of capital more profitable.

to the good society. He argued though, that the centrifugal forces of the free market and the inability of the free market to solve the problem of poverty required the presence of a properly ordered political system in order for the free market to make the *proper* contribution to the good society. The American political system does not have the required political order, as Hegel saw it, to guarantee the proper contribution of the free market. Both Lowi and Briefs have taught us how the free market *in fact* has transformed American capitalist society into an *unjust society* (Lowi) or a *society without* proper *concern* for the *common good* (Briefs). This is exactly the starting point for the Bishops' Pastoral on the American economy.

IV. The Bishop's Pastoral: A Religiously Based Economic Ethic

The Bishops' Pastoral letter starts a crucial moment of its document by praising the American system. The praise is formulated in a way that seems to approve of the American democratic capitalist arrangement of society. The document can therefore be seen as basically being in agreement with Hegel's view of the good society in the modern world. Thus the Pastoral letter states:[177]

> When we consider the performance of the American economy and its success in reflecting these basic economic rights, we see an encouraging record. In its comparatively short history, the United States has made impressive strides in the effort to provide material necessities, employment, health care, education, and social securities for its people. It has done this within a political system based on the precious value of freedom. (# 81)

Still, the Pastoral letter does not refrain from pointing to some very serious failures of the American economic system. Thus, in the same paragraph we read:

> While the United States can be rightfully proud of its achievements as a society, we know full well that there have been failures, some of them massive and ugly. Hunger persists in our country, as our Church-sponsored soup kitchens testify. Far too many people are homeless and must seek refuge from the cold in our church basements. As pastors we know the despair that

---

[177] The references are to the First Draft of the Bishops' Pastoral, "Catholic social Teaching and the U.S. Economy."

can devastate the individual families and whole communities when the plague of unemployment strikes. Inadequate funding for education puts a high mortgage on our economic future. Racial discrimination has devastating effects on the economic well-being of minorities. Inequality in employment opportunity, low wages for women and lack of sufficient child-care services can undermine family life. The blighted and decaying environment of some disadvantaged communities stands in stark contrast with the natural and architectural beauty of others. Real space for leisure, contemplation and prayer seem increasingly scarce in our driven society. (# 81)

The letter does not refrain from making a moral judgment about the factual failures. Indeed, in # 100 it states: "We believe that the level of inequality in income and wealth in our society and even more the inequality on the world scale today must be judged morally unacceptable." Or, "The fact that so many people are poor in a nation as wealthy as ours is a social and moral scandal that must not be ignored" (# 187); or finally, "In our judgment, the distribution of income and wealth in the United States is so inequitable that it violates this minimum standard of distributive justice" (# 202).

Lowi, Briefs, Olson, and Hegel all saw the problem of injustice (poverty in the midst of plenty) or collective inefficiency as arising from a society built upon a one-sided concept of freedom: liberty.[178] Lowi hoped for judicial democracy. Hegel hoped for institutional arrangements. Briefs indicated a moral task. What does the Pastoral letter introduce as novel elements?

The Pastoral letter uses the institutional authority of a major religious organization to introduce a religiously based ethic into the debate over the outcomes of a democratically organized free market. That ethic draws on two themes of the biblical vision of the human person. First, a human being created in the image and likeness of God has transcendent worth: there is something sacred about every person (## 23, 24). Second, the dignity of the human person is realized in community with others (## 23, 24). Based on that union, the letter demands from the economy not just productive efficiency, it demands that the economy "permit all persons that measure of active social and economic participation which befits their common membership in the human community" (# 73).

The letter does not consider this second goal as secondary in the sense that it is justifiable or desirable only if it helps the first goal of economic efficiency. The letter does not even consider the economic cost or economic benefit of imposing the participatory character on the economy. In-

---

[178] Olson calls it a view of the person taking only rational self-interest into account (1965, 64–65, 159–162).

stead it systematically spells out the implications of the communitarian demand. Thus, when enumerating the threefold moral significance of the economy, the letter mentions explicitly, "work should enable everyone to make a contribution to the human community to the extent each is able" (# 76). Or as reformulated in # 77: "it [the economy] should make possible the enhancement of unity and solidarity within the family, the nation and the world community."

This religiously-based economic ethic is then reformulated in the language of rights and in terms of a theory of justice. In terms of rights, three groups are enumerated. First, there are the rights to "food, clothing, shelter, rest, medical care" (# 79). Second, there are the rights "to free initiative in the economic field and the right to work" (# 79). Third, there are broader "rights which set moral constraints on the institutional ordering of the economy, such as the rights of labor unions and the rights of ownership" (# 79). The language of rights allows the letter to stress, in a language that is culturally understood, the demand that the economy must in *its outcomes* provide for the needs of all. The letter emphasizes this rhetorically when it states in italics some ten paragraphs later: "all persons really do have rights in the economic sphere" (# 79).

The language of justice is used to focus more specifically on the community building request issuing from a religiously based economic ethic. The letter presents several formulations, such as: "justice demands the establishment of minimum levels of participation by all persons in the life of the human community" (# 92); or, "justice demands that social institutions be ordered in a way that guarantees all persons the ability to participate actively in the economic, political and cultural life of the community" (# 94); or, "justice is not simply a matter of seeing to it that peoples' private needs are fulfilled. It is also matter of enabling them to be active and productive" (# 95).

The letter fully recognizes the difficulties in implementing the two major goals of fulfilling the basic needs of all (including those of the poor) and of increasing the participation of all in the economic process. Thus, it acknowledges that the American ethos does not give the same privileged position to economic rights as it gives to civil and political rights. In an eloquent paragraph we find the following statement:

> First, the philosophical tradition which helped form our national ethos gives pride of place to the protection of civil and political rights such as freedom of religion, speech and assembly. Economic rights (for example, adequate nutrition, housing and work), however, do not hold this privileged position in the cultural and legal tradition of our nation. (# 83)

Furthermore, the letter acknowledges that we do not know how to implement economic rights. Again, this is in sharp contrast to our institutional expertise in ensuring civil rights (# 84).

Finally, the letter sees difficulties for the implementation of its goals at the level of motivation. Thus, it states:

> There are forms of individual and group selfishness present in the nation that undermine social solidarity and efforts to protect the economic rights of all" or, "the sins of indifference and greed continue to block efforts to secure the minimum economic rights of all persons. This selfishness not only distorts the hearts of individuals, it has also become embedded in certain of the economic institutions, and cultured presuppositions of our society" (# 85).

The letter, therefore, almost naturally asks for "the formation of a new cultural consensus that all persons really do have rights in the economic sphere" (# 86). What this new cultural consensus entails is spelled out in the application program required by justice. It entails seeing that the "fulfillment of the basic needs of the poor is of the highest priority" (# 103), that the "increased economic participation for the marginalized takes priority over the preservation of privileged concentrations of power, wealth and income"(# 104) and that "meeting human needs and increasing participation should be priority targets in the investment of wealth, talent and human energy"(# 105).

In the part on "The Responsibilities and Rights of Diverse Economic Agents and Institutions," the letter introduces anthropological and politico-philosophical concepts to strengthen the weight of its demands made on the economy. Thus, the letter introduces, first, the anthropological concept of work as self-realization in the triple sense of fulfilling one's vocation as an individual, as a member of the human community and as a religious person, (# 109) or the idea that freedom requires the "capability to resist the pressures constantly to want to consume more" (# 141).

The second anthropological concept introduces the idea that private ownership must be subordinated to the "principles of stewardship and the common use of the goods of creation" (# 121).

The letter also introduces two principles of political philosophy. The first is that of subsidiarity. "This principle states that government should undertake only those initiatives necessary for protecting basic justice which exceeds the capacity of individuals or private groups acting independently" (# 127). The second principle is the principle of supra-national duty to the whole of the human family, even in the absence of international political authority (# 137).

But clearly, several of these principles are contrary to those that are operative in democratic capitalism. Indeed, at the anthropological level, capitalism has been heralded as the social arrangement that would tolerate, or even legitimize "interests," in order to extinguish some unacceptable vices.[179] However, arguing, that one must restrain the desire to consume or that one must acknowledge higher principles than private ownership, is situating oneself *outside* capitalism – as it was originally imagined and as it still legitimates itself at the popular imaginary level.

At the politico-philosophical level, matters might even be worse. Democratic capitalism clearly has an international dimension. But, the democratic aspect is tied to the nation state.

As Lowi and Briefs have shown, the democratic political order in the late capitalist phase is *not independent* of the interest groups that have emerged in the nation state. These interest groups actively interfere with ⁙⁙⁙⁙⁙⁙⁙ ⁙⁙⁙⁙ ⁙⁙ ⁙⁙⁙⁙⁙ ⁙⁙ ⁙⁙⁙ ⁙⁙⁙ ⁙⁙⁙⁙⁙⁙⁙ ⁙⁙⁙⁙⁙⁙⁙ ⁙⁙⁙⁙⁙⁙⁙ ⁙⁙ ⁙⁙ the Bishops' letter. Indeed, by their very nature, interest groups try to use the state to further their interests, and might therefore oppose international humanitarian objectives if these are perceived to be in conflict with the group's own interests. Even worse, in domestic policy, the refusal of interest groups to accept responsibility undermines the possible application of the subsidiarity principle, as Briefs argues, because the subsidiarity principle can only work if lower forms of organization are able and willing to take responsibility.

The Bishops' letter can thus be seen as an attempt to criticize some outcomes of American democratic capitalism on the basis of a religiously grounded economic ethic. This ethic goes against the implicit and explicit legitimation of self-interest in democratic capitalism, but it is a powerful challenge.

Conclusion

Studying the ideas of Lowi, Briefs, Olson, and Hegel allows us to reject some false opinions about American capitalism. Not all is well in a society that has embraced the principle of a constitutional free market. Both Lowi and Briefs argued that the constitutional free market society in the latter half of the twentieth century and American capitalism in particular, have become unjust. Olson argued that interest groups burden democracies with

---

[179] See Hirschman 1982, esp. "The Passions and the Interests" part I, "How the Interests were Called Upon to Counteract the Passions."

economic inefficiencies. In simple terms: democratic capitalism is not the realization of the good society. There is nothing in Hegel to contradict this conclusion. In fact there are several warnings in Hegel which point to the possibility that any constitutional free market society might degenerate.[180]

It is also possible to reject the opinion that the source of evil in late capitalistic societies is to be attributed to the technical organization of the economic order, (i.e. the free market mechanism). Indeed, Hegel presented convincing arguments to show that a good society must include the possibility for the exercise of the arbitrary will of individuals in important segments of our lives. The free market mechanism does present such an opportunity. Furthermore, of Lowi, Briefs, or Olson, none attributed the source of evil to the free market mechanism itself. Rather, they attributed it to the ethos pattern that has developed, and which permits or even encourages, the quasi-unrestricted pursuit of group self-interest.

Now that two false opinions are rejected, we are left with the question of whether we can come up with further insights. I believe we can stress at least two of them.

First, even if we grant that Hegel was far-sighted in his analysis of the political requirements of a good society within the context of the free market, we must deny that a hereditary monarch or an upper house whose members are composed of a landed aristocracy, is a valid correction to the contemporary situation. The popular sovereignty idea would simply not allow such a change in the political system. Furthermore, as Marx was the first to demonstrate (O'Malley 1970, 99–101), the purpose of introducing the free market as a necessary element of the good society was to promote freedom. Now, the landed aristocracy, in Hegel's view, would be deprived of freedom in the choice of profession. The oldest son, through primogeniture would be tied to the land of the family and, because of that, have a seat in the upper house. Such an arrangement would work against the principle of freedom which Hegel thought the free market helped to realize in the modern state.

Second, all three authors express the need for the explicit concern for moral values if the free market society is going to contribute to the good society. Hegel thinks that society would keep that moral concern because of the influence of the monarch and well-trained civil servants. Lowi believes that judicial democracy will force people to consider the moral quality of the rules that would be adopted. Briefs makes an explicit argument for the re-affirmation of values and ethics within a free-market society. Olson hopes that consolidation of interest groups will force those large interest groups to forgo free riding because they will see that the harm they

---

[180] *PR*, ## 243–245. The warnings concern the consequences for large masses of people of both poverty and "mechanical" work.

might do to society, for the purpose of promoting narrow group interests, will also perceptibly harm their own members – they have become so large that their behavior has a clearly visible impact on the well-being of the whole society.

There is a well-known theorem in economics which argues that in a competitive market everybody is paid his (marginal) contribution to the social product (Ferguson 1969, 377–80). Many accept such a distribution as morally correct. Our second conclusion rejects the idea that the free market distribution of goods and services (free market which is not always competitive) is a proper substitute for moral reflection upon the economic reality.

The Bishops' Pastoral is precisely an attempt to present an ethical reflection upon the economy. It is an ethical reflection based upon a religious
view of the human person and society. This view is quite different from the view of the human person legitimated within democratic capitalism – i.e. self-interest. Indeed, the religiously based economic ethic of the Pastoral demands restraints of consumer wishes, proposes restrictions on the absolute right of private ownership, and requires that economic activity promote the communitarian spirit. It should take some time before one can see if the religiously based economic ethic appeals to forces that can change society and how much change it can realize. But clearly, the Pastoral letter draws attention to a problem already delineated by academic thinkers such as Lowi, Briefs, Olson, and Hegel.

8. Unjust Redistribution in the American System

Abstract

In this chapter, I will argue that children are a special subgroup of society in that they represent an opportunity for gain for the whole society. Self-interested individuals acting atomistically are not motivated to contribute optimally, if they contribute at all, to the realization of this social opportunity. Societal opportunities can be approached as public goods, giving the government a positive role. However, I will argue that the financing of a public good by means of general taxation violates the public good argument. Such a financing method requires, in addition to the public goods argument, a moral or merit good argument. I will endeavor to provide such an argument. I will also explicitly argue that the current method of providing child support in the United States is defective, as it is neither efficient nor just.

I. An Opportunity for Collective Gains

A. An Argument Based on Expected Dollar Gains

On average, children have a potentially greater future ahead than those in other age groups. In that future they can either contribute to the productivity of society or become a financial burden, as in the case of criminals. Similarly, they may remain reasonably healthy or they might need expensive health services. My argument will concentrate on future productivity and future health requirements. Both present opportunities for collective gains that are more pronounced than for any other age group in society because current investment in children can expect a greater return than investment in any other age group.[181]

a. Potential Collective Gains from Investing in Children in Order to Promote Future Productivity

Most participants in the work force have both a luxury and a problem. The luxury is that they earn more than they consume: they normally have a surplus they can save. They also have a problem: they know that later, in old age, they will consume more than they can earn. Most participants in the work force thus have the problem of conserving current earnings for later consumption.

No one can buy the apples *now* that they will eat when they are old and retired. What one can do is save buying power, in the form of durable goods, precious metals or money, among others. Saving buying power in the form of money is more efficient for society than saving in other forms, because the use of money incurs fewer transaction costs. I will therefore build my argument upon the use of money as buying power for the future.

Let us assume for simplicity's sake an inflation-free, closed economy where the percentage of growth translates frictionless into the same percentage of real interest. An inflation-free society gives its population the opportunity to save its purchasing power risk-free over time. But what will that purchasing power buy, let us say, 36 years from now?

What that money will buy depends upon the productivity of society in the intervening 36 years. If there is no productivity increase during the 36 years, then $1.00 which could buy 1 pound of apples in 1995 will still buy 1 pound of apples 36 years later.

If we accept a 1 percent productivity increase per year for each of the 36 years then the national product will have increased by almost fifty percent in that time.[182] With no inflation the saved purchasing power of our $1.00 would now be able to buy 1.43 pound of apples. Society would be able to give 1 percent interest per year while holding inflation at 0 percent.

If society experiences a productivity increase of 2 percent per year, then the purchasing power would more than double after 36 years.[183] One dollar saved would, upon retirement, be able to buy about 2 pounds of apples.

---

[181] One exception might be pregnant mothers or mothers of very young children. However, the opportunity for collective gain by means of subsidizing these mothers is related in an essential way to the future well-being of their children. I take up this idea in section I.1.b of this chapter.

[182] $1.00 becomes $1.43 by compounding yearly at an interest rate of 1 percent.

[183] $1.00 becomes $2.04 by compounding yearly at an interest rate of 2 percent.

All persons facing retirement thus have a personal interest in seeing that the productivity of their own society increases. An important factor responsible for increases in productivity is the skill of the labor force.

Subsidies for children that are used for increasing the education and the training of the next generation in the work force contribute to an increase in the productivity of the future labor force and, thus, also increase the future purchasing power of every saved dollar.

In other words, subsidies for children, spent in a way to increase future productivity, provide a benefit to every consumer in society who saves purchasing power over time. Thus, every individual who will consume in the future on the basis of past savings will benefit from subsidies to children that increase future productivity. Subtracting the subsidies from the total discounted gains of future productivity increases gives us a measure of the net potential societal benefit that results from the undertaking of subsidies to children.[184]

Let us assume, as is often done (e.g., by neo-classical economic theory), that all individuals act atomistically and out of self-interest. Under those assumptions, each individual, by his own payment, can contribute only infinitesimally to the improved societal productivity. Therefore, it would be irrational for any individual to personally subsidize children in the hope of benefiting from the future societal productivity increase secured by that personal investment. Indeed, the increased purchasing power resulting from one individual's investment in children would be so infinitesimally small that it would not repay the cost of that investment. Nevertheless, there is a societal opportunity for gain. There is a potential societal gain to be made, but no atomistic individual, acting alone, could possibly be motivated by self-interest to contribute even minimally to the cost of realizing this potential gain. Thus, an economy relying on atomistic and self-interested individuals will forgo the potential societal benefit of future productivity created by subsidizing children.

b. Potential Collective Gains from Investing in Children in Order to Save in Future Health Insurance Costs

The United States has a health insurance system financed directly and indirectly by the contributions of individuals. If the cost of the health care system goes up, individuals end up paying, on the average, more for health insurance. It is true that the increased costs are not spread equally and are

---

[184] If the net societal benefit from increased productivity derived from subsidies to children is less than the subsidy itself then subsidy to children is not economically justified on productivity grounds.

sometimes hidden.[185] However, I want to make my argument on the basis of the average increase. Thus, if total health care costs increase, and we assume that co-payments are insignificant or are a fixed percentage of the total health care costs, then, by definition, an increase in health care costs leads to an increase in average health insurance costs. Conversely, if health care costs decline, the average health insurance premium will also decline. It is reasonable to assume that investment in basic prenatal and basic early infant care[186] will decrease future health care costs, and that such care will decrease those costs more than would a similar dollar amount of health care investment in another age group. The sum of discounted future savings in all individual health insurance premiums minus the cost of additional health care would give a measure of the net total societal benefit of additional spending on prenatal and early basic health care.[187]

As with future productivity, I wish to emphasize that the benefits accrue to individuals, not to a mythical entity called society. Again, no atomistic individual is rationally motivated to pay even minimally for increased current spending on health care for children because individual spending has such an infinitesimal consequence for future savings in health insurance costs that the benefit of that spending to the individual is much smaller (virtually infinitesimal) than the cost. And thus, as with the case of future productivity, there is a potential societal gain, but no atomistic individual is rationally motivated to buy the service that would realize that gain.[188]

B. An Argument Built Upon the Assumption of Intersubjective Utility Interdependence

Let me now turn to a softer argument. In recent decades authors have enlarged the concept of self-interest to include compassion and altruism as realistic elements of one's preference (Hochman & Rodgers 1969; Brennan 1974/75; Brennan & Walsh 1977; Sen 1977).[189] Human beings are not just interested in their own consumption of private goods – a sandwich – or of

---

[185] Unions may forgo wage increases in order to have the employers pay more for health benefits of employees, for example.

[186] Care for helping premature babies to survive is a more complicated matter.

[187] If the cost of additional health care for children were greater than the sum of discounted future savings in all individual health insurance premiums then subsidies for children based on potential savings in health costs would be economically unjustified.

[188] For the development of the full argument for this point see the last paragraph of section I.1.a. of this chapter and chapter 6.

[189] Sen argues that sympathy can be included in the concept of self-interest, but not commitment.

public goods – a bridge – but are interested in other people's consumption as well. Many feel pain when seeing or hearing about hungry and malnourished children. Let us concentrate on the actual number of hungry and malnourished children rather than on those that one happens to see oneself. By assumption, compassionate people with income are supposed to have a willingness to pay to satisfy their compassion or to remove their pain over the deprivation of children. Atomistic individuals, taking into account their compassion but acting to maximize their self-satisfaction, must compare the benefit from any spending out of compassion with other forms of spending such as buying private consumption goods, for example, more ice cream. Again, it should be noted that the result of the investment in deprived children that arises from *one* individual's willingness to pay for compassion's sake is so infinitesimal that, for the most part, it would not be worth it for any individual, acting alone, to pay out of compassion to diminish the hunger and malnourishment of children in the whole society. Still, acting together, individuals might consider that the personal satisfaction they would each derive from an overall reduction in hunger and malnourishment achieved by the contributions made by all individuals jointly is worth more than the cost that their *own share* would be in such a joint venture. It remains true, however, that individuals acting alone would not have any interest in paying for the reduction in hunger. There is a possible gain, but no individual alone is motivated, under neo-classical assumptions, to provide the money to materialize that gain (Brennan & Lomasky 1983, 198).[190] Thus, there is potential gain, but it will not be realized under neo-classical assumptions.

This argument based on compassion is a softer argument than the argument based on increased productivity because the argument from compassion assumes a certain willingness in the population to translate compassion into charitable giving. The argument based on increased productivity does not need to assume such a willingness, for it rests on already demonstrated dollar returns for gift dollars.

---

[190] "[H]ence all members of the paying group may vote for a governmental transfer program even though none would actually give one hundred dollars away unilaterally."

II. The Opportunity for Collective Gain is a Public Good

The most solid economic argument for a governmental role based on the motivation of self-interest is the public good argument. Let me summarize the argument already presented earlier in the book.[191] The public good argument is best formulated by means of the ideal concept of a pure public good. That concept is defined by the two characteristics of non-rivalness in consumption and the non-exclusion possibility. Non-rivalness in consumption refers to a good which, if provided by one person, can be enjoyed by all without the first person encountering any decrease in his enjoyment. By non-exclusion possibility, one means that the paying consumer is unable to withhold enjoyment of the good or the service from the other consumers even if they do not pay. The ideal, and thus unrealistic, character of the concept is, among other things, connected with the assumption that the provision of the good can be, first, enjoyed by *all* and, further, enjoyed by all *without the first person losing any enjoyment*. The theory, therefore, assumes non-crowdedness. Thus, busy bridges and roads can be given as examples of public goods, but they are not examples of pure public goods. An example that approaches the status of a pure public good is the provision of standards for weights and measures by the Bureau of Standards (now called the National Institute of Standards and Technology – NIST).

The concept of public good creates a problem for the economic theory of the free market. The problem arises because the economic theory of the free market assumes that economic decisions are made on a cost/benefit-calculus basis by individual actors. In the case of a public good, the benefits accrue to many individuals while the cost of providing the good falls upon the one or few individual decision-makers who decide to buy it. Assuming that the decision-maker(s) follows his self-interest, he will only consider his own benefit from this public good and not the benefit to all the other consumers. Let us call B^a_i the benefit of good **a** to consumer i. For simplicity's sake let us assume that all consumers are identical in their purchasing power and taste. Society (S) can be represented by S=Ni where N is the number of consumers in that society. The benefit of good **a** to society can then be represented by $\sum B^a_i$. If an individual i is deciding strictly atomistically then good **a** will not be bought if its total purchasing cost exceeds B^a_i, expressed in monetary terms. If, however, the total cost is less than $\sum B^a_i$ then society does not realize an opportunity for gains in total benefits, expressed as the difference between the cost of the good (which is

---

[191] See chapter 6 of this book.

too high for any individual to buy alone) and the summation of individual benefits over the set of all individuals. This opportunity loss will occur for every good **a, b, c...**where the benefit to the individual is less than the cost, but where $\sum B_i$ is larger than the cost.

What are some examples of goods having the above-described characteristic? There are many. Let me give some different types: national defense, provided that benefits include also losses with a negative sign; a light in an alley; a road; an airport; the Food and Drug Administration; a school system; police protection.

Libertarians argue that the role of the government should be restricted to what is normally called the minimal state: defense and police protection. In *Anarchy, State, and Utopia* Robert Nozick sums up his position by writing:

> We argued in Part I that the minimal state is morally legitimate; in Part II we argued that no more extensive state could be morally justified, that any more extensive state would (will) violate the rights of individuals. (Nozick 1974, 333)

However, if the above argument is correct, Nozick's theory prevents the government from helping the community realize an opportunity that atomistically self-interested individuals in the free market are unable to realize.

How can the opportunity gain for society present in some public goods be realized? Although several philosophers have written about the problem of public goods (De Jasay 1989; Schmidtz 1991), I find it useful to return to two economists, Samuelson and Olson, who provide two different approaches to the issue (Olson 1968, 1–3, 33–36; Samuelson 1954, 1955, 1958). Olson asks the question whether or not one can envision voluntary approaches that would go beyond atomistic strategies. He suggests that coming together or forming groups is the answer (Olson 1968, 5–52). The neighbors in an alley can come together and undertake a joint action. Workers can form a union and demand better and safer working conditions. Olson argues that the bigger the group the more numerous the difficulties that have to be overcome for joint action to succeed (Ibid., 132–35). Olson even argues that many very large groups in contemporary society are likely to fail in creating joint action (Ibid., 165–67). Families with children constitute a large group of people. These families will very likely fail to voluntarily join together in order to form a group. Let us therefore look to the Samuelson approach.

Samuelson sees very clearly the opportunity possibilities connected with public goods. He proposes a two stage plan of action.[192]   In each stage the government plays a role. Some political theories might accept one role and reject the other. The two stages of the analysis giving the government different roles should therefore be clearly differentiated.

The first stage of the analysis consists of the government collecting data for determining the presence of an opportunity gain. The government must ask every consumer how much he or she would be willing to pay for a particular public good. The declared willingness of all consumers should then be added up and this sum should be compared with the cost of providing the good as determined by the lowest bid. If the cost is lower than the sum of what individuals declared they were willing to pay, then the government has evidence of the presence of an opportunity for collective gain. The collective gain can be made evident to the atomistic consumers. Indeed, the government, in such cases, should be able to provide the public good at or below the price that each consumer is willing to pay. The concept of collective gain with reference to the concept of the public good is not a gain to a mythical entity called the collectivity. Rather, the collective gain is nothing but the sum of the surpluses experienced by each consumer separately when they subtract their share of the cost from their own personally experienced benefit of the good. Thus, in this first part of the analysis, Samuelson addresses solely the non-rivalry in consumption. He does not explicitly address the non-exclusion possibility.

In the first part of this chapter, I presented three arguments demonstrating the presence of an opportunity for collective gain by subsidizing children: future increased productivity benefiting every citizen who uses savings to finance consumption; diminished future health care costs benefiting all who will pay insurance premiums that reflect, however unevenly, expected costs; and, finally, increased satisfaction of one's sense of compassion from the decrease in hunger and malnourishment of children. Samuelson's theory of the pure public good is a theory designed to deal with unrealized opportunities for collective gain in public goods. The government should seize the initiative: it should realize an opportunity for collective gain and buy the services – in this case, the subsidizing of children.

The second stage of Samuelson's analysis consists of reflecting upon the implementation (and financing) of a program to realize the opportunity for gains with public goods. In this stage, Samuelson addresses the *non-exclusion possibility* characteristic of public goods. The first stage of the analysis gives us a list of public goods which possess opportunity gains. In

---

[192] "Efficient, inefficient, and socially optimal configurations can be theoretically defined...it will pay for each rational man to dissemble, trying to mask his preference for the public goods" (Samuelson 1958, 334).

order to realize these opportunity gains, the government needs to address the fact that individuals are not, by themselves, motivated to buy the good. Samuelson therefore proposes that the government use its taxation power to force people to pay according to the self-declared benefits they receive from the good. .But under such an arrangement, consumers are motivated by their self-interest to give false declarations to the government about their willingness to pay (Ibid.). Even if the government could devise clever interviewing strategies (Tideman & Tullock 1976),[193] it would remain the case that individual consumers are motivated to deceive the government about their true interest in the public good, because the government must rely on its power of taxation to deal with the non-exclusion possibility of public goods. The interests of the individual citizen and the interests of the government trying to realize an opportunity for joint gains do not coincide. This gives libertarians an opening to oppose government provision of public goods. But, successfully opposing government help in providing public goods leads to a collective opportunity loss.

Currently the government pays for its subsidies for children by using general revenue. The government does not ask its citizens to pay according to their declared willingness because of expected benefits. The government thus demands that some citizens pay more for the collective benefit of subsidizing children than they can expect that their share in personal benefits from this policy will be.[194] The government therefore forces some people to pay more for a collective good than it is worth to them. I interpret Musgrave's concept of merit good as capturing this idea. Indeed, a merit good is a good that is so meritorious that the government is justified in interfering with the preferences of consumers. I believe that the government can interfere both on the consumption side – providing the service below cost or even free of charge, with or without obligation to consume – and on the financing side – forcing some people to pay for what they have no interest in buying.

---

[193] See also the special supplement to *Public Choice*, vol. XXIX, 1977 devoted to demand revealing processes.
[194] Some authors use this point to object to the concept of public goods (Malkin & Wildavsky 1991, 355–78, particularly 372–73) or to limit the right of the government to provide public goods (Schmidtz 1991, 158–59). See chapter 6 for more detailed discussion of this point.

In my view, both the concept of public good and the concept of merit good are ideal concepts. Aspects of both can be present in concrete economic activity. A full justification of subsidies for children *paid for by general revenue* thus also requires a merit good argument (Priddat 1992, 246).[195] I will provide such an argument in the following section.

III. The Moral Argument

Clearly, such a standard needs to be defended. One can develop two lines of defense: one via a religious argument and the other via a secular argument. The secular argument relies heavily on the research of Mary Jo Bane and David T. Ellwood who write, "Almost 45% (40.9% plus 2.9%) of poor two-parent families had a full-time worker, and well over half of the poor families with two healthy parents had at least one full-time worker....work is no guarantee of success for those at the lower end of the wage spectrum" (1994, 11). They conclude, "Thus it is pay rates far more than unemployment which drives poverty among two-parent families" (Ibid., 12). If Ellwood and Bane are correct in their claims, I submit that they provide empirical support for the moral standard advocated in Catholic Social Thought.

The religious argument might run as follows. Human beings are created in the image of God. God is love. The family is the human institution where human love is most clearly present. Whatever undermines the family is a threat to the divine design for human beings.

The religious and the secular argument about the family, as far as I see it, reinforce each other. At the low end of the wage scale, family life is threatened. This should be avoided on religious as well as secular grounds, since studies show that such a low wage leads to poverty, which in turn leads to great costs later.

In short, both secular and religious arguments can be found to provide support for the claim of Catholic Social Doctrine that states that a society is unjust if it does not provide a family wage. But clearly, a competitive economic system using the market as its mechanism to determine prices

---

[195] Some authors argue that every public good voted for by a majority against the will of a minority must be considered as having a merit good aspect for the minority. That merit good aspect often relates to the financing system disliked by the defeated minority (Priddat 1992, 246). I made the same argument about financing methods for education in Chapter 5, Conclusion.

cannot guarantee a family wage. Who would hire workers who are more expensive simply because they have children?

Some have argued that the government should increase the minimum wage. That proposal has met with political resistance. Another important mechanism to transform the market wage into the moral category of the family wage is income support for dependents. As most dependents are children, I thus have discovered a moral argument for financing the public good of subsidies for children.[196] The public goods argument points to a collective opportunity gain that can be realized. The moral or merit good argument justifies financing the collective opportunity gain by means of general revenue rather than by the benefit principle – general revenue being collected often on the ability to pay principle. Without the moral or merit good argument, the financing method of child support is dubious, because it adds a redistributive dimension to the provision of a public good.

IV. The Current Method of Subsidizing Children in the United States

In the tax year 1994, subsidizing children was achieved in the United States 1) by allowing a pretax deduction of $2,450 for each qualifying dependent from the adjusted gross income in order to calculate taxable income; 2) by earned income credit; and 3) by child and dependent care expenses. I will address only the pretax deduction.[197] The 1994 tax code establishes five tax rates: 15%, 28%, 31%, 36%, and 39.6%.[198] As a consequence, the deduction of $2,450 for each dependent has a different actual net benefit for taxpayers in each of the five tax brackets. Not surprisingly, it turns out that it is worth more if one is in the higher tax bracket, i.e., if one has a higher income.[199]

---

[196] In the early 1990's, both the Clinton Democrats and the Gingrich Republicans defended new forms of child support. *Mandate for Change* (Kamarck and. Gallston 1993, 153–78), expressing the thinking of the Democratic Leadership Council, recommended an $800 per child tax credit for all preschool children. The fifth bill of the GOP's *Contract with America,* called "The American Dream Restoration Act," recommended, among other things, a $500 per child tax credit.

[197] I do not wish to address here whether my arguments could or could not be used for all methods of subsidizing dependents.

[198] See 1994, 1040. Form and Instructions. Washington, D.C.: U.S. Government Printing Office, 1994, p. 53.

[199] The actual benefit for a child deduction is obtained by multiplying the $2,450 deduction by the tax rate. The savings increase with income until taxable income reaches $167,700.

Subsidizing children by means of a tax exemption thus has the curious effect of giving a higher subsidy for children living in wealthier families and giving a lower subsidy for children living in poorer families.

I cannot imagine reasons based on considerations of either efficiency (i.e., public goods arguments) or justice (i.e., merit goods arguments) that would favor a method of subsidizing children whereby those in the upper income brackets receive what amounts to an $882.00 subsidy per child while lower income groups receive only $759.50, $686.00, $367.50or $0.00 per child.

A simple and straightforward alternative method of subsidizing children is to make the subsidy a refundable tax credit. The change in method can be made budget-neutral, and would, on a conservative estimate, probably fall between $400 and $500 for each dependent.

Beyond that income, the benefit of the deduction is slowly phased out by a formula requiring eight steps and described on p. 24 of the 1040 form. My calculation of how much the $2,450 deduction lowers the tax burden in 1994 for families with different incomes is as follows:

- between $0 and $367.50 for a family with taxable income between $0 and $2,450;
- $367.50 (15% of $2,450) for a family with taxable income between $2,450 and $38,000;
- $686.00 (28% of $2,450) for a family with taxable income between $38,001 and $91,850;
- $759.50 (31% of $2,450) for a family with taxable income between $91,851 and $140,00;
- $882.00 (36% of $2,450) for a family with taxable income between $140,001 and $167,700.

The benefit of the deduction slowly diminishes from $882.00 to $304.88 for a family earning between $167,701 and $250,000.

The benefit of the deduction diminishes from $330.37 to $0.00 for a family earning between $250,001 and $290,200.

Above $290,200 the benefit of the deduction is disallowed or worth $0.00.

If the deduction moves the taxable income into a lower tax bracket, then the actual benefit must be calculated in two steps. To calculate the benefit of the deduction applied to the higher tax bracket income, one must multiply this part of the deduction by the higher rate. The deduction applied to the lower tax bracket income must be multiplied by that lower rate. As a result, one could say that if the deduction straddles taxable income brackets, then the actual benefit of the deduction will be somewhere between the two appropriate values I calculated above. For example, a family filing jointly having taxable income of $39,000 before using the $2,450 tax deduction for their only child will end up with a taxable income of $36,500. Without that deduction they would have had to pay more taxes. For the part below $38,000 that would be $1,450 x .15 = $217.50. For the part above $38,000 that would be $1,000 x .28 = $280.00. The total benefit would be: $217.50 + $280.00 = $497.50. As stated, this benefit ($497.50) falls between the benefit of the 15% tax bracket ($367.50) and that of the 28% tax bracket ($686.00).

The net effect of the change would be to give the same dollar amount for every child, regardless of the tax bracket of the parent(s),[200] instead of giving a lesser subsidy to children of parents with a lower income.

This change in method would thus constitute a transfer of income from the upper income brackets to the lower ones, justifiable on grounds of both justice and efficiency. The new method of financing would be implemented explicitly as support for future labor productivity. As such, it would involve outlays that would have to be counted as investment, not as consumption. Compared with most other nations, the United States falls behind in investment. This change in the method of subsidizing children would thus also be a form of increased investment.[201]

On April 5, 1995, the House of Representatives voted in favor of a bill granting a $500 tax credit for every child to every family earning less than $200,000 per year.[202] This bill, however, leaves the right to a deduction for dependents intact. Furthermore, the bill does not make the tax credit refundable. Thus, children of parents earning so little that they owe the IRS less than $500 do not receive the full subsidy. My argument appeals to both efficiency and equity. On both grounds children of lower income families should be supported more, not less. Thus, the new bill fails to correct an objectionable practice of not subsidizing children of the lowest income parents on an equal basis as some other children of parents who earn more.

---

[200] The changes in method for subsidizing children could also include a phasing out of the subsidy above a certain taxable income, e.g., filing jointly and earning more than $75,000, $95,000, or $167,700. $167,700 is used as a benchmark for phasing out the subsidy in the 1994 tax code. Both the public and the merit good arguments would encourage increasing the subsidy for lower income families. Phasing out the subsidy for higher income families is one method of doing so. My general argument does not allow me to specify the method of such a phase-out. It does, however, allow me to argue for some kind of phase-out, and for a method resulting in a higher subsidy for children in lower income families. My personal preference would be that the subsidy not be phased out completely but phased down to say a $50 or $100 tax credit. All children deserve, in my opinion, at least a symbolic welcome into the world.

[201] This change in method could also simplify the tax code as the current phasing out requires eight different steps. (IRS 1994, 1040 Forms and Instructions, p. 24).

[202] The $200,000 limit is adjusted gross income. The $500 tax credit is phased out between $200,000 and $250,000, according to the office of Representative John T. Doolittle of California.

Conclusion

The United States political system through its tax laws makes collective decisions. Starting in 1995, its tax laws provide financial help for families with children in four ways: 1) a pretax deduction for a qualifying dependent. 2) a child credit. 3) earned income credit. 4) credits for child and dependent care expenses.

I have argued that the first two tax measures can be defended on economic and moral grounds. I have also argued that the specifics of those two tax measures are defective for both economic and moral reasons.

The economic reasons in favor of subsidies for families with children rest upon a public good argument. Children provide an opportunity of collective gain. I pointed to three economic reasons for the possible collective gain in subsidizing families with children: increased future productivity by money invested in education of the young; diminished health care costs derived from money invested in prenatal care and expanded health care costs to children; and greater collective pride and happiness derived from not seeing hungry, sick and neglected children. The above collective gain cannot be realized by a single individual, without the assured help of all other individuals. Legislation, for instance tax laws, can guarantee that all will properly contribute to the cost of realizing the potential collective gain.

For the moral argument I used Catholic social thought, the political manifestos of the Democrats' *Mandate for Change* and of the Republicans' *The American Dream Restoration Act*, and the academic work of Bane and Ellwood. Catholic social thought calls for the realization of a family wage defined as a one person wage which can support a whole family. The free market cannot be expected to produce such a morally desirable goal, since this would demand that a worker with children be given, under certain circumstances, a higher wage than a single person regardless of their respective economic performance. Hence the government is called upon to supplement wages by child subsidies in one or another form. This is precisely what both political manifestos are acknowledging by advocating a child tax credit, even though the two parties disagree on the amount. The research of Bane and Ellwood demonstrates that "well over half of the poor families...had at least one full-time worker....Thus it is pay rates...which drives poverty [even] among two-parent families" (1994, 11-12). If the free market cannot increase the lowest wages then the government must find methods to supplement incomes of the (working) poor. Some of these supplements need to be tied to the amount of children as the children increase the economic burden of a family.

The American political system listens to several ideas to guide its tax legislation. I demonstrated that these ideas lead to curious results, which I called both economically inefficient and morally unjustifiable. The American Congress allows itself to be guided by the economic argument that there is a potential collective gain that can be captured by subsidies to children, that is also morally praiseworthy. Thus in 1995 a law was passed granting a $500 tax credit for every child.[203]   In 2003 the tax credit for every child was increased to $1,000.[204]

The American political system is also regularly motivated to reduce taxes and to limit or diminish so-called hand-outs to the poor. This idea leads to a tax law that makes the child-credit purely a credit and not a re-fundable credit. Consequently, if a family has a tax bill that is less than the child credit, then those low income families do not receive the full benefit of the child credit or in the extreme case receive no benefit from the child credit tax bill. The same idea in favor of ideas promoting tax deductions also leads to a tax law with the right for an income deduction for each dependent. Given the fact of progressive taxation, it follows that a subsidy by means of a deduction results in a greater dollar benefit for higher income families and a lower dollar benefit for lower income families.

The two laws supporting children which are also influenced by the motive to reduce taxes are economically ineffective, because one should expect that subsidies would have a greater economic impact if provided to families with lower income than with higher income. These two results are also morally questionably. If it is morally desirable to give support to families with children, then it seems evident that it is morally desirable to help poorer families more than richer one. It would seem morally undesirable to help children of richer families more than those of poorer ones. The current American method of helping families with children through the tax system is thus defective on both economic and moral grounds.

---

[203] In 1995 the child tax credit was phased out for incomes above $200,000 (office of Representative John T. Doolittle of California). In 1999 calculations for the phasing out of the $500 child tax credit start at $110,000 income when married filling jointly (IRS 1999, 43).
[204] In 2003 the child tax credit was not phased out for high incomes (IRS 2003, 40–41).

Section II

Challenges in Transforming Command Economies

9. The Role of Religion and Civil Society in a Transformed Command Economy

Abstract

Both Marx and Hegel understood that there is a social question in the capitalist system: poverty of the labor class and the unemployed. Command economies used the all powerful state as an instrument to try to solve the social question in an industrial world. Command economies failed economically. Most command economies have now moved towards a free market system in which the state has abandoned its substantial powers to interfere and direct the economy. How can these societies deal with the social question, given that they have abandoned an important tool they used in the past: the all powerful state? Before addressing this question I provide arguments as to why the free market system is to be preferred to a command economy. Notwithstanding the arguments in favor of the free market, I argue that the free market itself cannot solve the social question. I then point out that command economies making the transition to the free market will have to take additional steps if they also want to keep addressing the social question. They will have to look for allies like organized religion. The move towards the free market therefore demands the promotion of intermediate institutions. This argument is then extended to some of the additional problems that a state, moving towards a free market, unavoidably faces (free trade hurting local industries, binding legal arrangements that eliminate abuses). Civil society is thereby given an essential role in a reformed command economy.

I. A Hidden Challenge in the Transition to the Free Market

Marx argued that the free market (or the capitalist system) is driven by the profit motive, that the profit motive requires the individual capitalist to obey the laws of Capital, and that these laws do not allow the capitalist to pay attention to human needs. Thus, Marx formulated the idea that there is a *social question* that emerges with the advent of capitalism.[205] He even went so far as to argue that capitalism was inherently contradictory and had to be replaced by another economic system. Marxian thought led to the creation of two kinds of economic systems: the command economies practiced in Eastern Europe, Russia, China, and some developing countries and the socialist economies promoted and defended by socialist parties all over the world. The most successful model of a socialist economy has been that of the Scandinavian countries.

The defenders of the idea of a command economy claimed to be the real heirs of Marx's thought. The theoreticians favoring a socialist economic system were aware that they were modifying Marx's ideas in essential ways. In this chapter, I will not address this modified Marxism.

The economists of the Austrian school are considered to be among the most important theoreticians of the pure free market. One of that school's members, Ludwig von Mises, argued already in 1920 in his article "Economic Calculation in the Socialist Commonwealth," that a command economy (a communist economy) is not a rational economy (Von Mises 1975, 104-105). Von Mises gave an argument for that view. A decade ago, Deng Xiaoping and Gorbachev acted and spoke in a way that amounts to a public confession that command economies are less than optimal ways of organizing economic life.

Marxism was an attempt to analyze and correct the failures of capitalism, in particular the massive suffering of the labor class. The low wages, the long working hours, the unhealthy conditions of many industrial work places, child labor, and the lack of security because of recurring unemployment are among the evils that Marxism perceived as inherent in capitalism. European historians refer to this problem as "the social question." However, trying to solve the social question by means of a command economy is a mistake, because a true solution requires that goods and services be produced in an efficient way. A command economy cannot produce efficiently and thus lacks the means to adequately remedy the suffering of the labor class.

Conclusions should always be modest. One should not overshoot. Marxist economic solutions to the social question have been a failure. Still, I am not prepared to argue that Marx was also mistaken in the problem he saw in an economy based on the free market.[206] Even Hegel, an ar-

---

[205] The Catholic Church, a major player in the organization of European society, has de facto recognized the correctness of the Marxian diagnosis by the publication of several encyclicals on this subject: *Rerum Novarum*, *Quadragesimo Anno*, and *Centesimus Annus*.

[206] Whereas in this chapter I restrict myself to Marx's way of dealing with the social question, one can find in the book by Louis Dupré (1983) a work that analyzes Marx's view on

dent supporter of the free market, sees the social question as a very serious problem for a society which uses the free market when he writes:

> It hence becomes apparent that despite an excess of wealth civil society is not rich enough, i.e. its own resources are insufficient to check excessive poverty and the creation of a penurious rabble. (*PR*, # 245)[207]

The above analysis dictates the points I will develop. First, I will discuss a number of arguments in favor of the free market. Then, I will articulate some reasons why the free market cannot avoid the social question diagnosed by Marx. Finally, I will give suggestions for a solution for the social question in a society moving away from a command economy.

II. Arguments in Favor of the Free Market

A. Primary Argument

The economy is a domain of social reality. There are other domains, such as the political, religious, recreational, and cultural domains. Each of these domains has primary goals. The organization of a domain should be judged, in the first place, by the way it contributes to or hinders the attainment of the primary goal. Thus, if the recreational domain is organized in such a way that it increases political loyalty or national income or religious feeling, while at the same time, it does not provide recreation, I would claim that such an organization of the recreational domain is defective. If this principle is accepted, then we have the first criterion for the proper organization of the economic domain. The primary goal of the economic domain is to produce the goods and services that are needed, desired, and demanded in society.

Now, the free market is a method of organizing the economic domain which, in fact, succeeds better in mobilizing the productive forces of soci-

---

the role of praxis for a more wholesome culture. Dupré acknowledges that Marx correctly saw a problem, but he also disputes that Marx saw the correct solution. See in particular "Conclusion: Culture reintegrated through Praxis" (Dupré 1983).

[207] In his book *Hegel's Theory of the Modern State*, Shlomo Avineri writes: "Hegel remarks that it [poverty] remains inherent and endemic to modern society" (p. 153). Avineri further comments that: "This is the only time in his system when Hegel raises a problem—and leaves it open" (p. 154). For an analysis of the arguments leading towards Hegel's pessimism see in this book: Chapter 3, Section III (towards the end) and Chapter 4, both Section IV (again towards the end) and the conclusion.

ety – and thus, in attaining the primary goal of the economic domain – than a command economy or a mercantilist economy. The free market economy succeeds better both for technical and motivational reasons.

The technical reason is that the pure competitive free market eliminates the ability of individuals (in particular politicians) to arbitrarily intervene in the production process.[208] Instead, it operates by means of a market-generated pricing mechanism combined with the freedom of individuals to buy and sell, produce, and consume. Neither prince, nor lord, nor bureaucrat can tell a member of the free market what to buy or sell, produce or consume. In the free market, the pricing mechanism is allowed to do its work of matching what people are capable of producing with what people are willing to buy. A necessary part of an effective market-generated pricing system is a monetary system in which payment gives economic actors the automatic right to a claim on real goods. It is inefficient and thus a violation of the first goal of the economic domain to produce goods at such a high cost that people are not interested in buying them or to price produced goods so low that the producers cannot profitably make them. A command economy constantly violates that first goal of the economic domain. A free-market economy obeying a pure competitive pricing system allows for the possibility of achieving that first goal. In a very strong statement, von Mises summarizes this point as follows: "Where there is no free market, there is no pricing mechanism; without a pricing mechanism, there is no economic calculation" (Mises 1973, 173, 105, 107, 110, and 130).

The motivational reason why a free-market economy succeeds better in realizing the first goal of the economic domain is that the free market imposes a rule on the economic domain that ties consumption to production. Indeed, the competitive free market is organized in such a way that it refuses the participants the means to buy anything unless they first produce

---

[208] Clearly, the emphasis here is on arbitrary intervention. That politicians need to intervene in the market was defended even by Adam Smith. Smith formulates the point this way:

> According to the system of natural liberty, the sovereign has only three duties to attend to; three duties of great importance, indeed, but plain and intelligible to common understandings: first, the duty of protecting the society from the violence and invasion of other independent societies; secondly, the duty of protecting, as far as possible, every member of society from the injustice or oppression of every other member of it, or the duty of establishing an exact administration of justice; and, thirdly, the duty of erecting and maintaining certain public works and certain public institutions, which it can never be for the interest of any individual or small number of individuals, though it may frequently do much more than repay it to a great society. (1937, 651)

something that others want to buy.[209] In the pure competitive free market someone who does not produce has nothing to sell to others. If one has nothing to sell one does not have any income. If one has no income one cannot buy anything. Similarly, if one produces things one likes to produce, but there are no buyers for them, then it follows that one cannot sell one's products. Again, one has no income and, thus, again one cannot buy what one wants and needs, even though the product was produced with great care, with great pleasure and even with great love. Thus, the rule dominating the competitive free market is a double rule: one must produce and one must produce what others want.

The binding character of this rule is expressed in one word: *must*. The binding character expressed in this word is of a totally different nature than Kant's categorical imperative. Whereas the binding character of the "must" implied in Kant's categorical imperative is purely moral, the binding character of the free market is more primitive. It has to do with survival. If you want to eat you must work.

The binding character present in the free market's rule that one must produce cannot be derived from the different motivations for which people work. Indeed, some people simply like to keep themselves busy. Others enjoy the pride that goes with being skillful. Others just love to work. However, none of these reasons produces a must. Rather, they tie work to the wishes or motivations of the workers. For an economic system, this is too contingent a motivation. The competitive free market is able to go beyond such contingent motivations and ground production in a "must." It does so by means of an anonymous threat that is executed automatically. The threat is that one will be granted access to goods and services needed for survival (food, lodging, clothing, medical care, etc.) only if one produces something that others want to buy. Given that everybody needs goods and services in order to survive and build a human life, the threat functions as a binding rule, a "must." Hence, even though the free market creates freedom of choice, it is based on a threat.[210]

The British economists of the 18th and 19th centuries did not stress very much the threat inherent in this basic rule of the free market. Rather, they stressed the socially beneficial results of that rule. When the rule is opera-

---

[209] Von Mises formulates the motivational argument, restricted to the role of the manager, as follows: "for in practice the propertyless manager can only be held morally responsible for losses incurred. And so ethical losses are juxtaposed with opportunities for material gain. The property owner on the other hand himself bears responsibility, as he himself must primarily feel the loss arising from unwisely conducted business. It is precisely in this that there is a characteristic difference between liberal and socialist production" (Id., 122).

[210] Hegel already understood this rule, in writing: "It follows that this unity is present here not as freedom but as necessity, since it is by compulsion that the particular rises to the form of universality and seeks and gains stability in that form" (*PR* # 186).

tive, the social system can disregard the motives of individuals. It need not expend resources to promote virtues such as high-mindedness and generosity. It can tolerate selfishness and greed. A social system obeying the basic rule of the free market ties the self-interest of the individual to the interests of the community. And thus, as by an invisible hand, this rule guarantees that the primary goal of the economy (production of what people need) will be satisfied.[211] And indeed, the free market has been recognized, even by its critics, as the type of societal organization that is best capable of mobilizing the productive forces of society (Marx & Engels 1948, 11–14).

B. Secondary Arguments

1. Freedom

The free market provides freedom of choice. A command economy restricts the range of choices. On the basis of this difference alone, there are three reasons to prefer the free market.

First, there is a moral argument. Human beings are essentially moral agents. To be a moral agent, it is required that one be able to make choices. The free market allows economic actors to make more choices than does the command economy. A command economy restricts the possibility of making choices to a limited number of political actors.

Second, there is an argument that can be made from an historical perspective. The modern period is the period in which the principle of subjectivity emerged. It emerged in philosophy with Descartes, in religion with Luther, in society-at-large with the arrival of the principle of individual insight required by the truth of natural sciences, and in morality with Kant. The principle that the subject is the grounding of truth and legitimation was applied to social organizations in Rousseau's political ideas. According to Hegel's analysis of the French Revolution, the application of the modern demand that the subject be the basis of political decisions was dis-

---

[211] This rule was given the poetic name of the "invisible hand" by Adam Smith. Let us quote him: "he [the individual] intends only his own gain, and he is in this, as in many other cases, led by an invisible hand to promote an end which was no part of his intention. Nor is it always the worse for the society that it was no part of it. By pursuing his own interest he frequently promotes that of the society more effectually than when he really intends to promote it" (1937, 423).

astrous: it led to the terror of Robespierre.[212] However, that modern principle of subjectivity is not disastrous if it is applied to the economic domain. The free market thus allows the modern spirit to find a social organization that gives it a proper embodiment.[213]

Third, there is the peculiar requirement inherent in freedom. In order to
be free one must feel free. To feel free one needs to have the opportunity
to make some arbitrary choices. It is, however, desirable that these arbitrary choices should not have grave negative consequences. (Thus the arbitrary wish to harm others obviously cannot be tolerated; the arbitrary
wish to have a direct say in making laws cannot be tolerated, because it
would bring the legislative process to a halt.) The free market provides the
opportunity to individuals to make arbitrary and mostly innocuous choices.
The free-market system restricts the damage that follows from such arbitrary choices. In this way, the free market contributes to an essential dimension of human freedom: a great deal of arbitrariness is tolerated, and
thus individuals are capable of feeling free.

2. The Economic System as an Ethical Institution

Both the free market and the command economy can be understood as
ways of ethically organizing the economic domain. Adam Smith presented
the argument for the ethical character of the free market. Marx presented
the argument for the command economy. The free market has the more
subtle – and, as I will argue, the better – argument. An ethical institution is
an objective embodiment of the moral intention and must, therefore, by
definition, incorporate the moral intention. The moral intention requires
two things: that one intends to do something good, and that one does so
freely. As for the first requirement of doing a good, we argued above that
the good of the economic domain is the production of goods and services
desired by consumers. The free market fulfills this first requirement better
than a command economy. With reference to the second requirement –
i.e., that good be done freely – one can point to the fact that, both in production and consumption, the free market allows many more actors the
freedom to decide and allows that freedom over a greater domain than does
the command economy. Because the two requirements of the moral intention are better preserved in the free market than in a command economy,

---

[212] Hegel 1967 c: "Absolute Freedom and Terror," 604: "Universal freedom can thus produce neither a positive achievement nor a deed; there is left for it only negative action; it is
merely the rage and fury of destruction." For a study of that claim see W. Ver Eecke 1975
a. I summarized that study in this book in Chapter 2 Section A "The Rejection of the Rousseau Type of Direct democracy."
[213] For an elaboration of this claim by Hegel see Chapter 2, Section C of this book.

one can claim that the free market represents a higher form of ethical organization of the economic domain. There is one complication. The command economy demands that the good – e.g., provision of housing, food, medical care, education to the total population – be directly targeted. The free market, on the other hand, does not require from its actors that they aim directly at the good. The free market, thus, has the appearance of lacking moral content. It allows its actors to aim at their personal benefit and relies on the theory of the invisible hand to guarantee the good (Smith, 423). If the invisible hand does not work, the free market, as economic system, is powerless and needs help from somewhere else. I will address this dilemma later in this chapter.

3. Labor in Its Harsh and Alienating Dimensions

Work and labor are humanizing. But work and labor also have their harsh, even alienating, aspects. Social conditions can improve or worsen the harsh and alienating aspects of work.[214] No degree of social engineering, however, can take away all of the harshness and alienation of work. There remains for each individual human being a psychological task of dealing with the ontological harshness of work.[215] The organization of a command economy provides individuals an excuse to point an accusing finger at the political system for the harshness and alienation connected with work (Chapter 3, Section II of this book). The free market, by contrast, invites individuals to accept the harshness of work as inherent in the human condition. The harshness of work that is needlessly created by the system is addressed in the free market by the politically tolerated institution of union protest and activity. A free market in which unionization has a place deals better with the harsh and alienating aspects of labor than a command economy does.

---

[214] Marx points out that work produces value that is not totally returned to the labor force. The labor force is thus alienated from the value it produces. In harsher language Marx calls this also theft. Hegel points to another form of alienation in work, particularly when work is service. In service persons are asked to execute the commands of another and are thus deprived of the possibility of expressing their minds in their work. Service is done nevertheless, because of a threat. In slavery it was the threat of death. In the capitalist system it is the threat of starvation or bankruptcy.

[215] The Christian tradition sees the harshness of labor as having an ontological dimension. Indeed, it attributes that harshness not to accidental sociological factors, but to the fall of Adam and Eve.

4. Precariousness of Moral Choice

Individuals might, from time to time, feel inclined to oppose the state on moral grounds. Sometimes such an opposition is morally desirable. However, in a struggle between an individual and the state, the power is unevenly divided: power resides overwhelmingly with the state. In a command economy the state has on top of this imbalance the power to deprive an individual of the possibility of earning a living. In a free-market economy, the state does not have this additional power. Moral opposition to the state thus has one less threat to face in a free market society.

III. The Social Question and the Limits of the Free Market

The free market as such does not solve the social question. Let me develop two reasons for this claim.

1. In every economy there are individuals who do not have the average capabilities necessary to earn a living. There are disadvantaged and handicapped people. Without special help such individuals can be condemned to unhuman conditions if only because they cannot make a living.

2. The free market is not fair in its distribution of hardship. There are at least three forms of economic harm that are not connected with moral vices in the individuals that are hurt. First, the free-market economy is cyclical: there are depressions as well as booms. The cyclical nature of the free-market economy is system-generated. The harm falls on individuals. Second, the political system sometimes needs to take action for the well-being of the whole even if that action hurts subgroups. Third, economic systems behave in unpredictable ways. Skills that were once very useful suddenly become outdated. If the system behaves in unpredictable ways, individuals cannot be faulted for lack of foresight.

These three factors can cause hurt to individuals through no fault of their own. Let me illustrate my claim with one concrete example. If the U.S. Federal Reserve Bank decides—let us assume for valid reasons—to increase interest rates in order to fight inflation, it follows that interest-sensitive sectors of the economy (e.g., housing construction and car manufacturing) will necessarily experience increased unemployment. This is system-generated unemployment. Individuals who are not the cause of unemployment are asked to suffer the penalty of that unemployment. In even stronger terms, unemployment is the predictable result of an economic action undertaken for the benefit of the whole society.

A society that suffers injustice is a society which is ill. Even if the illness is generated by an institution which produces many advantages, it remains an illness. Such an illness needs to be addressed. The question emerges as to how former communist countries will address that illness, given that these countries have conceded that the creation of a command economy is a defective way of dealing with social injustice.

Social injustice is, however, only one of the problems created by the introduction of the free market. I see three more problem areas that necessarily arise from the introduction of the free market.

First, the free market can provide its benefits only if it is competitive. However, every producer can envision great benefits from an escape from competition. The free market is not capable of enforcing competitiveness. Some other institution has to do so.

Second, the free market relies on a specific micro-economic mechanism to produce "as by an invisible hand" a socially desirable outcome. That micro-economic mechanism is self-interest (sometimes equated with the profit motive, though this equation is not quite correct, since the profit motive only covers producers and not consumers). But, if the market is guided by a micro-economic mechanism, then it clearly cannot be trusted to be self-regulating at the macro-economic level. The case of an economy in which there is a threat of unemployment provides an example of the limited ability of the market to deal with macro-economic phenomena. At the micro-economic level it is rational for individuals to react to the risk of unemployment by saving. But, saving means diminishing expenditures. Diminishing expenditures, at the micro-economic level, mean that at the macro-economic level there will be less demand for produced goods. But, less demand for produced goods means increased unemployment. We, thus, have here an example of a rational micro-economic reaction that leads to an increase in macro-economic problems. If the free market relies only on the micro-economic incentive of self-interest, then an institution, other than the free market, will have to be responsible for macro-economic stability.

Third, the free market is based on self-interest as perceived by the actors. The free market can, therefore, not be expected to produce the most socially or objectively desirable outcome. External costs and benefits will not automatically be taken into account, neither in production nor in consumption. If there are two production methods, one cheaper but more polluting, for example, then the competitive free market would encourage a producer to use the cheaper method. Increasing the risk of cancer to bystanders (passive smoking) does not deter the consumption of tobacco. This problem is normally dealt with under the heading of externalities, or more generally, public goods.

IV. To Which Institutions Should One Turn in Addressing the Social Question and Other Problems Arising from a Free Market?

I will focus my reflections in this chapter upon the social question: what to do with poverty, particularly with poverty of the working poor. It is my hope that the communist elite would still be concerned with the social question even when they have decided to go in the direction of a free market economy. In that case I believe that there is a common concern for dealing with the social question or more generally with the question of poverty between the communist elite in turning to the free market and my philosophical (Hegelian) understanding of the free market economy.

I wish to separate the two aspects I see in that question. The first aspect is the question of redistribution. This is normally associated with the question of justice. The second aspect is the problem of creating an economic pie which is big enough so that redistribution is meaningful. This raises the question of making the economy efficient.

A. The Redistributive Aspect of the Social Question

A society moving away from a command economy and incorporating free market principles is moving away from an all-powerful conception of the state. The question that arises immediately is: how will a state with diminished power perform the tasks for which it thought that absolute political power was necessary? My simple argument is that a state moving towards a free market should look for appropriate allies.[216]

In Hegelian terms the move from a command economy towards a free market is a move that recognizes the principle of modernity: subjectivity or individuality. The state will therefore have to find allies who accept and embody this new principle.[217]

---

[216] Michael Novak has argued that even the state in an existing free market as in the West needs to rely more on appropriate allies, i.e., intermediate institutions (1989, 201–08 and 281).

[217] In his encyclical *Centesimus Annus*, John Paul II reminds his audience that Catholic social thought since *Rerum Novarum* has stressed that the social nature of human beings is not completely fulfilled by the state. Various intermediate groups have their own functions. Interesting for our argument is that John Paul II claims that these intermediate groups represent the "subjectivity" of society. He further claims that both the subjectivity of the individual and the subjectivity of society were excluded by socialism. John Paul II thus arrives at the same conclusion as I did, though by means of a different framework (John Paul II 1991, # 13).

The social question is in the first place a moral question, although it does have, secondarily, economic consequences. Among the most important institutions concerned with morality are the churches. If a Marxist state moves towards a free-market economy and wishes to remain concerned with the social question, it should also introduce freedom of religion.[218] The communist elite incorporating free market principles can expect from a legal recognition of religion the emergence of intermediate institutions (organized churches) which have an inherent interest in the poor and thus in redistribution. The communist elite can also expect that organized religion will develop expertise in efficiently helping the poor.[219]

Having introduced a measure of freedom in society by accepting free market principles, the communist elite can expect that the church will understand that it now has a different function to perform. Instead of being a rallying point for symbolic and effective opposition against the repression of the state, the church will now likely see its task as heightening the moral conscience of the citizens so that they are willing to contribute towards the alleviation of the social question. The citizens will be asked to act as individuals: they will be asked to vote for government officials, to contribute to private charitable organizations, and to vote for programs in their private organizations (e.g., unions). Within this transformed society churches likely might concentrate on forming conscience, and providing moral impulses to the citizenry.

A similar argument can be made for other tasks of the government in a society which accepts free market principles. The government which has adopted free market principles will be a less powerful government. In confronting its many tasks, the new kind of government will need to appeal for help and support from appropriate legally recognized organizations. Some of the tasks of the government discussed in this book are the responsibility for economic policy. Economic policy includes dealing with property rights, creating anti-trust laws, providing measures to control business cycles, providing monetary policy, and drafting laws for the protection of the

---

[218] This technical conclusion supports and agrees with Dupré's work on Marx, where he praises Marx's original insight while deploring its narrow economic vision: "One cannot but regret this trend towards economism in a philosophy which contained such a profound and original theory of action...Its end is a messianic salvation of man so total that all need for a transcendent redemption ceases to exist" (Dupré 1966, 230) and also (Dupré 1993, 4).

[219] For empirical evidence see: Brown, D. M., & McKeown, E. *The Poor belong to us: Catholic Charities and American Welfare* and Morris, R., & Freund, M. (Editors). *Trends and Issues in Jewish Social Welfare in the United States, 1899–1952.*

environment.[220]   But, these policies will affect the lives of individuals. Here, too, the modern principle of subjectivity will have to be recognized.[221] The state will have to tolerate, to legitimize, and to encourage the formation of independent groups capable and willing to speak for the *worker*, the *consumer*, the *producer*, and the *environment*. Thus, the state will have to tolerate and *promote* professional organizations that typically try to support the values represented by their professions – the economic profession promoting economic efficiency, the legal profession promoting fair treatment under the law, the association of health providers, and the social workers promoting physical and mental well-being, etc. The state will need the help of these professional organizations in justifying to the broader public the wise and prudent use of its force to impose such measures as anti-trust laws, regulations to protect the environment, and fair-trade laws.

B. The Efficiency Aspect of the Social Question

If any state wants to alleviate poverty it needs to create an economy which is efficient enough to produce the means to alleviate poverty. A reasonable approach to the social question and the alleviation of poverty cannot be the creation of equality at such a cost to efficiency that a substantial part of the population is subject to famine.   This certainly is not a reasonable approach if an alternative approach would have created a measure of abundance.

I wish to discuss three ideas for the creation of an efficient economy: the question of motivation, the question of the necessary government tasks, and the question of the role of non-governmental community governance.

a. Self-Interest and Beyond

A communist elite accepting free market principles must and does indeed recognize and legitimize what Hegel calls the principle of subjectivity. In such a society the individuals are allowed to decide in more domains of

---

[220] In chapter 5, entitled "The Concept of 'Merit Good' and the History of Economic Thought," I defend the first three categories of governmental tasks and call them merit goods.

[221] In # 552 of the *Encyclopedia*, Hegel compares the state with religion. He argues that both relate to and are determined by the same Spirit. I would like to argue that it is not just the state and religion that are determined by the spirit of the times. All intermediate institutions, if they are to be effective, must accept the spirit of their times. In modern times that spirit is clearly the introduction of the principle of subjectivity.

their lives. Specifically, they are allowed to make for themselves most economic decisions as the economy is now a free market economy. Adam Smith argues that enlightened self-interest is an important motivation for the success and efficiency of the free market economy. Starting with a general observation, Adam Smith notices:

> In a civilized society he (any human being) stands at all times in need of the co-operation and assistance of great multitudes, while his whole life is scarce sufficient to gain the friendship of a few persons. (Smith, 14)

He argues that human beings will need more than friendship or benevolence to get from others what they want or even need. Adam Smith sees self-love or self-interest as a necessary motivation in modern society, or to put it differently, he sees the rationality of modern society in its capability to legitimize self-love or self-interest. He formulates his argument as follows:

> But man has almost constant occasion for the help of his brethren, and it is in vain for him to expect it from their benevolence only. He will be more likely to prevail if he can interest their self-love in his favour, and shew them that it is for their own advantage to do for him what he requires of them. (Smith, 14)

Adam Smith summarizes his argument rhetorically in his famous quote: "It is not from the benevolence of the butcher, the brewer, or the baker, that we expect our dinner, but from their own regard" (Id., 14).

However, a contemporary understanding of an efficient free market system points to the fact that there is a legitimate place for altruistic motivations and thus for motivations beyond self-interest. Here I wish to rely on the writings of Amartya Sen. Sen distinguishes motivation for action between self-interest, sympathy and commitment (1977, 326–29). He then focuses on commitment and writes that "commitment is, of course, closely connected with one's morals" (Id., 329). Commitment is something people feel they ought to do or not do, regardless of personal advantage. Hence, commitment "drives a wedge between personal choice and personal welfare" (Ibid.). Sen observes that "traditional economic theory relies on the identity of the two" (Ibid.). Sen then argues that there are two ways to demonstrate the erroneousness of the traditional economic theory of the all importance of self-interest. First, he points out that Adam Smith's argument only applies to the economic domain of exchange. Sen further asserts that a modern economy is not just exchange but production activity as well. Efficient production is done by corporations which rely on all kinds of co-operation. Sen enumerates: dutiful activity, unsupervised reliability and a concern for efficiency (1995, 25).

Second, Sen turns his attention to the domain of exchange in a modern economy. He points out that exclusive reliance on self-interest, where one expects that others might cheat as soon as it is in their interest to do so, would require an enormous and costly expansion of the use of the legal system. Trust in the domain of exchange is an efficient way to do economic exchanges.

Broadening his attack on the exclusive theoretical defense of self-interest in traditional economic theory, Sen points out that economic theory demonstrates that unrestrained self-interest leads necessarily to the under-provision of public goods such as education, health care and even public safety (Ibid., 27). Many of these public goods are nevertheless provided in the capitalist system by the creation of institutional arrangements. Sen's reflections on the importance of non-self-interest motives leads him to introduce the need for governmentally sanctioned institutional arrangements.[222]

b. Governmental Tasks

There is a long tradition in the economic literature about governmental tasks that is necessary for an efficient economic system. Let me make the argument first by means of an article by an economist, Richard R. Nelson. Nelson argues that the government has a necessary role in the organization of the economy for two different reasons. First, there are pure economic reasons, which Nelson lists as areas where the government has a role because of market failures caused by the presence of a public good or by asymmetries in information (2002, 225–232). Second, there are a number of non-economic reasons. Nelson argues that people do not want the free market to control the police, the army, or the foreign policy of a country. He further argues that it is the government's task to guide the economy in the direction that the population values, (e.g., subsidizing health and education, and legally stipulating who the stakeholders are in environmental disputes for the purpose of using the court system).

---

[222] Sen admiringly refers to Japan whose economic success was enhanced by co-operation. He then formulates this ironic paradox: "arguably the most successful capitalist nation in the world flourishes economically with a motivation structure that departs firmly from the pursuit of self-interest, which-we have been told-is the bedrock of capitalism" (Sen 1995, 28).

Having made his general claim, Nelson then draws attention to some questions of detail. He argues that in a modern economy it is not a matter of arguing for or against the role of the government but rather a matter of learning what mixture of government regulation and free market is appropriate for different areas of the economy. Thus the chemical and pharmaceutical industries are very dependent upon patent law (Ibid., 236), both the telegraph and railroad systems demanded government support to get started (Ibid., 235), the airline industry works under stringent safety controls and the medical profession works in a competitive environment with both controls and large forms of subsidy (medicare and medicaid). Nelson further argues that the government legitimately becomes the vehicle for the embodiment of societal values such as mandatory rest on Sundays or the prouoruo or absence of policies for conservation of oil products (Ibid., 234) and the promotion of constructive civil life (Ibid., 235).

Based on the ideas developed, for example, in the chapters in this book concerning the problem of merit and public goods I largely agree with Nelson's broad defense of the need for governmental tasks in the economy and of his description of the complexity of finding the proper balance of governmental intervention for every area of the economic domain. For my part, I argue for broadly defined categories of governmental tasks. I have come to see the need for eleven such broad categories.[223] The first broad category deals with property rights. The government has to specify property rights. The government also has to protect those rights by the creation of a justice system, a police force and even an army.[224] A second broad category of governmental tasks is the creation of institutional arrangements that promote the efficiency of the free market. Some of the well known tasks in this area are anti-trust legislation and natural monopoly controls, credit and bank regulations, promotion of transparency by the mandatory request of information on price and product content and more recently the improvement of customs.[225] A third broad category of governmental tasks is the development of human capital in the form of support and regulation

---

[223] See chapter 5 where I defend the first three categories of governmental tasks and call them merit goods.

[224] I rely on Adam Smith for arguments to defend the role of the government in the defense of property rights. I enlarge that tasks to the need for continuously to specify property rights in a changing economic and cultural environment, as in the current debate about intellectual property rights (Ver Eecke 2003).

[225] For the defense of this category of governmental tasks I rely on a group of economists, sometimes referred to as neo-liberals, particularly in the German literature. I make use of the writings of Walter Eucken, Friedrich Hayek and Henry Simons. See chapter 5 on merit goods in this book. For a summary of the argument for the great importance of improving customs, see: De Wulf and Sokol, IX.

of education and mental health.[226] A fourth broad category of governmental tasks deals with business cycles and their negative impact on economic growth and human well-being.[227] A fifth broad category is the creation of all kinds of social welfare measure.[228] A sixth broad category is the creation of a system promoting and providing health care.[229] A seventh broad category are the measures which promote a well functioning social contract particularly in societies with a very diverse population.[230] An eight category consists of those measures which promote transparency in the economic domain and thus help prevent corruption.[231] A ninth category consists of wise investment decisions and strategic planning.[232] The tenth category is the protection of the environment. The eleventh and last category consists in measures protecting the cultural heritage.[233] Of course,

---

[226] For an interesting illustration of the connection between education and economic progress in Finland as reported in the Washington Post read the following claim: "Superb schools symbolize the modern transformation of Finland, a poor and agrarian nation half a century ago, and today one of the world's most prosperous, modern and adaptable countries" (Kaiser & Perkins).

[227] For the defense of this category I rely on the theories of John Maynard Keynes (Ver Eecke 1975 b).

[228] Musgrave introduced the concept of merit good in order to have a conceptual home for such redistributive measures as free education, free or subsidized health-care, free school lunches, or lost-cost housing (Musgrave 1957, 1959). In a OECD publication on social indicators we find a much more comprehensive list of social welfare measures (OECD 1982).

[229] Musgrave gave as one of his early examples of merit goods: free health measures (1959, 13).

[230] I became aware of the importance of this category after studying the economic miracle of Singapore. Its economic growth was promoted by removing the growth threatening phenomenon of civil unrest between the Malay minority and the Chinese majority (The official policy can be found at Singapore HDB InfoWEB (the official Website for Housing Policy). Mark Hong, a Singapore official, presents a short summary (2000). A discussion of the policy can be found in: Ooi et al., Chih, and Tan).

The lack of economic growth in the Democratic Republic of Congo is caused, among others, by the many areas of civil unrest in that country. After the riots in Los Angeles, the United States implemented several measures to diminish the tensions in the inner cities with the African American minority ("Los Angeles riot still echoes a decade later," http://archives.cnn.com/2002/US/04/28/la.riot.anniversary/index.html).

[231] The World Bank has "identified corruption as among the greatest obstacles to economic and social development" http://web.worldbank.org/wbsite/external/topics/extpublicsectorandgovernance/extanticorruption.

[232] This category is present in classic economic theory under the name of "infant industry protection." A modern nation needs to do more than think about wise decisions in the selection of infant industries it wants to protect. For a study on how the economic success of a nation (Singapore) depended upon wise investment decisions and wise strategic planning see: Ghesquiere 2007.

[233] Even though this category of merit goods is economically less crucial, Musgrave, towards the end of his life, explicitly mentioned this category (1987, 452).

these governmental tasks can be done more or less intelligently and can contribute to increased or diminished efficiency.

c. Neither Government nor Pure Market: Creating Space for Community Governance

Economic theory includes a specialized domain called the theory of "market failures." The theory of market failures seems to open the door for legitimate governmental functions. In reaction to this conclusion a group of economists, specifically economists connected with the theory of public choice, have argued that it might be true that the market cannot guarantee, in certain circumstances, Pareto optimality, but in many cases the alternative of government controlled economic activity results in ever greater inefficiencies. Is there a way out when neither the free market nor the government can handle activities in an economically efficient manner? The answer requires the betting on social capital or letting community governance play a role.[234]

A number of studies have shown that communities can solve problems more efficiently than the market or the government can. Residents of some neighborhoods can "speak sternly to youngsters skipping school, creating a disturbance, or decorating walls with graffiti" (Bowles and Gintis, F421). Fishermen can pool their shrimp boats and their knowledge in order to share the risks of trying new fishing grounds and educate all with the best and latest techniques (Ibid., F422). Co-operative ownership of a plywood factory can contribute to a higher level of work dedication, a

---

[234] Social capital and community governance are not identical, but they are intimately connected. Social capital refers to a certain number of virtues possessed by some people. When these virtues facilitate economic interactions they can be compared to other skills which improve economic productivity. Investment in computer skills and organizational skills is justified economically on the same ground as investment in physical capital. An economist looks where the marginal utility of a dollar of investment is the greatest regardless of whether it is in physical assets or human skills. Hence the introduction of the term: human capital. However, economic productivity can be increased both by skills and virtues. In as much as both are factors which are important for economic productivity, both deserve the name of human capital. Among the virtues normally assumed under such an understanding of human capital are: "trust, concern for one's associates, a willingness to live by the norms of one's community and to punish those who do not" (Bowles and Gintis, F419). However, these virtues are virtues about how people interact with each other. This form of human capital is only productive when interaction of people is a crucial factor in economic performance. Furthermore, these virtues come more or less alive depending upon the way people are allowed or succeed in interacting. To capture the fact that it is virtues as they are allowed to play in human interaction patterns some authors introduce a new concept: community governance. In it these virtues are expected to play an important role (Bowles and Gintis, F420).

lesser need for supervision and a willingness to share the burdens of a recession as opposed to fire some workers and thus create unemployment (Ibid.). In these three cases, there was a market failure because economic efficiency depended upon some public good which the market could not and is known not to be able to provide efficiently. In these three cases too the government, represented by judges, police, or government bureaucrats, did not have the information nor a readily available method to deal with the problems. Who are the youths that need to be punished and how do they need to be punished? What new fishing grounds should be tried and what techniques should be taught? And, how much should be paid to entice the fishers to act as such? Finally, government intervention is not known to improve work dedication as co-operatives ostensibly do. Furthermore, when the government would like to provide the equivalent of the insurance schemes originally provided by the co-operative ventures of fishermen or the co-operative ownership of plywood workers, the theory argues and the evidence shows that there is a problem of moral hazard. Once insured, the motive to work is diminished.

The domain of successful community governance deals with the fact that "the nature of social interactions of the goods and services being transacted makes contracting highly incomplete or costly" (Ibid., F424). Effective community governance has two great advantages over the market and the government as a whole. Its members have a lot of pertinent and detailed information. Its members make effective usage of a broad range of motivations not normally considered in economic theory such as: trust, solidarity, reciprocity, reputation, personal pride, respect, vengeance, and retribution (Ibid.).

There are at least two kinds of failures associated with community governance. The first is that community governance, by its very nature, is limited in scope. Furthermore, it concerns a limitation in principle: both the market and the government develop ways to deal with strangers and can thus expand their range almost infinitely. Community governance relies upon close relations for both its information and its enforcement success . The second limitation is that community governance tends to promote homogeneous membership leading to parochialism with some very negative consequences. It creates an insider-outsider mentality or an "us" versus "them" strategy. When community creation is based upon race or ethnicity, it can produce hostility. When it is based on wealth and power, it can lead to exploitation of the poor and the powerless (Ibid., F427–8).

The importance of human capital and community governance was stressed by Joseph Stiglitz (Stiglitz 1999), when he tried to understand a graph of the 1997 GDP as a percentage of the 1989 GDP of the countries that belonged to the Soviet Union and the communist countries of Eastern

Europe. Only Poland produced more in 1997 than in 1989 – all of the rest had significantly *lower* GDPs. These countries with lower GDPs were the ones that followed the advice of Western economists, from the IMF in particular. Stiglitz points out that countries that did not follow that advice, such as China, India and to some extend Malaysia, often had double digit growth numbers over the same period of time. Stiglitz points out that the Gini coefficient of inequality in Russia during that same period doubled. Stiglitz then asks what do Western economists misunderstand about the economy. As I see it, Stiglitz argues that Western economists do not fully understand the functions of institutions and legal regulations that are necessary for an economy to function efficiently and justly. Thus, Stiglitz focuses on the need for tax collection so that the government can perform its many functions. He also points to the need for intelligent bankruptcy laws, an efficient banking system and measures that can prevent corruption.[235]

Related to our current argument, Stiglitz also argues that Western advisers underestimated the function of social capital and community governance in the creation of flourishing economies. Thus he points out that a market economy must accept the reality of what Schumpeter called "creative destruction." In order to have an efficient economy, inefficient enterprises must be allowed to disappear. However, so argues Stiglitz, for bankruptcy to contribute to a more efficient economy, it is necessary that other more efficient enterprises are created than the dying inefficient ones. This requires entrepreneurial talent.

Stiglitz agrees that there was plenty of entrepreneurial talent in the Former Soviet Union, but argues that the social capital in entrepreneurs was largely inapplicable for creating efficient market oriented firms. Entrepreneurs in the Former Soviet Union, so he writes, "had acquired skills in evading government regulations, in arbitraging away some of the inefficiencies in government regulations for private profit, and in operating at the interstices between the legal and illegal world" (Stiglitz 1999, 7). Stiglitz therefore concludes that there was a deficiency in market oriented entrepreneurial talent.

Stiglitz further argues that the transformation of the FSU created the additional problem of undoing the "social glue" that is necessary for any society and economy to work. He sees the social institutions, the trust in them, and the accepted norms of doing daily tasks as part of this social glue. (Ibid., 8). Stiglitz argues that a better route for economic transformation in the FSU would have been to build on existing social capital as it exists everywhere such as in local workplaces, local township governments,

---

[235] For a more detailed analysis of the ides of Stiglitz, see Chapter 10, Section III in this book.

unions, schools, colleges, co-operatives, mutual aid associations, guilds, professional associations, churches, veterans' associations, clubs, and extended family groups (Ibid., 9). Stiglitz further argues that reform by means of privatization without a proper institutional framework and a lack of proper social capital could have gone another and better route, the one of planned decentralization. He points to the fact that by 1992 some ten thousand enterprises in the Soviet Union had become "leasehold enterprises" (Ibid., 25). Leasehold enterprises were work collectives that could "lease enterprises from the state and run them as more or less private entities, according to the market logic" (Ibid., 24). Such decentralized enterprises had or were acquiring at the time the social capital necessary for running efficient businesses (Ibid., 18, 25). We thus see in Stiglitz's analysis of the failures evident in the attempts to transform the command economies of the FSU into a market economies a confirmation of the claim that, not withstanding neo-classical economic theory, it is important to pay attention to human capital and local or community governance.

C. Putting the Arguments Together

If the communist elite in accepting a transition to the free market remains concerned with the social question and thus the alleviation of poverty, it will have to recognize that the state has less power than when it controlled the economy almost completely. I have argued that the state still has many important functions to perform. But, since the state is not so powerful any more, it will have to legitimatize intermediate institutions and rely on them for support for its tasks. For its different functions it may have to rely on the association of economists, of lawyers, and of engineers. I have argued that for the specific concern of alleviating poverty a communist state introducing free market principles should legitimize a natural ally for this concern: religion.

I have also argued that concern for alleviating poverty must include concern for economic efficiency. I have argued that there are a number of oversight functions, institutional obligations and regulatory duties that the government must perform in order to create an efficient economy. I have also argued that an efficient economic system requires the promotion and protection of social capital and the possibility of using community governance. There I discovered and argued for non-self-interest motives such as trust, acceptance of norms, and the dedication to moral commitments. Interestingly enough, some authors have pointed out that community governance works better in societies that are not suffering from extreme inequality ((Bowles and Gintis, F434). Put more positively, several authors tie the economic success of the East Asian countries to the fact that they created a commitment to share broadly the benefits of economic growth (Campos and Root, 177) which in turn made the co-operative spirit possible (Sen 1993, 27–28). Concern for alleviating poverty can thus go hand in hand with economic growth.

Conclusion

For a society moving away from a command economy, I see a basic challenge. It must introduce the principle of subjectivity in societal organizations. That principle has its privileges, but it also has its duties. It still requires organizations. For it to work effectively, there are some limited but important functions that must be performed by the state. The state should be able to rely on intermediate institutions to perform those multiple functions with less absolute power than before. But in order to be able to rely on intermediate institutions, the state will have to tolerate and promote them.

By concentrating my argument on the assumed interest of the communist elite in the social question – i.e., alleviating poverty – I was able to rely on my Hegelian understanding of an ethical free market. Such an ethical free market necessarily has a redistributive aspect. However, the redistributive aspect must go together with effective efficiency. The latter demands not only the introduction of the free market principle, but also the assumption by the government of a number of institutional and regulatory functions. In addition it requires giving systematic space for non-egoistic motives such as trust and co-operation and for appropriate community governance opportunities.[236]

---

[236] In this chapter I did not address the question of foreign direct investment which plays a big role in the economic growth in both Singapore and China.

Section III

Philosophy of Economics and Catholic Social Thought

10. Overlapping Ideas: Catholic Social Thought and Recent Nobel Laureates in Economics

Abstract

Economic doctrine is interested in the efficient use of resources for production and consumption. It often uses mathematical and geometric arguments in order to speak authoritatively. Catholic Social Thought and most religious ethics are more directly concerned with what the economy does to people, particularly to the poor. These traditions use the message of sacred texts or moral reasoning to make authoritative demands. I will demonstrate that, notwithstanding their different methods and interests, there are important areas where these different discourses about the economy acknowledge each other's authority. I will begin by emphasizing the obvious difference between these two discourses about the economy and end by pointing to multiple forms of overlapping concerns.

I. Multiple Authorities in Economics

A. The Authority of Economic Theory

As economics is the study of the efficient use of scarce resources, it is a science which cannot avoid making recommendations. Economics is a science with prescriptive goals.[237] The development of economic theory

---

[237] Of course, economists do a lot of descriptive work. They provide reports on price levels. They also provide reports on quantities produced in many sectors of the economy, such as the agricultural sector, the service sector, the health sector, and so on. Economists also provide reports that have implicit or explicit recommendations. Thus, a report on the mortgage interest rates charged by different banks leads to the recommendation that taking the lowest interest rate – other things being equal – is the only efficient course of action. For

is the attempt to make such recommendations authoritative. Economic theory has for that purpose developed mathematical and geometric models. In order to build mathematical or geometric models, economists need to specify their model. They need to make a number of assumptions, and these assumptions limit the applicability of conclusions drawn from the model to those parts of the reality that fit the assumptions. Economists interpret the idea of "fit" as "fit reasonably well for the purpose at hand." The application of an economic model to a concrete case thus demands that the economist judge that the reality is sufficiently close to the model so that the model's conclusions apply to the reality under consideration. Such judgments can vary from claims that the assumptions of the model are generally acceptable (apples, bananas, and pears are presented in the markets in units that are close enough to the assumption of the theory that units of production and sale are infinitely divisible), to claims that the assumptions are generally not accepted (distance and time separating producer from ultimate consumer do matter even if the model has no space and time variable). The question then arises: who has the authority to make the decision that the assumptions of the model are close enough to the reality to accept the recommendations of the model in a concrete situation?

To illustrate the difficulties involved, recall that there is an economic correlation called the "Phillips curve" that claims that there is a significant relation between the percentage change in money wages and the level of unemployment (increase the money wages and unemployment can be expected to increase). According to the standard interpretation of the model, if one judges the price elasticity of demand for labor to have a value greater than one, then it follows that an increase in the minimum wage will result not only in an increase in unemployment but also in a decrease of the total wage income of the affected workers. A policy to increase the minimum wage under such circumstances would therefore have two undesirable consequences. However, were one to judge that in the particular case the price elasticity of the demand for labor is zero, then economic reasoning tells us that no one would lose a job as a consequence of the policy and that all workers involved would earn more.[238] The need for a judgment about the applicability of economic models sets a limit to the absolute authority of economic models: Economic models have absolute authority

---

an illustration of the descriptive work done by economists see any publication of the US Census Bureau.

[238] For a recent article questioning the general validity of the Phillips curve and the proposition that minimum wage legislation necessarily increases unemployment, see Prasch & Sheth 1999.

only for the conclusions of the model, not for the applicability of the conclusions to the reality.

I will now show that economic theory demonstrates that there are crucial limitations to its own authority not just in the application of models, but in the construction and interpretation of models. I take as the focus of my argument an influential paper by Francis Bator, wherein he neatly summarizes the theory of welfare economics: "The simple analytics of welfare maximization" (Bator 1957). As the title suggests, Bator makes a number of recommendations concerning how a society could maximize its welfare. More than two thousand years before Bator, Plato had already considered maximization of welfare to be an integral part of justice. Indeed, any interference with the possibility of producing the maximum welfare in society results in there being less resources available within society to share or to distribute. Some people could therefore receive less than they could have received if welfare maximization had not been impeded. Plato considered such interference a form of injustice. Bator's model must therefore be given ethical authority in matters of economics.

Bator's model makes a number of simplifying assumptions – e.g., Bator reduces his economy to two persons, two input factors (land and labor), and two products (apples and nuts). Bator's model also includes a number of less obvious assumptions – explained in a footnote[239] – such as the idea that the two inputs are perfectly divisible, homogeneous, and inelastically supplied. Or, in other words, he assumes that all production functions have a "smooth curvature...[and] neoclassical generalized diminishing returns obtain in all but one dimension – returns to scale are assumed [to be] constant" (Bator 23).[240]

By means of his model, Bator is able to demonstrate that three rules must be obeyed in order to maximize social welfare. One rule relates to

---

[239] The assumption of smooth curvature implies that all inputs and outputs are infinitely divisible. Thus the model has the option of using land in increments of one acre, half an acre, a tenth of an acre, a square foot, half a square foot, etc. The model also has the option of using labor in increments of one laborer, half a laborer, one month's work, one week's work, one day's work, etc. The model also assumes that apples can be produced in increments of, say, one hundred pounds, ten pounds, one pound, half a pound, one apple – and here the unrealistic dimension of the assumption emerges – half an apple, one fourth of an apple, etc. One could therefore describe physically impossible situations where all of the land is turned over to the production of nuts except for one square inch upon which part of an apple tree is supposed to grow and which is supposed to produce some minute fraction of an apple. The neoclassical assumption of generalized diminishing returns means that for a fixed amount of one production factor, say land, the use of a third laborer will lead to a greater production of apples than the use of two laborers, but that the increase in production due to the third laborer's work is postulated to be less than the previous production increase made possible by the hiring of the second laborer.

[240] For an enumeration of these and other assumptions see Bator 23.

production, another rule relates to consumption, and a third rule relates to the co-ordination of production and consumption. I will summarize Bator's arguments for each of these three rules below and state the appropriate rule at the end of each argument.[241]

Let us start by analyzing the production rule. In Bator's model there are two products: apples and nuts. The only resources available to produce these are land and labor. No third factor, say fertilizer, can be used. If the model calls for the production of a thousand pounds of apples and further assigns 100 acres for apple production, then a good farmer will know exactly how many hours of labor are required to produce the desired quantity of apples. Bator captures the knowledge of the farmer by referring to a production function, that stipulates what inputs are required for given outputs under current technology. Having fixed the input and output levels for the production of apples, all remaining resources of land and labor are dedicated to the production of nuts. If some quantity of land or labor is not used when it could be used productively, then the economy does not produce at its possible maximum.[242] However, even if all land and all labor is used most production decisions would still be inefficient.[243]

---

[241] Advice to non-economists: the validity of these three rules is what the reader needs to understand or accept. I spend the most time with the argument for the first rule because there is a great similarity in the arguments for the three rules.

[242] If using one more laborer to pick apples would mean that the other laborers are hindered more than the last laborer contributes to production then it may be efficient to leave that laborer unemployed.

[243] The line called "Pareto Efficient Production Line" represents the only points that are efficient. Clearly, most production decisions can lead to inefficient results.

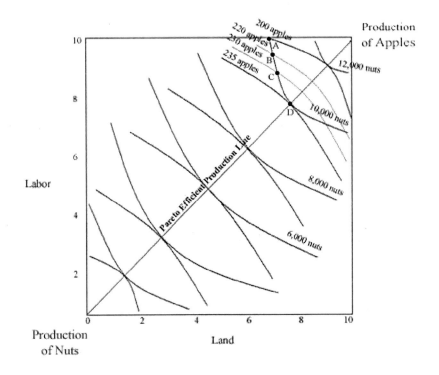

Figure 1.

Let us take the simple example of a model that devotes half of 10 acres
land to nuts, the remaining 5 acres to growing apples, and assigns all
workers (10) to picking nuts (Point A). Obviously the model would produce zero apples and some quantity (let us say 10,000) of nuts. An economist would suggest that one worker be reassigned from picking nuts to
picking apples. Having lost one worker in nut production overall nut production would decline unless additional land (say 1/2 acre) be dedicated to
nuts. As a consequence of the economist's advice nut production lost one
worker and gained 1/2 acre of land (Point B). This judicious change in input mix (more of one input; less of the other) leaves the nut production at
the original level. However, apple production increases drastically from
zero to, say, 220 apples. This increase comes about because apple production is assigned a laborer for the first time. Losing 1/2 acre of land for apple production is more than compensated for by the gain of one laborer.
The economist again advices that we shift one of the nine nut laborers
away from nut production to apple production and recoup the loss in nut
production with land – say, that the total amount of rededicated land is

brought to .55acres – so that nut production stays the same (Point C). Apple production again increases, with a total of, say, 230 apples being produced. The economist will offer the same advice of decreasing laborers working in nut production, reassigning them to apple production, and taking just enough land away from apple production to maintain current levels of nut production. As long as the nut production stays the same and the shift in input mix leads to an increase in apple production, the previous mix is considered to be inefficient. However, if a small shift in input mix leads to a decrease in apple production while nut production stays the same then we know that the previous mix was more efficient. Efficient production is achieved when changing minimally the mix of inputs leaves the output of both products unchanged (Point D). Technically speaking, efficiency is reached when the rate at which one input must be substituted for another to keep production levels unchanged is the same for both products. In the present model this occurs when the farmer produces 10,000 nuts and 235 apples because for the production of both nuts and apples .57 acres need to be added to compensate for losing one laborer or vice versa. This is called the marginal rate of substitution of production factors.

In our example we started out by giving half of the land (5 acres) and all of the workers to the production of nuts. We could now start our reasoning all over again, reserving some number of acres (e.g., 6, 7, 8, 2, 3, or 4 acres) to the production of nuts and then work out, for each different starting point, what amount of labor is necessary for maintaining the original level of nut production. Each different starting position leads to a different efficient result. The points of efficient input mix for production is called the Pareto efficient production possibility curve. In such an efficient production point the model shows that more production of one output necessarily leads to diminished production of the other output. The miracle of efficiency by which one produces, with the same inputs, more of one output without diminishing the other output is not possible any more at an efficient production point.

If producers are profit motivated and operate in a perfectly competitive environment, it is believed that the producers are automatically motivated to look for such efficient production solutions.

The second rule relates to consumption choices. Given a fixed amount of consumable goods produced by the production process, the question arises as to how the consumer goods should be divided between the two consumers so as to maximize their satisfaction. Again, we can start by giving half of one consumption product – say, nuts – to each of the consumers. All of the apples are then given all to Jane (consumer X); John (consumer Y) receives none.

As economists need to compare things quantitatively – even if only ordinally – they need a unit of consumer satisfaction. In an imaginative move they call the unit of consumer satisfaction a "util." When comparing quantities of utils – say, 200 utils to 400 utils – the rule is that more utils is better. However, while 400 utils is definitely better than 200 utils, one is not allowed to draw the further inference that 400 utils is twice as good as 200 utils. Utils are calculated in ordinal numbers, not in cardinal numbers. Moreover, quantities of utils are not intersubjectively comparable. Thus, if X has 200 utils and Y 400, economists do not allow one to say that Y is better off than X.

Let us now assume that Jane has a satisfaction level of 10,000 utils and John a satisfaction level of 2,000. Suppose John receives 100 nuts from Jane, and Jane needs in return a certain number of apples – say, one – to maintain her present satisfaction level. In other words, Jane is effectively declaring that she is equally satisfied by a basket of 5,000 nuts and 237 apples and a basket of 4,900 nuts and 236 apples. If John now declares that having one apple now, when he had none before, makes him feel better even though he has to give up 100 nuts, then we have moved to a situation where Jane feels equally good and John feels better. Thus trading between Jane and John improved the situation of John and did not worsen the situation of Jane. The after-trade situation may be characterized as more efficient. So long as a trade of one consumer good for another consumer good leaves one person equally well off and improves the well being of the other consumer the pre-trade situation was not optimal. The trade situation becomes optimal when no consumer can be made better without making another one worse off. This is because for both consumers the same amount of nuts is required to make them feel equally well off after having given up one apple. The number of nuts required to substitute for one apple is called the marginal (i.e., at the margin) rate of substitution in consumption.

The original pre-trade situation gave 5,000 nuts to each consumer. We now could give Jane 4,000; 3,000; 2,000; or 6,000; 7,000; 8,000; 9,000 or any amount of nuts in between and start the search for the optimal trade result. Each search would give one point on what is called the utility-possibility frontier. Points on the utility-possibility frontier can be reached only if the consumers benefit in their society from efficient production (i.e., if production has reached the production possibility frontier as defined above).

If consumers are self-interested utility maximizers and no external effects are present (Veblen effect,[244] envy) then it is assumed that private

---

[244] Thornstein Veblen is famous for his description of the phenomenon of conspicuous consumption. This leads to a phenomenon known to happen in up-scale stores: a product does

property combined with freedom in consumption and in trade will automatically result in society reaching the utility frontier.

The third rule concerns the co-ordination of production and consumption. Production can be efficient at many points. It is possible to achieve efficient results with the production of no apples and all nuts or with all apples and no nuts and for all the maximally feasible combinations in between.

Trading consumption goods for maximum satisfaction too can be efficient at many points depending upon the starting point. If Jane starts off possessing almost all resources the efficient trade outcome would be that Jane ends up with almost all of both nuts and apples. If John starts off possessing almost everything then efficient trade would end up with him having almost all of both apples and nuts. Many different positions in between are likewise possible.

To each efficient production outcome there corresponds an infinite number of efficient trade outcomes. As there are an infinite amount of efficient production outcomes possible the number of possible efficient trade outcomes is thus infinity times infinity.

How does economic theory find a rule that selects an efficient coordination? The solution lies in the following observation. At each efficient production solution the producer has the option of giving up the input factors required for producing one product – say, one apple – and of rededicating those freed up resources to the production of all the nuts that can be produced efficiently. The number of nuts that can be produced by giving up one apple is called the (marginal) rate of transformation of apples in nuts. It is this rate which is crucial for co-ordinating production and consumption. Efficient co-ordination of production and consumption requires that the (marginal) rate of transformation in production be equal to the (marginal) rate of substitution in consumption. Indeed, if this equivalence did not hold, one would encounter a situation in which consumers feel that they are indifferent to either one apple or 90 nuts and in which producers would be able to give up producing one apple and produce instead 95 nuts. In this case production and consumption are not efficiently co-ordinated even though both production and consumer trade might be efficient. Overall satisfaction would be increased in our example by asking consumers to give up one apple and redeploying the freed-up resources instead to pro-

---

not sell well at a particular price but sells much better when the price is doubled. Veblen explains this phenomenon by pointing out that a conspicuous consumer does not so much enjoy the intrinsic qualities of a good as the knowledge that the good is expensive. The logic behind the phenomenon seems to be that the conspicuous consumer feels the more important the more expensive the good is that he or she is consuming. Goods that sell more when the price is increased are said to be subject to the Veblen effect (Veblen 1934).

duce 95 nuts. Ninety nuts would be sufficient to make consumers feel equally well off. Five nuts would remain to make one or both consumers better off. Efficient co-ordination requires that the (marginal) rate of transformation in production be equal to the (marginal) rate of substitution in consumption. For each efficient production point there is an efficient trade point where that equality is true. The sum of all efficiently co-ordinated production-consumption points gives rise to the grand utility-possibility frontier. No trade or change in production choices could make it possible for one consumer to be better off without making another consumer worse off.

In conclusion, economic theory is able to show that by varying production and consumption decisions and by co-ordinating production with consumption, the economy can improve the satisfaction of some consumers without hurting other consumers. This is considered to be an unambiguous improvement in economic efficiency.

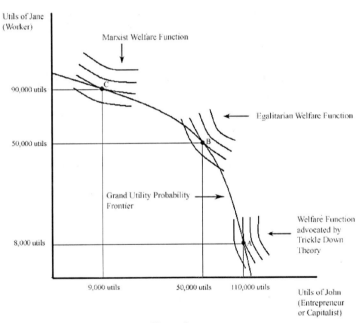

Figure 2.

One more decision has to be made. Bator's economic model tries to give its authoritative approval to a concrete economic reality. Bator clearly demonstrates the limits of economic authority, when confronted with that last necessary decision. The grand-utility possibility frontier is a line showing the joint welfare of two consumers. Examples of points on that line are Jane experiences 50,000 utils (Jane feels a utility level called 50,000 utils) and John experiences 60,000 utils (point B). Other possibilities are Jane at 8,000 and John at 110,000 (point A); Jane at 90,000 and John at 9,000 (point C); there are an infinite number of other possibilities, i.e., all the points on the grand-utility possibility frontier. To decide that the economy must result in situation A would give preference to John – say, an entrepreneur or a capitalist – whereas deciding in favor of B would be favoring a more egalitarian society and deciding in favor of C would be favoring Jane – say, a worker. Such decisions demand that one evaluate the worthiness of the satisfaction of different consumers. Economic theory professes that such an evaluation is not part of its job description. In order to complete its analysis, economic theory assumes that it will be furnished with what it calls a social welfare function by philosophers, politicians, or other people in charge of normatively evaluating human affairs.

In the model discussed, production decisions, consumption decisions, and co-ordination of production and consumption are to be guided by economic rationality. The determination of a welfare function must come from outside the domain that is subject to economic authority.

The implementation of the welfare function can be done by specifying the original endowments. There are only two original endowments or inputs: land and labor. One way to influence the outcome of the grand-utility possibility frontier is to specify the ownership of land (e.g., by land reform, inheritance taxes). If one were to broaden the model one could talk about the ownership of all assets (i.e., property rights in general). The other way to influence the outcome is to see what can be done with labor. Bator's model assumes that labor is fixed and homogeneous. But, clearly it is not. There are disabled persons. Furthermore, the productive value of labor can be greatly increased by training and education.

A different approach to influence the outcome requires the modification of the relative buying power of labor and land (assets). This could be done, for instance, through minimum wage laws, taxes on luxury goods, and differential taxes on labor and assets.

The Bator model gives us enough information to start discussing some disputes of authority about economic matters:

1.) Ironically, the Bator model seems to justify a Marxist line of thinking which argues that property rights are one of the most important factors determining justice in a modern economy. However, Ludwig von Mises had already in 1920 presented an argument for why the socialization of the means of production is an economically bad strategy. Von Mises argued that a central authority could not gather all the information necessary to create an efficient economy requiring the satisfaction of the three rules found in the Bator model. Furthermore, a central authority would not have the motivation (either a profit motive or self-satisfaction) to implement the three rules even if it had the necessary information (Mises 1975). This suggests that other approaches to the problem of property rights, as they relate to issues of justice, need to be considered.

2.) Bator assumes that consumption choices are made efficiently. Actions that thwart efficient consumption choices thus become morally relevant because they hinder the morally desirable goal of economic efficiency. (Examples would include deceptive advertising and deceptive sales practices (including deceptive privatization schemes)). The same can be said of situations that make efficient consumer choices difficult (e.g., lack of easily-available consumer information). Equally morally relevant are irrational consumption choices (e.g., driving when drunk). These are three kinds of events or situations that are to be avoided in order to reach the economically and morally desired efficiency. Some ethical theorists (libertarians) argue that it is morally unacceptable to violate property rights in order to achieve greater efficiency (Nozick 1974).

3.) Production is assumed to be done competitively and motivated by the desire for profit. But what is an economist to advise us to do in situations where the profit motive dictates anti-competitive moves? This raises the possibility of economic and moral justifications of anti-trust legislation and legislation about fair-trade practices. Again, some theorists (economists and ethicists) argue that state intervention in such matters is either not wise or not permissible.

4.) The economy is more complex than Bator's model suggests.[245] There are all kind of transaction costs both in production and in consumption. A proper banking system is one important institutional arrangement to diminish transactions costs. However, pointing towards the need for a banking system introduces the idea of implementing some appropriate governmental regulation of economic institutions.

Let us conclude this section by noting that economic reasoning unavoidably gets entangled in moral questions. These moral questions emerge from within economic reasoning itself and are in no way foreign to it.

---

[245] See below in the section on Stiglitz.

B. Religious Authority and Economics

1. U.S. Bishops' Pastoral Justice for All

a. Non-Economic Authority in Economic Matters

This document appeals to two forms of authority: the biblical vision and the natural law tradition.

From the biblical tradition the Pastoral derives the claim that "no dimension of human life lies beyond God's care and concern" (# 31). As men and women are made in God's image and as the creation belongs to God, the gift of creation belongs to all men and women (# 31). Being made in God's image makes all human beings free, responsible for co-creation and worthy of sharing in the fruits of the earth's gifts (# 36). Human beings are therefore asked to work productively and to do so in social co-ordination. The vulnerable and the poor are said to deserve special attention.

Turning to natural law, the Pastoral develops the concept of justice, distinguishing between commutative, distributive, and social justice and thereby stressing fairness in transactions, compassion for the poor. Finally, the Pastoral points to the need for institutional arrangements that promote the participation of all in economic life.

b. The Pastoral Letter Makes Use of Its Authority

The Pastoral letter makes use of its special authority in economic matters with sharp rhetorical language. Thus we find the following statements (emphasis mine):

1.) "Harsh poverty *plagues* our country despite its great wealth" (# 16)

2.) "That so many people are poor in a nation as rich as ours is a *social and moral scandal* that we cannot ignore" (# 16).

3.) "Discrimination in job opportunities or income levels on the basis of race, sex or other arbitrary standards can never be justified. It is a *scandal* that such discrimination continues in the United States today" (# 73).

4.) "Among black teenagers unemployment reaches the *scandalous rate* of more than one in three" (# 140).

5.) "It is *patently unjust* to deny workers any role in shaping the outcome of these difficult choices" (# 303).

c. The Pastoral Letter Limits Its Own Authority

There are several indications that the authors of the Pastoral letter accept limitations to their moral authority.

1.) The Pastoral letter explicitly acknowledges the authority of technical economic thinking in the following text: "This document is not a *technical blueprint for economic reform*. Rather, it is an attempt to foster a serious moral analysis leading to a more just economy" (133). Does this mean that a technical economic model has also authority? Which authority has priority? Over what issues?

2.) The Pastoral letter implies a third authority, which is neither that of economic reasoning nor that of religious ethics, even though it might be influenced by both. This third authority is what Hegel called "Geist" (spirit) and is cultural and political in nature. We find the following text: "The first step in such an effort is the development of a *new cultural consensus* that the basic economic conditions of human welfare are essential to human dignity and are due persons by right" (# 83).

3.) When analyzing concrete economic problems with a view toward assessing their moral relevance, the Pastoral letter often mixes two kinds of arguments. The letter clearly advances moral or meritorious goals. However, it also uses public good arguments which are economic arguments based on rational self-interest. And, public goods arguments also entail arguments for limiting the provision of moral goals up to the amount justified by rational self-interest.

2. John Paul II and Centesimus Annus

This document is more favorable to the free market than most other official Catholic documents. Still, John Paul II argues that the economic domain needs to be subordinated to the political domain. I interpret John Paul II as assigning three quite different functions to the state. First, he assigns to the state a necessary structuring function. This structuring function is evident when he writes:

> Economic activity, especially the activity of a market economy, cannot be conducted in an institutional, juridical or political vacuum. On the contrary, it presupposes sure guarantees of individual freedom and private property, as well as a stable currency and efficient public services. (# 48)

Second, John Paul II assigns the state a role in helping the economy reach full employment. This role is described when he argues for the more traditional Catholic – and Keynesian – position that "the state has a duty to sustain business activities by creating conditions which will ensure job opportunities, by stimulating those activities where they are lacking or supporting them in moments of crisis" (# 48).

Third, John Paul II introduces the central idea of Catholic Social Thought – subsidiarity – which allows him to limit the authority of the state. He draws a new application of that idea. Thus he writes:

> in exceptional circumstances the State can also exercise a *substitute function*, when social sectors or business systems are too weak or are just getting under way, and are not equal to the task at hand....Such supplementary interventions, which are justified by urgent reasons touching the common good, must be as brief as possible, so as to avoid removing permanently from society and business systems the functions which are properly theirs, and so as to avoid enlarging excessively the sphere of State intervention to the detriment of both economic and civil freedom. (# 48)

John Paul II chooses to introduce the principle of subsidiarity when discussing the "Welfare State," which is also called the "Social Assistance State" (# 48). In matters of welfare John Paul II argues that the state is not the sole agency responsible; rather, the state should only have a helping function. Individuals and private organizations must be allowed to exercise private charity (# 49). Where individuals and private organizations fail, there the state needs to help. Thus, according to my reading of *Centesimus Annus*, John Paul II differentiates the nature of authority of the state in economic matters into three different kinds. First, there are matters that fall unconditionally under the authority of the state (property rights, stable currency). Second, there are matters where the state is the crucial helper for an economy which performs defectively (business cycle policies). Third, there are matters where the state has a subsidiary function. Here, the state cannot take charge. If the state takes charge, it deprives individuals and private organizations of opportunities. Moreover, the state performs the welfare function inefficiently, and it is unavoidable that it so performs.

II. Overlapping Authority

A. Beyond the Bator Model: More Moral Options in Economic Reasoning[246]

The assumption of infinite divisibility of both outputs and inputs and the assumption that consumption excludes "external effects" means that public goods are not conceptualized in Bator's model (Bator 43, 44 note 44). Samuelson addresses that problem and defined a pure public good as a good that can be consumed by other consumers without the first consumer losing any satisfaction (Samuelson 1954, 387). For private goods that is not possible. If my colleague eats my sandwich, I cannot enjoy it. However, if I buy and install a light in a dark alley, my neighbor can enjoy the safety of the light while I loose none of my own feeling of safety. When goods are public goods, efficient provision of those goods requires in many cases some form of collective action. Samuelson proposes that the state ask citizens how much they would be willing to pay and asks entrepreneurs how much they would charge. If the payment demanded by the entrepreneur is less than the willingness of the citizens to pay then the state should buy the public good and use its taxation power to force the citizens to pay for the public good. If the state does not perform this function then society forgoes an opportunity and thus operates at less than optimal efficiency. In other cases, individuals might come together and take joint private action by, for instance, creating an exclusive club (e.g., for recreation).

At least three kinds of important difficulties have been discussed in the literature with the provision of public goods.[247] If the government takes the initiative, it intends to help citizens to achieve a consumption satisfaction that they might not be able to achieve on their own. The government needs to know what the citizens want and how much they are willing to pay. This information is required for the government to make the calculus as to whether the citizens want the particular public good strongly enough to warrant its provision. This information is then also used to differentially tax the various individuals involved. A taxi driver will have more utility from a bridge than a bicyclist and therefore can be expected to pay more for the cost of building the bridge than the bicyclist. But, given that the

---

[246] I am here summarizing arguments more fully developed in chapters 5 and 6 in which I present respectively the arguments about merit and public goods.
[247] For a survey of the many difficulties connected with the concept of public good see chapter 6 of this book.

government will use the information about the citizens as a basis for taxation, citizens have a selfish interest in hiding (i.e., lying about) their real interest in public goods. In the provision of public goods, there is an unavoidable information problem (Ibid., 389).

Again, if the public good is provided by private initiative then the exclusionary practice of a club provision of public goods raises the question of discrimination. This is clearly a domain for the moral exercise of state authority.

Lately, a new problem has emerged. Many public goods provided by the state are financed by general revenue. Thus, the decision to provide or not to provide a public good is a political choice (Stretton & Orchard 1994). In the best of circumstances, one may hope that the government makes a list of projects that are economically justified. Given a limited budget, the government must chose which economically-justified public goods should be provided. Will it be a new highway or improved education? Different citizens will benefit differently from the two projects. There will even be a distributive effect. Some public goods benefit the lower classes more; others benefit the well-to-do more. Thus, the decision as to which public goods deserve to be provided has both economic and moral aspects.

Musgrave is credited with having pointed out that there is a third kind of economic good that is neither a private good nor a public good. He calls this third type of good a merit or demerit good (Musgrave 1959, 13–14). Musgrave gives as examples of merit goods: subsidized low cost housing, free hospital care for the poor, and obligatory education. He gives as examples of demerit goods: the prohibition of alcohol and tobacco consumption. He defines a (de)merit good as a good that is so (de)meritorious that the government is justified in interfering with consumer wishes by deciding that the level of consumption is either too low (merit good) or too high (demerit good). Clearly, the concept of a merit good does not respect the consumer sovereignty tradition. Moral arguments will therefore be needed to justify such government interventions. Musgrave finds the cases of economic events requiring moral justification important enough to create a special concept for them.[248]

---

[248] Musgrave consistently limits the applicability of his new concept. On philosophical grounds I argued for an expansion of the concept (Chapter 5 of this book).

B. Religious Documents Use (Submit to) Economic Reasoning

Some moral documents about the economy mix public good and merit good arguments. A merit good argument points to moral arguments as having authority over the economy. A public good argument points to self-interest and thus to a strictly economic argument as having authority in economic matters. One might therefore wonder whether moral documents that employ public good arguments effectively subordinate their moral arguments to purely economic arguments. Let us survey some examples of such mixed argumentation.

The Pastoral letter *Justice for All* points to "Full employment [as] the foundation of a just economy" (# 136). The document then points to documented losses from unemployment. "It gives rise to family quarrels, greater consumption of alcohol, child abuse, spouse abuse, divorce and higher rates of infant mortality" (# 141). The "strains of job loss may drive individuals to suicide" (# 141). "Jobless people pay little or no taxes, thus lowering the revenues for cities, states and the federal government" (# 142). "[R]ising unemployment requires greater expenditures for unemployment compensation, food stamps, welfare and other assistance" (# 142). "The Federal Bureau of Prisons reports that increases in unemployment have been followed by increases in the prison population" (# 142). The public goods argument is then summarized as follows: "we simply cannot afford to have millions of able-bodied men and women unemployed. We cannot afford the economic costs, the social dislocation and the enormous human tragedies caused by unemployment" (# 143). However, the public goods argument (as developed by Samuelson) would demand that one ask citizens how much they are willing to pay to increase the level of employment – taking all advantages of employment into account – and that one then calculate the costs of public works or public subsidies for increasing employment. However, such an approach implies that one is willing to limit the commitment of funds to those that the public is willing to pay and thus that one is willing to live with the unemployment level resulting from the limitation of funding.

At this point the Pastoral shifts gears. It introduces a merit good argument which does not seem to accept a tolerable level of unemployment. Rather the authors of the Pastoral present a moral argument and make a moral appeal. The moral argument is articulated thus: "In the end, however, what we can least afford is the assault on human dignity that occurs when millions are left without adequate employment" (# 143). The moral appeal is formulated as: "current levels of unemployment are intolerable, and they impose on us a moral obligation to work for policies that will reduce joblessness"(# 143) or "We must make it possible as a nation for *everyone* who is seeking a job to find employment *within a reasonable amount of time*" (# 136) (Emphasis is mine). The argument for such an appeal is based on a moral claim: "human work has a special dignity and is a key to achieving justice in society" (# 136); and again "work has a threefold moral significance" (# 97). The recommendation is not to find the efficient level at which willingness to pay matches the costs of increased employment. The demand is that unemployment be eliminated. As cost considerations are not determinative, such a demand does not aim at economic efficiency.

The Pastoral also points to poverty as a moral scandal (# 16). One method advocated for fighting poverty is to ensure just wages through, for instance, increasing the minimum wage (# 197). For that idea the Pastoral presents a public good argument: "the persistence of poverty harms the larger society because the depressed purchasing power of the poor contributes to the periodic cycles of stagnation in the economy" (# 196). Another method advocated for fighting poverty is the use of education because "lack of adequate education, especially in the inner-city setting, prevents many poor people from escaping poverty" (# 203). For that idea, too, the Pastoral presents a public good argument: "Working to improve education in our society is an investment in the future" (# 204). However, the Pastoral does not seem to be willing to limit assistance to the poor to the limits dictated by public goods arguments. Public goods arguments insist on limiting the cost connected with an increase in the minimum wage to the sum total of benefits that result from the increase and thus benefit the whole economy. These arguments limit investment in education of the poor to what can be defended as investment in the future. At the moment when investment in machinery or in medical schools leads to a greater expected return on investment then investment in the education of the poor would have to be halted. However, the Pastoral seems to have a different attitude toward poverty. The Pastoral does not advocate that poverty be remedied to the extent that it is economically beneficial. Rather, the authors move from a public good argument to a merit good argument when they write that "Dealing with poverty is...a moral imperative of the highest priority" (# 170) and "The themes of human dignity and the preferential option for the poor ... compel us to confront the issue of poverty with a real sense of urgency" (186). One of the causes of poverty is that: "Many poor people are working, but at wages insufficient to lift them out of poverty" (# 174). John Paul II defines sufficient wages as wages that "enable [a workman] to support himself, his wife and his children," i.e., as a family wage (John Paul II 1991, p.18, no 8). The Pastoral and John Paul II have in mind a moral or meritorious goal: establishing just (family) wages and completely eradicating poverty. The public good arguments appear as preliminary steps toward the more ambitious moral and/or meritorious goals of full employment, just wages, and the eradication of poverty.

Is mixing public good and merit good arguments hypocritical? The Pastoral explicitly appeals to an argument (public goods) which has build-in limits and whose limits it does not accept. I believe that there is a more constructive way of viewing the Pastoral's mix of argumentation. The Pastoral is primarily motivated by a moral or meritorious goal. The authors of the Pastoral Letter are aware that moral motivation is a scarce commodity. Therefore, they look for other motivations that can nudge the members of the community in the direction of their goal. Motivation is achieved by appeals to enlightened self-interest as it is embedded in public good arguments. Not implementing the recommendations of economic public good arguments is missing an opportunity for gain. If a public good argument points the community in the direction of a moral goal then the scarce resources of moral motivation will have to shoulder a lighter burden. Such an argumentative strategy also makes it possible for those who are morally motivated to take the first necessary social steps in communion with the larger community. Fostering such solidarity with one's fellows in the pursuit of the common good is itself a worthwhile moral goal.

III. Economists and Catholic Social Thought

A. Buchanan and the Moral Idea of Fairness in Starting Positions

Buchanan is very sensitive to insights derivable from Bator's model: the competitive free market is motivated to push automatically towards the grand utility frontier and thus all interference with the market process should be avoided. On the other hand, Buchanan acknowledges that there is a question of fairness. Buchanan captures the American principles of fairness by referring to the White House Easter hunt (Buchanan 1983, 59–

60). In order to make the hunt fair, small children are given an advantage and older children are handicapped. The purpose is to make sure that all have an equal opportunity. Similarly, Buchanan accepts the idea of fairness as equal opportunity for all in the American economy. He distinguishes four factors in the success of individuals: good choices, luck, effort, and birth (Id., 58). Good choices and effort deserve to be rewarded. Luck cannot be controlled. That leaves birth. Buchanan argues that birth is an important factor in the success of an individual. One can be born with native intelligence or one can be disabled. One can be born into poverty or into great wealth. Buchanan argues that the American conception of fairness demands that one address such inherent forms of unequal opportunity. Interfering with the market process by legislating minimum wages or providing low income housing are, for Buchanan, all interventions that violate the rule of market efficiency. On the basis of economic arguments, help is only allowed as a re-arrangement of initial conditions. Bator's original model presented two initial factors of production: land (which can be generalized as wealth) and labor. Buchanan proposes that inheritances be heavily taxed so as to make the material starting conditions of all citizens more equal. He then proposes to use the revenue from inheritance taxes to finance public education. Free public education equalizes the earning potential of all citizens.

Buchanan himself greatly stresses that his proposal cannot be understood in the light of or be justified by appeals to the concept of public good (Buchanan 1983, 65). Indeed, the public good argument for education is based on the joint or collective consumption of education. Buchanan's argument for making education public is his concern for "potential adjustments in starting positions...making the game 'fair'" (Ibid.). Buchanan's argument for publicly financing education is thus a moral or a merit-based argument. His suggestions aim at handicapping some privileged individuals and improving the chances of others so as to create more equal opportunities for all.

Public education as a commodity whose general provision is justified by a public good argument should be limited to what the people want to pay for and should ideally be financed by user fees (tuition). Indeed, the central idea of a public good is that people take joint action because there is joint consumption. The goal of the joint action is that nobody should be worse off and that some should be better off. Public education justified by a moral or meritorious argument is not limited to what people are voluntarily willing to pay. A moral or meritorious goal is aimed at a result that is deemed (morally) good and some citizens will be charged more than they get back in return.

Buchanan's view on education is similar to the view developed in the Pastoral letter in that both want to use public financing of education as a means to a moral goal. Buchanan wants to achieve a more equal starting position for all citizens and the Pastoral wants to lift the poor out of poverty.

B. Stiglitz: Criticizing Economic Theory in the Name of both Economic and Moral Goals

Joseph E. Stiglitz argues in his "Whither Reform? Ten Years of the Transition" that the Washington consensus, as it is based on conventional neoclassical economics, misunderstands the working of the modern economy. As a consequence, the transition from a command economy to a market economy in Eastern-Europe and the former Soviet Union has been badly mismanaged. Let me briefly summarize again the facts which form the basis for Stiglitz's reasoning.[249] Stiglitz presents a chart comparing the 1989 and 1997 GDPs (Gross Domestic Product) of these countries. Only Poland had a slightly higher GDP in 1997. All other countries had a lower GDP in 1997 than in 1989 (Stiglitz's Figure 3). Countries such as China and India, which regularly violate the recommendations of Western economic theory increased their GDP each year, sometimes with double digit numbers. Also alarming is that Russia not only lost about half its GDP in that period, but the Gini coefficient of inequality[250] in that time period roughly doubled (Stiglitz's Figure 2).

The basic thesis of Stiglitz is that "conventional neoclassical economics are likely to underestimate the importance of informational problems, including those arising from the problems of corporate governance; of social and organizational capital; and of the institutional and legal infrastructure required to make an effective market economy" (Stiglitz, Abstract). Put in another way, Stiglitz argues that it is true that the success of the market economy is connected to the fact that prices are used as signals to coordinate production.[251] However, "Prices do not convey all the relevant in

---

[249] For the development of Stiglitz's ideas about the misunderstood role of entrepreneurial talent in the countries of the FSU see Chapter 9, Section IV.

[250] The Gini index of inequality is a number between zero and one that indicates the inequality of income in a country. A Gini index approaching zero indicates that the country approaches almost total equality of income). A Gini index approaching one indicates that the country has almost complete inequality of income (one person having almost all income).

[251] The publications of Arrow and Debreu have proven this insight mathematically (Arrow & Debreu 1954).

formation" (Stiglitz 4).[252] Let us concentrate on one of the author's arguments: institutional and legal infrastructure in the economy.

Stiglitz refers approvingly to Schumpeter's idea of creative destruction in a well-functioning economy. Some factories or corporations use resources (material and labor) in such an inefficient way (because they produce inefficiently or because they produce unwanted gadgets) that they must be allowed to go bankrupt. Bankruptcy of an inefficient corporation allows for those resources to be redeployed for more efficient usage, creating a total economy that operates more efficiently. The pain of bankruptcy is a necessary condition for moving the total economy to a higher utility frontier. However, Stiglitz rightly points to the legal and social institutions required for the destructive part of bankruptcy to become creative.

A first condition for bankruptcy to become a positive move toward improvement for the total economy is that there be more efficient alternatives available. If there are no better alternatives available, then the inefficiently-used resources will not be re-employed more efficiently; rather, they will become idle. Large-scale unemployment means that the economy allows inefficiently used resources to not be used at all. Making no use of resources is not an improvement relative to the meager yet still positive productivity of inefficiently-used ones (Stiglitz 6).[253] Where there is large scale unemployment Stiglitz argues (in a manner consonant with Catholic Social Thought) that "Vigorous programs of employment creation and maintenance [even if partially inefficient!], through promotion of entrepreneurship and/or by Keynesian stimuli, must go hand in hand, if not precede, bankruptcy-induced restructuring" (Stiglitz 8).

A second condition for the destructive aspect of bankruptcy to become creative is that the two pillars of creative economics be solidly in place: entrepreneurship and banking. Entrepreneurship existed in former communist countries. However, under communist regimes workers had acquired skills that are not useful for "creating new businesses and compet-

---

[252] Stiglitz refers to the following authors who point to important economic information not conveyed by prices: Marshall, Keynes, Berle and Means, Galbraith, Baumol.

[253] Martin Summers, the East European Desk Officer for the Catholic Fund for Overseas Development in Great Britain presented similar ideas in the November 10–13, 1993 Zagreb Conference on the usefulness of Catholic Social Thought for the transition from a command economy to the free market. He explicitly warned: "Post-Communist countries are, however, as vulnerable as any to the disempowering process of the de-regulated international market." (Summers 1994, 244). He also writes: "the upsurge of New Economic approaches...does hold out the promise of a significant re-localization of economic activity" (Ibid., 245). His suggestions are micro-suggestions which do not form an overall plan for economic reform in Eastern Europe. Summers shows unease with the then-prevailing hope that international competition will do the job and he makes some modest alternative suggestions. Summers argues tentatively for what Stiglitz now argues for forcefully.

ing in the international market place" (Stiglitz 7). Indeed, good entrepreneurs under communism "acquired skills in evading government regulations, in arbitraging away some of the inefficiencies in government regulations for private profit, and in operating at the interstices between the legal and the illegal world" (Ibid.). In communist countries there were institutions that were called banks. But that "banking system had no experience in screening and monitoring loans" and few banks "actually got into the business of providing funds to new, small enterprises" (Stiglitz 7). Thus the lack of the proper experience in the banking institutions resulted in entrepreneurs with good ideas not receiving the capital necessary for realizing possible innovations and thus employing more productively the resources idled by bankruptcies.

A third condition for the potential creative dimension of bankruptcy is a legal framework that includes bankruptcy laws and judges capable of applying those laws. In bankruptcy there is a conflict between creditor and debtor. Stiglitz refers approvingly to Supreme Court Justice William O. Douglas and Henry Clay when they claim that the interest of the State in bankruptcy is "in all the faculties of its members, moral and physical" (Stiglitz 7). The speed and manner in which the "assets can be re-engaged in productive use" is a crucial consideration. (Ibid., 7). The advice that in ex-communist countries one should simply enforce bankruptcy laws is therefore empty advice. Bankruptcy laws barely existed and were rarely applied under communism. Neither the law nor the experience of judges existed to promote the creative redeployment of the resources of bankrupt enterprises.

Stiglitz argues that reformers cannot hope that the imposition of pure free market competition in the absence of appropriate legal and institutional arrangements will be effective. He concludes that one first will have to create "the implicit social contract, necessary to a market economy" (Stiglitz 8). This is a theme that is also stressed in Catholic Social Thought.

Conclusion

Adam Smith sometimes argues that the economy is a natural system (651). He seems to imply that economics and nature have the same ontology: they are both governed by immutable laws. Violating these immutable laws of economics leads to unproductive usage of resources, as Adam Smith argues was the case with societies where governments intervened (improperly) in the name of mercantilism or physiocratic economic theories (650–51).

Hegel, on the other hand, looks upon the economy as an ethical institution (Hegel 1967 a, ## 182–256; Ver Eecke 1983; Chapter 3 in this book). The economy has an important role to play in the promotion of freedom. A successful economy liberates human beings from the tyranny of nature by preventing starvation and by elevating natural needs to cultural events (meals as social gatherings, clothing as cultural expressions). A successful economy also provides a domain where human beings can realize important aspects of their freedom: it allows individuals to achieve dignity in and through work. Finally, a successful economy encourages individuals to transcend their individuality and realize the social vocation of human beings. The economy gives rise to many morally desirable forms of social interaction, to the formation of social groups, and to the exercise of some types of social caring. Hegel agrees that economic activity is carried out within a double form of determinism: the determinism of nature and the determinism of social interaction. Hegel would thus reject a purely voluntarist moral view of the economy but would also reject a purely deterministic approach devoid of moral responsibility.

Like Hegel, Adam Smith, in his concrete analyses, also assigns moral responsibility to economic agents and argues in favor of responsible actions but against irresponsible ones.[254]

Given that the economic domain is a domain of natural laws and a domain of moral responsibility,[255] it is not surprising to have discovered that, *de facto*, both the economic and the moral discourse about the economy are discovering and respecting the dual ontological nature of the economy. What some might criticize as an illegitimate confusion in the two discourses on the economy should rather be applauded as the discovery of and manifestation of a proper respect for the ontological complexity of the economic domain.

---

[254] For a general argument in favor of responsible intervention in the economy see Adam Smith's considerations about public works and public institutions (651 and Book V, Ch I, Part III). For a general argument against irresponsible intervention in the economy see Adam Smith's argument against the use of government regulations for the creation of private benefit (250).

[255] Goetz Briefs concludes his masterful essay on the history of the influence of ethics on economics as follows: "A degree of freedom exists, and there are functions of the state that are vital. But we realize now as never before the existence both of a realm of necessity ruled by economic laws and of a variable zone of freedom. Because of this freedom, ethics again has a place in economic life... [and] a place in economics proper"(Briefs 1983, 298).

Conclusion

In reflecting philosophically about the economy and its management I made use of ideas about the proper organization of the economy in order for the economy to be able to make its contribution to the morally good society as developed by Adam Smith, Hegel and Catholic Social Thought. My position can best be understood as that of an admiring but rebellious child of Adam Smith. I accept as true the ideas of Adam Smith as developed in his *Wealth of Nations*, but I am convinced that Adam Smith underestimated the broad applicability of the positive role of the government in managing the economy, which he relegated to the fringes of his system.

Followers of Adam Smith who insist, against my arguments, that the ideas about the positive role of the government advocated by Adam Smith should not be given a more expansive role than he gives them, can rightly see this book as a radical rejection of Adam Smith's thought. I do not see my book in that light. Let me spell out my five conclusions.

First, I believe that Adam Smith introduced new ideas about the economy that authoritarian regimes and authoritarian ways of thinking are afraid of. I will highlight my agreement with Adam Smith's novel insights.

Second, as a sophisticated thinker, Adam Smith also included in his *Wealth of Nations* ideas that contradicted his main thesis, i.e., ideas that refer to the positive roles of the government in the economy. He referred to them as exceptions to his general thesis. I will stress the importance of these ideas even if Adam Smith marginalized them.

Third, Adam Smith made a general claim about the inherent danger of the government. I agree with this warning but at the same time I argue that one can expect great rewards for societies that can find an artful solution for the dangers pointed out by Adam Smith.

Fourth, economic theory can be generalized to illustrate the functions of government in the economy which Adam Smith already noticed but minimized.

Fifth, the moral demands made by Adam Smith regarding the government can also be generalized instead of keeping them at a minimum, thus rejecting his ontological view of the economy as being mostly a natural system

The first two conclusions thus show my dependence upon Adam Smith. The three other conclusions show where I go beyond Adam Smith. I like to think that I only stretch the arguments of Adam Smith. Others might think that I reject Adam Smith. I personally think that I do not reject Adam Smith's practical thinking about the economy. I agree that I explicitly reject Adam Smith's views on the ontology of the economy. He sees the economy more as a natural system like nature. He thus sees economic theory much like a natural science. I see the economy both as obeying some iron laws much like laws of nature (using scarce resources is paid for by forgoing alternative usages of these resources) and as providing moral opportunities (should work be made safe, how safe and at what cost?) which require economic theory to deal with all the complexities of moral freedom. For articulating that dimension of economics, I find much more guidance in authors other than Adam Smith.

1. In this book I take for granted a number of ideas which were revolutionary when Adam Smith wrote them down. These ideas are consonant with those of another philosopher whose ideas guided me: Hegel. Modern society discovered and accepted the crucial role of the individual for science, for religion and for the organization of society (Chapter 2 of this book). Hegel credits the British economists (Steuart and Adam Smith) with the ability to articulate the legitimate role of the individual in economics. Smith's arguments, known as the invisible hand theory, are that self-interest and self-responsibility of individuals will create a productive economic system responsive to the needs of people (651). Smith argues that neither government planning nor the moral virtues of friendship or benevolence can be relied upon to provide the thousands of economic transactions that people rely on everyday (14). Self-interest is also credited as promoting economic growth by means of technological inventions and division of labor. Adam Smith uses the example of the pin factory and the ingenuity of the boy working with fire-engines to make his point (3-10). The failure of command economies can be attributed to the fear of those societies for the freedom of individuals. Repression and restriction of freedom led to poor economic outcomes. I relied on the ideas of von Mises to show that command economies could, in principle, not succeed in mobilizing self-interest so as to create a successful economy (Chapters 9 and 10). I relied on the ideas of Hegel and of Catholic Social Thought, particularly as formulated by John Paul II in his *Centesimus Annus*, to connect self-interest with the idea of individual freedom. Both Hegel and John Paul II use the connection between self-interest and freedom as the stepping stone to argue that individual freedom requires a proper social environment (Chapter 3, 4, 9 and 10). I use these ideas to go beyond the insights of Adam Smith.

2. In this book I make use of insights by Adam Smith that many of his admirers overlook or tend to minimize. They are arguments in favor of governmental tasks if not duties that economists need to understand and accept. A first argument is a defense of the government's role in the provision of public goods which has great similarity with Samuelson's view of the matter (Chapter 6 and 9). A second argument concerns several cases of what I call merit good arguments. The government intervenes in the economy on merit good grounds if it lacks a public goods argument (self-interest argument) and/or a public good's method of financing (nobody is worse off after the government's intervention). Adam Smith produces arguments in favor of property rights and justice, in favor of conscription, and in favor of subsidized education which are not in tune with the public good's argument. I see them as providing justification for the concept of merit good as introduced by Musgrave and defended in chapter 5 of this book. A third argument for a role of the government is Adam Smith's method of dealing with dangers to the emerging banking sector. In order to prevent the lack of trust in the banking sector Adam Smith agrees that the government can violate the claims of "natural liberty." He crafts his argument skillfully. He agrees to two restrictions on bankers. They cannot issue notes below a certain amount and they must commit themselves to immediate and unconditional payment of their notes (313). He gives as argument for the restriction of "natural liberty" the interest (security) of the whole community (308). It is this argument which I see as having broad applicability for my own reflection. The disagreement lies in how to interpret the reasons for limiting the "natural liberty" of individuals. Adam Smith literally writes that the argument concerns security. I interpret the word 'security' in the context used by Adam Smith to mean: any very important interest. These interests must be so important that they are morally relevant. Finally, Adam Smith stresses that any economic activity should be left as free as [reasonably] possible (313). I agree with this recommendation.

3. Adam Smith provides a socio-economic analysis of politics. He argues that both the landowners and the labor class have economic interests which are similar if not identical to those of the society at large. However, their daily work or non-work (landowners) results in a lack of understanding of the complexities of a modern economy. On the other hand, the daily activities of the third class – the employers – make this class very knowledgeable in economic affairs. Unfortunately, their interests are often in conflict with the interests of society at large. Adam Smith concludes that any law proposed by this class should be looked at with suspicion (250). I agree with this warning about all proposed legislation. In his wisdom Adam Smith does not conclude that new governmental laws and regulations should be rejected. He advises that they be carefully scrutinized (Ibid.). In my book I point to the rewards for the whole society if the government's tasks have been done well or the losses if these tasks have not been done or have been done badly. I defend a number of tasks which the government should undertake without going into a debate on what and how precisely these tasks should be performed. I limit my tasks to arguing where the government has a responsibility. I do not discuss how these tasks have to be discharged except that I agree with the recommendation of Adam Smith that maximum reasonable freedom should be aimed at in economic activity.

4. I go beyond Adam Smith by generalizing Adam Smith's arguments in favor of the government's tasks with reference to public and merit goods. About public goods one can argue that Samuelson's approach is consonant with the ideas of Adam Smith. Samuelson, though, demonstrates that using the government in order to solve the public good's problem is not that simple. We reported on Samuelson's point that self-interested consumers-citizens have an interest in falsifying their reported interest in the public good for which the government is going to charge them according to their declared interest in the good. The government must thus make decisions about the provision of public goods without full knowledge. Other authors, like Stretton and Orchard, argue that, in practice, government is oftentimes forced to choose between economically worthwhile public goods because of competing budget priorities. Libertarian authors, such as Schmidtz, point out that the provision of public goods requires the violation of property rights of some consumers (confiscation of land for building highways or bridges; levying taxes to raise the funds for providing public goods). I solve these problems theoretically by arguing that the concept of public good is an ideal concept which is most often only partly realized in any economic event, because that same economic event might have aspects of several economic concepts including the concept of merit good. Confiscating the land of the farmer against his objections is, in my opinion, not justifiable on public goods grounds, even if compensated at market price. However, a public good might have such a great social value such that, in Adam Smith's words, "natural liberty" may be violated in favor of the security (interest, in my view) of society. It thus has a merit good dimension. Libertarians want to restrict the right to violate "natural liberty" to cases of survival of society. I argue that less dramatic arguments than survival of society can justify societal interventions in private property rights.

I also pointed out that there are two other methods for of dealing with the problem of public goods. The first method is the one promulgated by Olson that analyzes the formation of groups (interest or lobbying groups) for the purpose of providing public goods of interest to the group members. This method of securing public goods leads to either over-provision (a feast) of the public good if the interest group can mobilize itself or to under-provision or no provision at all (famine) if the interest group cannot mobilize itself. The government might be asked to violate "natural liberty" if the public good that is under-provided or not provided is of great importance to society such as safety in the work place. Here the government is asked to create laws that provide the private incentives for interested members to become a member of the interest group such as union shop legislation.

The second method for providing public goods not considered by Adam Smith is the creation of club goods in which the good (recreation) is provided only to the members. This method of addressing the problem of public goods rests on the use of exclusion of non-members to the good provided. This method has the by-product of allowing discrimination which is recently considered so morally sensitive in the USA that the government has severely restricted the "natural liberty" of creating club goods as one sees fit.

Each of the three methods of providing public goods includes on the fringes of its implementation actions that either restrict or demand restriction of our "natural liberty." On the fringes, the implementation of public goods demands, as I see it, help from the concept of merit good (Chapter 6).

With regard to the concept of merit good I feel that Adam Smith understood the three aspects of the concept without using the name of the concept (Chapter 5). He understood that there was an infringement on the "natural liberty" of some persons, which is not the case with the concept of public good. His clearest example is that of induction in the army. He understood that merit goods would need to find a different financing method than public goods. Thus the payment cannot be tied to one's personal enjoyment (utility). Instead, Adam Smith proposed as financing method for paying for what we now call merit goods: taxation according to ability to pay. Finally, Adam Smith understood that one needed serious arguments for the provision of merit goods in as much that they always included some infringement on "natural liberty." In some cases he appealed to the security of the whole society in support of his argument (308). In other cases he appealed implicitly to some moral value like courage (as partial justification for obligatory induction on the army) or respect for the importance of the mind of all people including the poor (to justify subsidized education for the poor) in order to justify merit goods activity. For my development of broad categories of merit goods I build upon Adam Smith's arguments for the necessity of the institution of private property and its protection by a justice system against thieves and an army against foreign invasions. Adam Smith provides a minor argument for the government's role in the banking system. The neo-liberals provide a much broader series of arguments. Adam Smith mentions the worthiness of education for receiving subsidies, yet he seems to restrict his justification to education for the poor. Since the middle of the nineteenth century education has become much more central to the well functioning of society as documented by A. Heri. Since the great depression, dealing with business cycles has been another recognized task of the government, advocated with great persuasion by Keynes. I also argue for the importance of measures sometimes grouped under the title of safety net or welfare state measures. They include help for the disabled, the sick, the unemployed and the retired. Further categories deal with health issues, with a workable social contract that avoids the need for civil unrest in its many economically disastrous forms, with the protection of the environment, with the promotion of strategic investments and, finally, with the protection of symbols of cultural identity (Chapters 5 and 9).

My reflections on the concepts of both public and merit good can be understood as a further elaboration of thoughts already present in Adam Smith, even though Adam Smith minimizes their importance.

5. I disagree with Adam Smith when he sees the economic domain as being mostly a natural system, implying that economic science is like a natural science. Instead, I see the competitive free market as an institutional arrangement which recognizes that there are strict economic laws (see the Bator model) but which also recognizes freedom at work (free economic agents create cartels and trusts to escape the harshness of the competitive free market). I like the conclusion of Briefs', stating:

> A degree of freedom exists, and there are functions of the state that are vital. But we realize now as never before the existence both of a realm of necessity ruled by economic laws and of a variable zone of freedom. Because of this freedom, ethics again has a place in economic life and hence...a place in economics proper. The era of determinism accommodated by silent and implicit ethical assumptions is over. (Briefs 1983, 298)

In my opinion the free competitive market recognizes the "realm of necessity ruled by economic laws" by creating an institutional arrangement based on the harsh rule that individuals have a right to a share of the goods and services produced in the economy only if they themselves produce something that others want. If they do not, then the institutional arrangement deprives them automatically of any rights to a share of those goods and services. Such individuals are thus faced with bankruptcy, starvation, or both.

Understanding the harshness of the competitive free market leads to two consequences. The first consequence is that it is unreasonable to expect that the free market will operate properly on its own initiative. Given its harshness it needs to be imposed. Adam Smith saw this very well when he argued that property rights need to be installed and enforced for the free market to take off. The neo-liberals understood that the enforcement of the preconditions of free market exchanges (property rights) was not enough to have the theoretically desirable outcome expected from the competitive free market. The neo-liberals knew that many would try to evade the harshness of the system in a way that would diminish the attractiveness of the institutional arrangement. They focused on the efficiency expected from the competitive arrangement and argued that the government should prevent the erosion of the competitive arrangement (anti-trust legislation) and simultaneously create additional arrangements (banking regulations) in order to positively promote the efficiency of the economic system (Chapter 4).

The second consequence of understanding the harsh dimension of the competitive free market arrangement is the idea that, for moral reasons, at least some catastrophic consequences of that harshness need to be avoided or mitigated (starvation is unacceptable; poverty needs to be mitigated). Hegel pointed out, however, that mitigating the harshness of the competitive system is not costless and will have to be paid for by those who are subjected to its harshness. Those asked to pay to alleviate poverty and avoid starvation might therefore feel cheated. Such enforced charity will meet with resentment and will, so Hegel argued, put up a barrier on how much the harshness of the competitive system can be remedied.

One of the main purposes of introducing and defending the concept of merit good by Musgrave was to deal with the limits to the welfare state. Musgrave argued that if the rich and the well-off, who are asked to pay for the alleviation of poverty, can control what their money is used for, there might be a greater willingness to support the poor. One way to let them exercise such a control is to donate goods in kind to the poor rather than simply give money. The goods considered worthy of being given to the poor are called merit goods (free school lunches, subsidized housing, free hospital care). Restricted to this usage, the provision of merit goods is a tool for public policy to weaken the formation of resentment that could limit the implementation of the morally desirable goal of redistribution within the harsh environment of the competitive free market.

The insight that the competitive free market needs institutional arrangements implies the involvement of politics in the economy. However, economic actors also try to influence politics. This interconnection of politics and economics has both promises and risks. The promise is that politics can influence the ethical goals realized by the economy. The government is assigned the task of protecting legitimate property rights. The government is also asked to create the institutional arrangements that make economic transactions fair and efficient. Finally, the government is called upon to create a safety net in order to soften the harshness of the competitive system. On the other hand, the interconnection of politics and economics also has its risks against which Adam Smith already warned us. The government can become an instrument of interest groups, particularly if interest groups have an important electoral influence. As a consequence, governmental action can undermine several ethical goals of the economic system. It leads to inefficiency (Olson), to injustice (Lowi), and lack of concern for the common good (Briefs).

Our first conclusion about the free market as a socio-political entity obeying moral demands pointed towards the presence of resentment as a limiting factor for even a minimal safety net. Our second conclusion pointed towards the risk of undue influence of politics in economics and of economic actors in political decisions. Thoughtful constitutional arrangements are important to deal with these two negative possibilities of the interconnection of politics and economics. The current development of capitalism, with the emergence of both interest groups and a bargaining form of democracy, creates a defective way of structurally relating politics with economics. Some (Lowi) believe that this structural deficiency is more pronounced in the United States than in other Western countries. Hegel and Catholic Social Thought argue that there is an inevitable deficiency in the competitive economic system, even if it is combined with a constitutional government (resentment will limit the extent of an ethically required safety net). An effective ethical discourse (including pronouncements of churches on justice in the economy) might provide additional help to partially remedy the two deficiencies of our competitive free market. I believe it to be both unrealistic and defeatist to hope for improvements only from constitutional changes. It is defeatist in that it minimizes the efficacy of ethical discourse; it is also defeatist in that it confesses to have no remedy at all for the malady of modern society pointed out by Hegel: resentment for government organized redistribution. The exclusive hope in constitutional arrangements is unrealistic in the sense that it is hoping for an all or nothing solution. In anticipation of an ideal constitutional arrangement, which Hegel argued we cannot hope for, one finds oneself in a defective situation that cannot be changed. Betting on at least partial efficacy of ethical discourse on the economy allows one to work for steady if minimal improvement and it might also create the moral motivation for meaningful constitutional changes if that proves desirable.

References

Works Cited

Adams, R. D., & McCormick, K. (1993). The Traditional Distinction between Public and Private Goods Needs to be Expanded, not Abandoned. *American Journal of Political Science, 5* (1), 109–116.

Andel, N. (1968/69, March). Zur Diskussion über Musgraves Begriff der 'Merit Wants.' *Finanzarchiv, N.F.*, pp. 209–213.

Andel, N. (1984). Zum Konzept der meritorischen Güter. *Finanzarchiv, N.F., 42*, 630–648.

Anderson, K., & Martin, W. (2005). Agricultural Market Access: The Key to Doha Success [Trade Note 23. The World Bank Group] (pp. 1–5). Http://siteresources.worldbank.org/INTRANETTRADE/Resources/Pubs/TradeNote23.pdf.

Angehrn, E. (1977). *Freiheit und System bei Hegel*. Berlin: de Gruyter.

Arrow, K., & Debreu, G. (1954). Existence of an Equilibrium for a Competitive Economy. *Econometrica*, 265–290.

Arrow, K. J., & Hahn, F. H. (1971). *General Competitive Analysis*. San Francisco: Holden-Day.

Audi, R. (General Editor). (1995). *The Cambridge Dictionary of Philosophy*. Cambridge: Cambridge University Press.

Avineri, S. (1972). The Political Economy of Modern Society. In *Hegel's Theory of Modern State*. New York: Cambridge University Press.

Avineri, S. (1972). *Hegel's Theory of the Modern State*. Cambridge: Cambridge University Press.

Bane, M. J., & Ellwood, D. (1993). One Fifth of the Nation's Children: Why are they Poor? *Manuscript*, 1–25.

Bane, M. J., & Ellwood, D. (1994). *Welfare Realities: From Rhetoric to Reform*. Cambridge, MA: Harvard University Press.

Bator, F. M. (1957, March). The Simple Analytics of Welfare Maximization. *American Economic Review*, pp. 22–59.

Bird, R. M., & Head, J. G. (Editors). (1972). *Modern Fiscal Issues: Essays in Honor of Carl S. Shoup*. Toronto: University of Toronto Press.

Bishops Pastoral. (1984, November 15). Catholic Social Teaching and the U.S. Economy. *Origins*, pp. 337–338.

Boey, C. (1970). *L'Aliénation dans "La Phénoménologie de l'Esprit" de G.W.F. Hegel*. Paris-Bruges: Desclée De Brouwer.

Bohm, P. (1997). *The Economics of Environmental Protection: Theory and Demand Revelation*. Cheltenham, UK: Edward Elgar.

Bowles, S., & Gintis, H. (2002). Social Capital and Community Governance. *Economic Journal, 112*, F419–F436.

Brennan, G. (1974/75). Pareto Optimal Redistribution: A Perspective. *Finanzarchiv, N.F., 33*, 237–271.

Brennan, G. (1990). Irrational Action, Individual Sovereignty and Political Process: Why there is a Coherent 'Merit Goods' Argument. In G. Brennan & C. Walsh (Eds.), *Rationality, Individualism and Public Policy*. Canberra: The Australian National University.

Brennan, G., & Lomasky, L. (1983). Institutional Aspects of 'Merit Goods' Analysis. *Finanzarchiv, N.F., 41*, 183–206.

Brennan, G., & Lomasky, L. (1993). Paternalism, Self-Paternalism, and the State. In *Democracy and Decision: The Pure Theory of Electorral Preference* (pp. 143–166). Cambridge: Cambridge University Press.

Brennan, G., & Walsh, C. (Editors). (1990). *Rationality, Individualism and Public Policy* (p. XII+256). Canberra: The Australian National University.

Briefs, G. A. (1957, March). The Ethos Problem in the Present Pluralistic Society. *Review of Social Economy*, pp. 47–75 (Reprinted in *Review of Social Economy*, 61 (3), Dec. 1983, pp. 281–299.).

Briefs, G. A. (1957). Grenzmoral in der pluralistichen Gesellschaft. In E. Beckerath, Meyer (Ed.), *Wirtschaftsfragen der freien Welt (In honor of Ludwig Erhard)*. Frankfurt A.M.: Knapp.

Briefs, G. A. (editor). (1966). *Laissez-faire Pluralismus*. Berlin: Duncker & Humblot.

Briefs, G. A. (1966). Staat und Wirtschaft im Zeitalter der Interessenverbände. In G. Briefs (Ed.), *Laissez-faire-Pluralismus. Demokratie und Wirtschaft des gegenwärtigen Zeitalters* (pp. 1–317). Berlin: Duncker & Humblot.

Briefs, G. A. (1983, Dec.). Marginal Ethics in the Pluralistic Society. *Review of Social Economy*, pp. 259–270.

Brown, D. M., & McKeown. (1977). *The Poor Belong To Us: Catholic Charities and American Welfare*. Cambridge, MA: Harvard University Press.

Buchanan, J. M. (1974). Hegel on the Calculus of Voting. *Public Choice, 17* (Spring).

Buchanan, J. M. (1975). *The Limits of Liberty: Between Anarchy and Leviathan*. Chicago: University of Chicago Press.

Buchanan, J. M. (1983). Fairness, Hope and Justice. In R. Skurski (Ed.), *New Directions in Economic Justice* (pp. 53–89). Notre Dame: University of Notre Dame Press.

Byers, D. M. (Editor). (1985). *Justice in the Marketplace*. Washington.C.: United States Catholic Conference.

Campos, J. E., & Root, H. (1996). *The Key to the Asian Miracle*. Washington, D.C: Brookings Institute.

Catholic Bishops of the United States. (1975). The Economy: Human Dimensions. In D. M. Byers (Ed.), *Justice in the Marketplace*. Washington, D.C.: United States Catholic Conference.

Chamley, P. (1963). *Économie Politique et Philosphie chez Steuart et Hegel*. Paris: Dalloz.

Charles, S., & Westaway, T. (1981). Ignorance and Merit Wants. *Finanzarchiv, N.F., 39*(1), 74-78.

Chih, H. S. (2003). The Politics of Ethnic Integration in Singapore: Malay 'Regrouping'as an Ideological Construct. *International Journal of Urban and Regional Research, 27*(3), 527–544.

Cornes, R., & Sandler, T. (1994). Are Public Goods Myths? *Journal of Theoretical Politics, 6* (3), 369-385.

Cristi, F. R. (1978). Hegel on Possession and Property. *Canadian Journal of Political and Social Theory, 2* (3), 111–124.

Cristi, F. R. (1983). The Hegelsche Mitte and Hegel's Monarch. *Political Theory, 11* (4), 601–622.

Cullen, B. (1979). *Hegel's Social and Political Thought: An Introduction*. New York: St. Martin's Press.

Culyer, A. J. (1971). Merit Goods and the Welfare Economics of Coercion. *Public Finance, 26* (4), 546–570.

Deboeck, G. (Editor). (1994). *Trading on the Edge. Neurl, Genetic, and Fuzzy Systems for Chaotic Financial Markets*. New York: John Wiley & Sons, Inc.

Denis, H. (1984). *Logique Hegelienne et Systèmes Économiques*. Paris: Presses Universitaires de France.

Desan, W. (1972). *The Planetary Man* (Vol. Volumes 1 and 2). New York: The Macmillan Company.

de Jasay, A. (1989). *Social Contract, Free Ride: A Study of the Free Goods Problem*. Oxford: Clarendon Press.

De Wulf, L., & Sokol, J. B. (2005). *Customs. Modernization Handbook*. Washington, DC: The World Bank.

Douglass, R. B. (Editor). (1986). *The Deeper Meaning of Economic Life*. Washington, D.C.: Georgetown University Press.

Douglass, R. B. (1986). First Things First: The Letter and the Common Good Tradition. In R. B. Douglass (Ed.), *The Deeper Meaning of Economic Life.* Washington, D.C.: Georgetown University Press.

Dubouchet, P. (1995). *La Philosophie du Droit de Hegel: Essay de Lecture des "Principes."* Lyon: L'Hermes.

Dudley, W. (1997). Freedom and the Need for Protection from Myself. *The Owl of Minerva, 29* (1), 39–67.

Dupré, L. (1966). *The Philosophical Foundations of Marxism.* New York: Harcourt, Brace & World.

Dupré, L. (1983). *Marx's Social Critique of Culture.* New Haven: Yale University Press.

Economic Justice for All. Pastoral Letter on Catholic Social Teaching and the U.S. Economy. (1986). Washington, D.C.: National Conference of Catholic Bishops.

Economic Justice for All. Pastoral Letter on Catholic Social Teaching and the U.S. Economy [Tenth Anniversary Edition of]. (1997). Washinton, D.C.: United States Catholic Conference, Inc.

The Economy: Human Dimensions. (1975). In *A Statement of the Catholic Bishops of the United States.* Washington, D.C.: United States Catholic Conference.

Edwards, P. (Editor). (1972). *The Encyclopedia of Philosophy* (P. Edwards, Ed.) (Vol. 1–8). New York: Macmillan Publishing Co., Inc. & The Free Press.

Eucken, W. (1982). A Policy for Establishing a System of Free Enterprise (Derek Rutter, Trans.). In W. Stützel, C. Watrin, H. Willgerodt & K. Hohmann (Eds.), *Standard Texts on the Social Market Economy.* Stuggart, New York: Gustav Fischer Verlag.

Evans, M. K. (1969). *Macroeconomic Activity: Theory, Forecasting, and Control.* New York: Harper and Row.

Feehan, J. P. (1990). A Simple Model for Merit Good Arguments. *Journal of Public Economics, 43,* 127–129.

Ferguson, C. E. (1969). *Micro-economic Theory.* Homewood: Richard D. Irwin, Inc.

Fleischmann, E. (1964). *La Philosophie Politique de Hegel; Sous Forme d'un Commentaire des Fondements de la Philosophie du Droit.* Paris: Plon.

Foley, D. K. (1967, Spring). Resource Allocation and the Public Sector. *Yale Economic Essays,* pp. 43–98.

Foley, D. K. (1970, January). Lindahl's Solution and the Core of an Economy with Public Goods. *Econometrica,* pp. 66–72.

Folkers, C. (1974). Meritorische Güter als Problem der normativen Theorie öffentliche Ausgaben. *Jahrbuch für Sozialwissenschaft, 25,* 1–29.

Friedman, M. (1962). *Capitalism and Freedom*. Chicago: University of Chicago Press.

Fritsch, M. (1980). Staatseingriff und "Meritorität." Überlegungen des Konzeptes der "meritorischen Güter.". In *Wirtschaftswissenschaftlichen Dokumentation. Disk. Pap.* (Vol. 53). Berlin: Technische Universität Berlin.

Galbraith, J. K. (1958). *The Affluent Society*. Boston: Houghton-Mifflin.

Ghesquiere, H. (2007). *Singapore's Success. Engineering Economic Growth*. Singapore: Thomson.

Godwin, K. R. (1991). Charges for Merit Goods: Third World Family Planning. *Journal of Public Policy, 11* (4), 415–429.

Gossman, L. (1961). Rousseau's Idealism. *Romanic review, 52*(3), 173–182.

Green, D. G. (1993). *Reinventing Civil Society: The Rediscovery of Welfare without Politics*. London: IEA Health and Welfare Unit.

Harada, T. (1989). *Politische Ökonomie des Idealismus und der Romantik: Korporatismus von Fichte, Muller und Hegel*. Berlin: Duncker & Humblot.

Hardimon, M. O. (1994). *Hegel's Social Philosophy; The Project of Reconciliation*. Cambridge: Cambridge University Press.

Hausman, D. (2001). Review of Women and Human Development: The Capabilities Approach. *Journal of Economic Literature, 39* (2), 599–600.

Hausman, D. M., & McPherson, M. S. (1996). *Economic Analysis and Moral Philosophy*. Cambridge; New York: Cambridge University Press.

Hayek, F. A. (1944). *The Road to Serfdom*. Chicago: University of Chicago Press.

Hayek, F. A. (1960). *The Constitution of Liberty*. Chicago: University of Chicago Press.

Hayek, F. A. (1967). *Studies in Philosophy, Politics and Economics*. Chicago: University of Chicago Press.

Hayek, F. A. (Editor). (1975). *Collectivist Economic Planning*. Clifton, NJ: Augustus M. Kelley Publishers.

Hayek, F. A. (1978). *New Studies in Philosophy, Politics, Economics and the History of Ideas*. London: Routledge & Kegan Paul.

Head, J. G. (1966, March). On Merit Goods. *Finanzarchiv, N.F.*, pp. 1–29 (Also published in Head, John. *Public Goods and Public Welfare*.1974, 214–247.).

Head, J. G. (1968). The Theory of Public Goods. *Rivista di diritto finanziario e scienza finanze, 27*(2), 209-36 (Also published in Head, John. *Public Goods and Public Welfare*. 1974, 68–92).

Head, J. G. (1969, March). Merit Goods Revisited. *Finanzarchiv, N.F.*, pp. 214–225 (Also published in Head, John. *Public Goods and Public Welfare.* 1974, 248–261.).

Head, J. G. (1974). *Public Goods and Public Welfare.* Durham, NC: Duke University Press.

Head, J. G. (1988). On Merit Wants: Reflections on the Evolution, Normative Status and Policy Relevance of a Controversial Public Finance Concept. *Finanzarchiv, N.F., 46*, 1-37 (Also published in *Rationality, Individualism and Public Policy.* Geoffrey Brennan and Cliff Walsh, Eds.Canberra:Australian National University, 1990, 211–44.).

Head, J. G. (1990). On Merit Wants: Reflections on the Evolution, Normative Status and Policy Relevance of a Controversial Public Finance ᴸᵒⁿᶜᵉᵖᵗ. ⁱⁿ ᴸ. ᵐᵒⁿⁿⁱⁿⁿ ᵃⁱ ⁱ. ᵂᵃⁱᵇⁱ (ᴱᵈⁱ), ᴿⁱⁱⁱⁱⁱⁱⁱⁱⁱᵗⁱⁱⁱ, ⁱⁱⁱⁱⁱⁱⁱⁱⁱⁱⁱⁱⁱⁱⁱⁱ *and Public Policy* (pp. 210–244). Canberra: The Australian National University.

Hegel, G. (1955). *Grundlinien der Philosophie des Rechts.* In *Philosophische Bibliothek, 124 a.* Hamburg: Felix Meiner.

Hegel, G. (1959). *Enzyklopädia der Philosophischen Wissenschaften.* In *Philosophische Bibliothek, 33.* Hamburg: Felix Meiner.

Hegel, G. (1967 a). *Hegel's Philosophy of Right* (T. Knox, Trans.). Oxford: Oxford University Press. Abbreviated as PR.

Hegel, G. (1967 b). *Jenaer Realphilosophie. Vorlesungsmanuskripte zur Philosophie der Natur und des Geistes von 1805-1806.* In *Philosophische Bibliothek 47* [Reprint of "Jenenser Realphilosophie II"] (J.Hoffmeister, Ed.). Hamburg: Felix Meiner.

Hegel, G. (1967 c). *The Phenomenology of Mind* (J. B. Baillie, Trans.). New York: Harper Torchbooks. Abbreviated as PhG.

Hegel, G. (1971). *Hegel's Philosophy of Mind* (W. Wallace & A. Miller, Trans.). Oxford: Clarendon Press. Abbreviated as PM.

Hegel, G. (1977 a). *Early Theological Writings* (T. Knox, Trans.). Philadelphia: University of Pennsylvania Press.

Hegel, G. (1977 b). *Phenomenology of Spirit* (A. Miller, Trans.) (p. xxxv+595). Oxford: Oxford University Press (Analysis of the text and Foreword by J.N. Findlay).

Hegel, G. (1990). *The Phenomenology of Mind* [Machine readable version] (J. Baillie, Trans.). Washington, D.C.: Georgetown University.

Hegel, G. (1991). *Elements of the Philosophy of Right* (A. W. Wood, Ed.) (N. Nisbet, Trans.). Cambridge: Cambridge University Press.

Henrich, D., & Horstmann, R. (Editors). (1982). *Hegels Philosophie des Rechts: Die Theorie der Rechtsformen und ihre Logik.* Stuttgart: Klett-Cotta.

Hirschman, A. O. (1977). *The Passions and the Interests*. Princeton, NJ: Princeton University Press.

Hirschman, A. O. (1982, December). Rival Interpretations of Market Society: Civilising, Destructive, or Feeble? *Journal of Economic Literature*, pp. 1463–1484.

Hochman, H., & Rodgers, J. (1969). Pareto Optimal Redistribution. *American Economic Review, 59*, 542–557.

Hochman, H., & Rodgers, J. (1969). Pareto Optimal Redistribution. *American Economic Review, 59*, 542–557.

Hong, M. (2000). Singapore's Sucess in Creating Racial and Religious Harmony. Http://sam11.moe.gov.sg/racialharmony/download%5CRacial_Religious_Harmony_final.pdf.

Horace. (1997). *Carmina. English & Latin* (D. Ferry, Trans.). New York: Farrar, Strauss and Giroux.

Hyppolite, J. (1939). La Signification de la Révolution Française dans la 'Phénoménologie de Hegel. *Revue philosophique de la France et de l'Etranger, 128*.

IRS. (1994). *1994 1040. Forms and Instructions*. Washington, D.C.: US Government Printing Office.

IRS. (1999). *1999 1040. Forms and Instructions*. Washington, D.C.: US Government Printing Office.

IRS. (2003). *2003 1040. Forms and Instructions*. Washington, D.C.: US Government Printing Office.

Jarczyk, G., & Labarrière, P. (1986). *Hegeliana*. Paris: Presses Universitaires de France.

Jermann, C. (Editor). (1987). *Anspruch und Leistung von Hegels Rechtsphilososphie*. Stuttgart-Bad Cannstatt: Frommann-Holzboog.

John Paul II. (1991). *Centesimus Annus*. Washington, D.C.: U.S. Catholic Conference.

Kainz, H. (1974). *Hegel's Philosophy of Right, with Marx's Commentary: A Handbook for Students*. The Hague: Martinus Nijhoff.

Kaiser Robert G., & Perkins, L. (2006, October 4, 2005). Finland Diary. Focus on Schools Helps Finns Build Showcase Nation. Http://blogs.washingtpost.com/finlanddiary/education/index.html.

Kamarck, E. &., Gallston. (1993). A Progressive Family Policy for the 1990's. In W. &. Marschall, Schram (Ed.), *Mandate for Change*. New York: Berkeley Books.

Kant, I. (1956). *Critique of Practical Reason* (L. W. Beck, Trans.). Indianapolis: The Bobbs-Merrill Company.

Kaul, I., Grunberg, I., & Stern, A. M. (1999). *Global Public Goos: International Cooperation in the 21 st Century*. New York: Oxford University Press.

Keynes, J. M. (1963). *Essays in Persuasion*. New York: W.W. Norton.

Keynes, J. M. (1965). *The General Theory of Employment, Interest, and Money*. New York: Harcourt, Brace & World, Inc.

Kiesling, H. (1992). *Taxation and Public Goods: A Welfare Economic Critique of Tax Policy Analysis*. Ann Arbor, MI: The Universtiy of Michigan Press.

Kraus, J. B. (1931/1932). Wirtschaft und Gesellschaft bei Hegel. *Archiv für Rechts- und Wirstschaftsphilosophie, 25*.

Langan, J. (1977, June). Rawls, Nozick and the Search for Social Justice. *Theological Studies*, pp. 346–358.

Langan, J. (1986). The American Context of the U.S. Bishops' Pastoral Letter on the Economy. In R. B. Douglass (Ed.), *The Deeper Meaning of Economic Life*. Washington, D.C.: Georgetown University Press.

Levine, D. P. (1977). *Economic Studies: Contributions to the Critique of Economic theory*. London: Routledge & Kegan Paul.

Levine, D. P. (1988). *Needs, Rights, and the Market*. Boulder and London: Lynne Riener Publishers.

Levine, D. P. (1995). *Wealth and Freedom: An Introduction to Political Economy*. Cambridge: Cambridge University Press.

Levine, D. P. (2001). *Normative Political Economy: Subjective Freedom, the Market, and the State*. London: Routledge.

Lowi, T. J. (1979). *The End of Liberalism: The Second Republic of the United States* (2nd edition). New York: W. W. Norton & Co.

Lucas, H., & Pöggeler, O. (Editors). (1986). *Hegels Rechtsphilosophie im Zusammenhang der Europäischen Verfassungsgeschichte*. Stuttgart-Bad Cannstatt: Frommann-Holzboog.

Lukacs, G. (1973). *Der junge Hegel*. Frankfurt am Main: Suhrkamp.

Mackscheidt, K. (1974). Meritorische Güter: Musgraves Idee und deren Konsequenzen. *WISU-Das Wirtschaftsstudium, 3*, 237–241.

Mackscheidt, K. (1981). Die Entfaltung von privater und kollektiver Initiative durch meritorische Güter. Meritorische Güter zwishen Marktwirtschaft und Staatswirtschaft. *Archiv für öffentliche und freigemeinnützige Unternehmen, 13*, 257–267.

Mackscheidt, K. (1997). Letter with course notes. Kóln.

Maker, W. (Editor). (1987). *Hegel on Economics and Freedom*. Macon: Mercer University Press.

Malkin, J., & Wildavsky, A. (1991). Why the Traditional Distinction Between Public and Private Goods Should Be Abandoned. *Journal of Theoretical Politics, 3*(4), 355–78.

Marx, K. (1977). *Critique of Hegel's Philosphy of Right* (J. O'Malley, Trans.). Cambridge: Cambridge University Press.

Marx, K., & Engels, F. (1948). *Manifesto of the Communist Party* (F. Engels, Ed.). New York: International Publishers.

McLure, C. E. (1968, June). Merit Wants: A Normative Empty Box. *Finanzarchiv, N.F.*, pp. 474–483.

McLure, C. E. (1990). Merit Wants. In G. Brennan & C. Walsh (Eds.), *Rationality, Individualism and Public Policy*. Canberra: The Australian National University.

Mensbrugghe, D. v., der. (No date). Estimating the Benefits of Trade Reform: Why Numbers Change (pp. 59–75). Http://siteresources.world bank.org/INTRANETTRADE/Resources/239054-1126812419270/4. EstimatingThe.pdf.

Mises, L. v. (1963). *Human Action. A Treatise on Economics*. New Haven: Yale University Press.

Mises, L. v. (1975). Economic Calculation in the Socialist Commonwealth. In F. A. Hayek (Ed.), *Collectivist Economic Planning* (pp. 87–130). Clifton, New Jersey: Augustus M. Kelley Publishers.

Molitor, B. (1988). Meritorisierung des Gutes "Sicherheit?". In K. Hohman, D. Schönwitz, H. Weber & H. F. Wünsche (Eds.), *Grundtexte zur Sozialen Marktwirtschaft. Vol. II.* Stuttgart, New York: Gustav Fischer Verlag.

Molitor, B. (1989). *Wirtschaftsethik*. München: Verlag Franz Vahlen.

Morris, R., & Freund, M. (Editors). (1966). *Trends and Issues in Jewish Social Welfare in the United States, 1899-1952*. Philadelphia: The Jewish Publication Society of America.

Mueller, D. C. (1979). *Public Choice*. Cambridge: Cambridge University Press.

Murphy, J. B. (1994). A Natural Law of Human Labor. *The American Journal of Jurisprudence, 39*, 71–95.

Murray, P. (Editor). (1997). *Reflections on Commercial Life. An Anthology of Classical Texts from Plato to the Present*. New York: Routledge.

Musgrave, R. A. (1956, September). A Multiple Theory of Budget Determination. *Finanzarchiv, N.F.*, pp. 333–343.

Musgrave, R. A. (1957). Principles of Budget Determination. In Joint Economic Committeee (Ed.), *Federal Expenditure Policy for Economic Growth and Stability* (pp. 108-115). Washington, D.C.: Government Printing Office.

Musgrave, R. A. (1959). *The Theory of Public Finance* [Musgrave at Harvard University]. New York: McGraw-Hill Book Company.

Musgrave, R. A. (1959). *The Theory of Public Finance* [Musgrave at Michigan University]. New York: McGraw-Hill Book Company.

Musgrave, R. A. (1969). Provision for Social Goods. In J. Margolis & H. Guitton (Eds.), *Public Economics*. London: Macmillan Press Ltd.

Musgrave, R. A. (1971). Provision for Social Goods in the Market System. *Public Finance, 26,* 304–320.

Musgrave, R. A. (1980). Theories of Fiscal Crisis. In Aaron. H. (Ed.), *The Economics of Taxation.* Washington, D.C.: Brookings Institution.

Musgrave, R. A. (1987). Merit Goods. In J. Eatwell, M. Milgate & P. Newman (Eds.), *The New Palgrave: A Dictionary of Economics* (Vol. 3). London: Macmillan.

Musgrave, R. A. (1990). Merit Goods. In G. Brennan & C. Walsh (Eds.), *Rationality, Individualism and Public Policy* (pp. 207–210). Canberra: The Australian National University.

Musgrave, R. A. (1993). Crossing Traditions. In H. Hagemann (Ed.), *Zur deutschsprachigen wirtschafttlichen Emigration nach 1933* (pp. 63–79). Marburg: Metropolis.

Musgrave, R. A. (1996). Public Finance and Finanzwissenschaft Traditions Compared. *Finanzarchiv, N.F., 53*(2), 145–193.

Musgrave, R. A. (1997). Crossing Traditions. In H. Hagemann (Ed.), *Zur deutschsprachigen wirtschafttlichen Emigration nach 1933* (pp. 63–79). Marburg: Metropolis.

Musgrave, R. A., & Musgrave, P. (1973). *Public Finance in Theory and Practice.* New York: McGraw-Hilll Book Company.

Nawroth, E. E. (1961). *Die Sozial- und Wirtschaftsphilosophie des Neoliberalismus.* Heidelberg: F. H. Kerle Verlag.

Nelson, R. R. (1987). Roles of Government in a Mixed Economy. *Journal of Policy Analysis and Management, 6* (4), 541–557.

Nelson, R. R. (2002). The Problem of Market Bias in Modern Capitalist Economies. *Industrial and Corporate Change, 11* (2), 207–244.

Novak, M. (1981). A Theology of the Corporation. In M. &. Novak, Cooper (Ed.), *The Corporation: A Theological Inquiry.* Washington, D.C.: American Enterprise Institute.

Novak, M. (1982). *The Spirit of Democratic Capitalism.* Lanham,MD: Madison Books.

Novak, M. (1989). *Catholic Social Thought & Liberal Institutions: Freedom with Justice.* New Brunswick: Transaction Publishers.

Nozick, R. (1974). *Anarchy, State, and Utopia.* New York: Basic Books.

OECD. (1982). *The OECD List of Social Indicators.* Paris: Organization for Economic Co-operation and Development.

Olson, M., Jr. (1968). *The Logic of Collective Action.* New York: Schocken Books.

Olson, M., Jr. (1982). *The Rise and Decline of Nations.* New Haven and London: Yale University Press.

Olson, M., Jr. (1983). The Political Economy of Comparative Growth Rates. In D. C. Muller (Ed.), *The Political Economy of Growth* (pp. 7–52). New Haven: Yale University Press.

Ooi, G. L., Siddique, S., & Soh, K. C. (1993). *The Management of Ethnic Relations in Public Housing Estates.* Singapore: Times Academic Press for IPS.

Ostrom, V., & Ostrom, E. (1991). Public Goods and Public Choices: The Emergence of Public Economies and Industry Structures. In V. Ostrom (Ed.), *The Meaning of American Federalism* (pp. 163–197, 276). San Francisco: Institute for Contemporary Studies.

Ostrom, V., Tiebout, C. M., & Warren, R. (1991). The Organization of Government in Metropolitan Areas: A Theoretical Inquiry. In V. Ostrom (Ed.), *The Meaning of American Federalism* (pp. 137–161, 275). San Francisco: Institute for Contemporary Studies.

O'Malley, J. (1970). Editor's Introduction. In *Critique of Hegel's `Philosophy of Right' by Karl Marx* (pp. IX-LXVII). Cambridge: Cambridge University Press.

Pelczynski, Z. (Editor). (1984). *The State & Civil Society.* Cambridge: University of Cambridge Press.

The Penguin Dictionary of Economics (G. Bannock, R. Baxter, & R. Rees, Eds.). (1972). Middlesex: Penguin Books Ltd.

Plato. (1979). *The Republic* (F. M. Cornford, Trans.). New York: Oxford University Press.

Pogge, T. W. (1989). *Realizing Rawls.* Ithaca, NY: Cornell University Press.

Prasch, R. E., & Sheth, F. A. (1999). The Economics and Ethics of Minimum Wage Legislation. *Review of Social Economy, 57* (4), 466–487.

Priddat, B. P. (1990). *Hegel als Ökonom.* Berlin: Duncker & Humblot.

Priddat, B. P. (1992). Zur Ökonomie der Gemeinschaftsbedürfnise: Neuere Versuche einer ethischen Begründung der Theorie meritorischer Güter. *Zeitschrift für Wirtschafts- u. Sozialwissenschaften, 112,* 239–59.

Priddat, B. P. (1994). Moderne Ökonomische Staatsbegründung: Zur Theorie Meritorischer Güter. In *Diskussionspapiere* (pp. 1–45). Witten: Universität Witten/Herdecke.

Pulsipher, A. G. (1971/72). The Properties and Relevancy of Merit Goods. *Finanzarchiv, 30,* 266–286.

Rahner, K. (Editor). (1968–70). *Sacramentum Mundi. An Encyclopedia of Theology. 6 Vols.* New York: Herder and Herder.

Rawls, J. (1971). *A Theory of Justice.* Cambridge, Mass.: Harvard University Press.

Rees, A. (1970). The Phillips Curve as a Menu for Policy Choice. *Economica, 37*(147), 227–38.

Reyburn, H. A. (1967). *The Ethical Theory of Hegel: A Study of the Philosophy of Right*. Oxford: Clarendon Press.

Richardson, H. (1989, January). The Logical Structure of Sittlichkeit: A Reading of Hegel's Philosophy of Right. *Idealistic Studies*, pp. 62–78.

Riedel, M. (Editor). (1975). *Materialien zu Hegels Rechtsphilosophie* (Vol. Vol I–II). Frankfurt am Main: Suhrkamp Verlag.

Ritter, J. (1982). *Hegel and the French Revolution: Essays on the Philosophy of Right* (R. D. Winfield, Trans.). Cambridge: MIT Press.

Ritter, J. (1982). Morality and Ethical Life (Richard D. Winfield, Trans.). In *Hegel and the French Revolution* (pp. 183–191). Cambridge: MIT Press.

Roth, K. (1989). *Freiheit und Institutionen in der politischen Philosophie* ꜰꭔꞟ꜔꜖ꜟ ꞟ ꞟꞟꞟꞟꞟꞟꞟꞟ ꞟꞟꞟꞟꞟꞟ.

Samuelson, P. A. (1954, Nov.). The Pure Theory of Public Expenditure. *Review of Economics and Statistics*, pp. 387–389.

Samuelson, P. A. (1955, Nov.). Diagrammatic Exposition of a Theory of Public Expenditure. *Review of Economics and Statistics*, pp. 350–356.

Samuelson, P. A. (1958, Nov.). Aspects of Public Expenditure Theories. *Review of Economics and Statistics*, pp. 332–338.

Samuelson, P. A. (1969). Pure Theory of Public Expenditure and Taxation. In J. Margolis & H. Guitton (Eds.), *Public Economics*. London: Macmillan Press Ltd.

Sandler, T. (1992). *Collective Action: Theory and Applications*. Ann Arbor, MI: University of Michigan Press.

Sartre, J. (1958). *No Exit. A Play in One Act* [Adapted from the French by Paul Bowles]. New York: Samuel French, Inc.

Scheer, C. (1975). *Sozialstaat und öffentliche Finanzen*. Köln: Peter Hanstein Verlag GmbH.

Schmidtz, D. (1991). *The Limits of Government: An Essay on the Public Goods Argument*. Boulder. CO: Westview Press.

Schmidtz, D., & Goodin, R. (1998). *Social Welfare and Individual Responsibility*. Cambridge: Cambridge University Press.

Schumpeter, J. A. (1954). *Capitalism, Socialism, and Democracy*. London: George Allen & Unwin.

Schumpeter, J. A. (1968). *A History of Economic Analysis*. New York: Oxford University Press.

Schumpeter, J. A. (1969). *The Theory of Economic Development*. Oxford: Oxford University Press.

Seeberger, W. (1961). *Hegel oder die Entwicklung des Geistes zur Freiheit*. Stuttgart: Ernst Klett.

Sen, A. (1977). Rational Fools: A Critique of the Behavioural Foundations of Economic Theory. *Philosophy and Public Affairs*, 6, 317–344.

Sen, A. (1985). Moral Standing of the Market. *Social Philosophy and Policy*, *2*(2), 1–19.

Sen, A. (1995). Moral Codes and Economic Success. In S. Brittan & A. Hamlin (Eds.), *Market Capitalism and Moral Values: Proceedings of Selection F (Economics) of the British Association for the Advancement of Science. Keele 1993*. Vermont: Edward Elgar.

Simons, H. C. (1948). *Economic Policy for a Free Society*. Chicago: University of Chicago Press.

Singapore HDB InfoWEB. (2007). Housing & Development Board. Http://www.hdb.gov.sg/fi10/fi10203p.nsf/WPDis/Selling%20Your%20 FlatEthnic%20Group%20Eligibility?OpenDocument.

Smith, A. (1937). *The Wealth of Nations*. New York: The Modern Library.

Smith, S. B. (1989). *Hegel's Critique of Liberalism. Rights in Context*. Chicago: University of Chicago.

Steinberger, P. J. (1988). *Logic and Politics: Hegel's Philosophy of Right*. New Haven: Yale University Press.

Stevens, J. B. (1993). *The Economics of Collective Choice*. Boulder, CO: Westview Press.

Stiglitz, J. E. (1999). Whither Reform? Ten Years of the Transition. *World Bank, WEB*, 1-32.

Stretton, H., & Orchard, L. (1994). *Public Goods, Public Enterprise, Public Choice: Theoretical Foundations of the Contemporary Attack on Government*. New York, NY: St. Martin's Press.

Summers, M. (1994). An Economic Alternative [Croatian Conference. Special Issue]. *The Chesterton Review*, *2–3*, 239–245.

Summers, M. (1994). An Economic Alternative [Croatian Conference. Special Issue]. *The Chesterton Review*, *2–3*, 239–245.

Tan, E. (2005). Multiracialism Engineered: The Limits of Electoral and Spacial Integration in Singapore. *Ethnopolitics*, *4* (4), 413–428.

Taylor, C. (1990). Irreducibly Social Goods. In G. Brennan & C. Walsh (Eds.), *Rationality, Individualism and Public Policy*. Canberra: The Australian National University.

Tideman, T., & Tullock, G. (1976). A New and Superior Principle for Collective Choice, or, how to Plan. *Journal of Political Economy*.

US Census Bureau. (2004). *Public Education Finances: 2002*. Washington, DC: U.S. Department of Commerce. http://ftp2.census.gov/ govs/school/02f33pub.pdf.

Ver Eecke, W. (1975 a). Hegel's Dialectic Analysis of the French Revolution. *Hegel Jahrbuch*, 561–67.

Ver Eecke, W. (1975 b). Keynes, of de Prijs voor een Humanitair Doel in een Economisch Bestel. In *Liber Amicorum Professor Dr. Gaston Eyskens* (pp. 431–446). Leuven: Universitaire Pers Leuven.

Ver Eecke, W. (1983). Hegel on Economics and Freedom. *Archiv für Rechts- und Sozialphilosophie, 69* (2), 187–215.

Ver Eecke, W. (1984). The State: Ethics and Economics. In Rocco Porreco (Ed.), *The Georgetown Symposium on Ethics. Essays in Honor of Henry Babcock Veatch* (pp. 195–203). Lanham, New York, London: University Press of America.

Ver Eecke, W. (1998). The Concept of a 'Merit Good': The Ethical Dimension in Economic Theory and the History of Economic Thought or the Transformation of Economics into Socio-Economics. *Journal of Socio-Economics, 27* (1), 133–53.

Ver Eecke, W. (1999). Public Goods: An Ideal Concept. *Journal of Socio-Economics, 28* (3), 139–156.

Ver Eecke, W. (2001). Le Concept de "Bien Méritoire" ou la Nécessité Epistémologique d'un Concept Ethique dans la Science Economique. *Laval Théologique et Philosophique, 57* (1), 23–40.

Ver Eecke, W. (2003). Adam Smith and Musgrave's Concept of Merit Good. *Journal of Socio-Economics, 31*, 701–720.

Ver Eecke, W. (2007). *An Anthology Regarding Merit Goods. The Unfinished Ethical Revolution in Economic Thought*. West Lafayette, IN: Purdue University Press.

Walsh, C. (1990). Individual Irrationality and Public Policy: In Search of Merit/Demerit Policies. In G. Brennan & C. Walsh (Eds.), *Rationality, Individualism and Public Policy*. Canberra: The Australian National University.

Waszek, N. (1988). *The Scottish Enlightenment and Hegel's Account of "Civil Society."* Dordrecht: Kluwer Academic Publishers.

Whitebook, J. (1977). *Economics and Ethical Life: A Study of Aristotle and Hegel*. Ann Arbor: University Microfilms.

Wildavsky, A. (1979). Opportunity Costs and Merit Wants. In *Speaking Truth to Power: The Art and Craft of Policy Analysis* [Chapter 7]. Somerset, NJ; Previously, Boston and Toronto: Transaction Publishers; Previously, Little, Brown and Company.

Winfield, R. D. (1988). *Reason and Justice*. Albany: State University of New York Press.

Winfield, R. D. (1990). *The Just Economy*. New York: Routledge.

Wolfowitz, P. (2005). Trading for Results? Realizing the Promise of Doha. Keio University, Tokyo, Japan.

Wood, A. (1990). *Hegel's Ethical Thought*. Cambridge: Cambridge University Press.

World Bank. (1993). *The East Asian Miracle: Economic Growth and Public Policy*. New York: Oxford University Press.

World Bank. (1996). *World Development Report 1996: From Plan to Market.* New York: Oxford University Press.

World Bank. (1997). World Development Report 1997: The State in a Changing World. New York: Oxford University Press.

Indices

Proper Names

Subjects

A

B

C

U

Studies in Economics Ethics and Philosophy

P. Koslowski (Ed.)
Ethics in Economics, Business,
and Economic Policy
X, 178 pages. 1992
ISBN 978-3-540-55359-5 (out of print)

P. Koslowski and Y. Shionoya (Eds.)
The Good and the Economical:
Ethical Choices in Economics
and Management
X, 202 pages. 1993.
ISBN 978-3-540-57339-5 (out of print)

H. De Geer (Ed.)
Business Ethics in Progress?
IX, 124 pages. 1994
ISBN 978-3-540-57758-4

P. Koslowski (Ed.)
The Theory of Ethical Economy
in the Historical School
XI, 343 pages. 1995, reprint 1997
ISBN 978-3-540-59070-5

A. Argandoña (Ed.)
The Ethical Dimension
of Financial Institutions and Markets
XI, 263 pages. 1995
ISBN 978-3-540-59209-9 (out of print)

G. K. Becker (Ed.)
Ethics in Business and Society
Chinese and Western Perspectives
VIII, 233 pages. 1996
ISBN 978-3-540-60773-1

P. Koslowski (Ed.)
Ethics of Capitalism and Critique
of Sociobiology. Two Essays with
a Comment by James M. Buchanan
IX, 142 pages. 1996
ISBN 978-3-540-61035-9

F. Neil Brady (Ed.)
Ethical Universals in International Business
X, 246 pages. 1996
ISBN 978-3-540-61588-0

P. Koslowski and A. Føllesdal (Eds.)
Restructuring the Welfare State.
Theory and Reform of Social Policy
VII, 402 pages. 1997
ISBN 978-3-540-62035-8 (out of print)

G. Erreygers and T. Vandevelde (Eds.)
Is Inheritance Legitimate?
Ethical and Economic Aspects
of Wealth Transfer
X, 236 pages. 1997
ISBN 978-3-540-62725-8

P. Koslowski (Ed.)
Business Ethics in East Central Europe
XII, 151 pages. 1997
ISBN 978-3-540-63367-9

P. Koslowski (Ed.)
Methodology of the Social Sciences, Ethics,
and Economics in the Newer
Historical School.
From Max Weber and Rickert
to Sombart and Rothacker
XII, 565 pages. 1997
ISBN 978-3-540-63458-4

A. Føllesdal and P. Koslowski (Eds.)
Democracy and the European Union
X, 309 pages. 1998
ISBN 978-3-540-63457-7

P. Koslowski (Ed.)
The Social Market Economy.
Theory and Ethics of the Economic Order
XII, 360 pages. 1998
ISBN 978-3-540-64043-1

Amitai Etzioni
Essays in Socio-Economics
XII, 182 pages. 1999
ISBN 978-3-540-64466-8

P. Koslowski (Ed.)
Sociobiology and Bioeconomics.
The Theory of Evolution in Biological
and Economic Theory
X, 341 pages. 1999
ISBN 978-3-540-65380-6

Studies in Economics Ethics and Philosophy

J. Kuçuradi (Ed.)
The Ethics of the Professions:
Medicine, Business, Media, Law
X, 172 pages. 1999
ISBN 978-3-540-65726-2

S. K. Chakraborty and S. R. Chatterjee (Eds.)
Applied Ethics in Management.
Towards New Perspectives
X, 298 pages. 1999
ISBN 978-3-540-65724-8

P. Koslowski (Ed.)
The Theory of Capitalism
in the German Economic Tradition.
Historism, Ordo-Liberalism,
Critical Theory, Solidarism
XII, 577 pages. 2000
ISBN 978-3-540-66674-5

P. Koslowski (Ed.)
Contemporary Economic Ethics
and Business Ethics
IX, 265 pages. 2000
ISBN 978-3-540-66665-3

L. Sacconi
The Social Contract of the Firm.
Economics, Ethics and Organisation
XV, 229 pages. 2000
ISBN 978-3-540-67219-7

M. Casson and A. Godley (Eds.)
Cultural Factors in Economic Growth
VIII, 244 pages. 2001
ISBN 978-3-540-66293-8

Y. Shionoya and K. Yagi (Eds.)
Competition, Trust, and Cooperation
IX, 252 pages. 2001
ISBN 978-3-540-67870-0

B. Hodgson
Economics as Moral Science
XIV, 380 pages. 2001
ISBN 978-3-540-41062-1

A. Labrousse and J.-D. Weisz (Eds.)
Institutional Economics in France
and Germany.
German Ordoliberalsm versus
the French Regulation School
IX, 384 pages. 2001
ISBN 978-3-540-67855-7

F. Vandenbroucke
Social Justice and Individual Ethics
in an Open Society.
Equality, Responsibility, and Incentives
XIII, 305 pages. 2001
ISBN 978-3-540-41636-4

G. Brennan, H. Kliemt and R. D. Tollison
(Eds.)
Method and Morals
in Constitutional Economics.
Essays in Honor of James M. Buchanan
XVI, 571 pages. 2002
ISBN 978-3-540-41970-9

H. H. Nau and B. Schefold (Eds.)
The Historicity of Economics.
Continuities and Discontinuities
of Historical Thought
in 19th and 20th Century Economics
X, 245 pages. 2002
ISBN 978-3-540-42765-0

J. Wieland (Ed.)
Standards and Audits
for Ethics Management Systems
VIII, 253 pages. 2003
ISBN 978-3-540-40206-0

P. Koslowski, C. Hubig and P. Fischer (Eds.)
Business Ethics and the Electronic Economy
IX, 248 pages. 2004
ISBN 978-3-540-22150-0

B. Hodgson (Ed.)
The Invisible Hand and the Common Good
XVI, 463 pages. 2004
ISBN 978-3-540-22353-5

P. Koslowski (Ed.)
The Discovery of Historicity
in German Idealism and Historism
VIII, 291 pages. 2005
ISBN 978-3-540-24393-9

W. Ver Eecke
Ethical Dimensions of the Economy
Making Use of Hegel and the Concepts
of Public and Merit Goods
XIV, 301 pages. 2008
ISBN 978-3-540-77110-4

Printed in the United Kingdom
by Lightning Source UK Ltd.
132295UK00002B/49-129/P